MW01039099

The Global Frontier

THE NEW AMERICAN CANON

The Iowa Series in Contemporary Literature and Culture

Samuel Cohen, series editor

THE GLOBAL FRONTIER

Postwar Travel

in American Literature

ERIC STRAND

UNIVERSITY OF IOWA PRESS | IOWA CITY

University of Iowa Press, Iowa City 52242
Copyright © 2023 by University of Iowa Press
uipress.uiowa.edu
Printed in the United States of America

ISBN 978-1-60938-901-7 (pbk)
ISBN 978-1-60938-902-4 (ebk)

Design and typesetting by April Leidig

Printed on acid-free paper

Cataloging-in-Publication data is on file
with the Library of Congress.

For Mom, Dad, Leif, and Kyle

Contents

Acknowledgments

This book is inescapably a response to the job-market meltdown—let's put it this way: if I narrated my experiences, it would make Rebecca Schuman's "Thesis Hatement" look measured and restrained—and I feel that my career has lacked professional coherence, even as I've been lucky to receive far more support than I deserve. Michael P. Clark was my mentor and dissertation committee chair, and he has gone beyond the call of duty in providing feedback and advice long after I left graduate school. I'm extremely grateful to Ersu Ding, a true cosmopolitan intellectual who believed in my scholarly potential when it seemed that no one else did, and who finally gave me the chance to live and work in Asia. The University of Iowa Press's commitment to this project has been a godsend, and I'm indebted to the editor of the New American Canon series, Samuel Cohen, and two anonymous readers for their rigorous peer reviews. Stephen Schryer has been a valuable colleague and a generous friend. I hope it's not arrogant to say that this book is an attempt to globalize his profound contribution to the study of twentieth-century American literature, *Fantasies of the New Class* (2011).

This book is informed by my years in the Sociology Department at the University of Stony Brook, which generously admitted me to their doctoral program even though my bachelor's degree was in English. Diane Barthel-Bouchier, John Gagnon, Michael Kimmel, and Andrea Tyree were especially supportive. Erich Goode taught me about history and politics as well as sociology, supervised my MA thesis, and gave me valuable advice about professionalization. As a teaching assistant, I was a member of the Communication Workers of America, and I'm grateful to my union, as well as to New York state taxpayers, for supporting my graduate education. I suppose this is the overindulgent welfare state that Saul Bellow demonized in *Mr. Sammler's Planet*, but I think 1930s-era Bellow would have been more sympathetic.

Despite 2008, I've never regretted pursuing a PhD at UC Irvine. I'd like to thank Linda Georgianna for welcoming me back into the fold of literary studies, and arranging a first-year fellowship. Natalka Freeland's seminar in Victorian literature introduced me to cultural anthropology, which informs

chapter three of this book. Jerome Christensen was an awesome HoD, Ann
Van Sant provided encouraging words, and Nancy Benay and Arielle Read
were supportive department managers. I'm especially indebted to Hugh Roberts, whose seminar in Romanticism stimulated my first academic publication, an article on Lord Byron and tourism that eventually morphed into this
book's approach to postwar American literature. The Donald and Dorothy
Strauss Dissertation Fellowship not only enabled the writing of my dissertation but also the completion of my PhD. A few people were helpful during one
of the most painful experiences of my life, when I had a job offer withdrawn—
twice! This was the strange and sad tale of the white commoner who tried to
become part of Sky Castle's royal bloodline (so much more dramatic than
any TV show). I think there should have been an intervention at the administrative level, which would have saved me from falling on the wrong side of
an emergent color line in what some scholars call the Transpacific, and the
many years of unhappiness that followed. Most of all, there would never have
been an imaginary Euro-American who didn't show up for his presentation at
the ELLAK conference, and who angrily said he wasn't coming when an un-
named person called him on the phone. Nevertheless, I'm grateful to Nancy
for putting a roof over my head when I had to leave Verano Place housing upon
award of the PhD, and to Mike Clark and James Steintrager for securing me
adjunct work at UCI.

Along with Mike, Brook Thomas and Richard Godden supervised the dissertation that finally became this book, and I'm thankful for their feedback
as well as their inspiring models of scholarship. John Carlos Rowe moved on
to USC while I was at UCI but has continued to provide mentoring; I wonder
how he manages so many commitments with such warmth. I'd like to thank
my supervisors in the Composition Program, Lynda Haas, Ellen Strenski, and
the late Carla Copenhaven. For many years, I supported myself by teaching
the courses that they designed. In particular, Ellen's award-winning Writing
39C asked students to research a social problem, and then advocate for the passage of a congressional bill or policy plan designed to address the problem—
an inspiring, albeit also sobering, way of relating research in the supposed
ivory tower to politics, and one that made my own political stances less pre-
tentious. Andrew Newman and Peter Leman, PhDs who made good, gave
me job-seeking advice. Ariane Simard proved that a charismatic creative writing MFA and a fusty literary scholar can be friends during the Program Era.
I'm nostalgic about the seminars I took with Aaron Winter, and his parody

newspaper for our English department, *The Ant Farm*; I'm convinced that its successor, *ML Ade*, would have been the *Onion* of our profession. I'm probably not the only one who's wondered if this profession is really worth pursuing if he's not a part of it.

After some rough years on the job market, I was lucky to work at the University of Cape Town. Carrol Clarkson and Meg Samuelson were supportive HoDs who did an extremely difficult job with strength and integrity. Victoria Collis-Buthelezi, John Higgins, and Christopher Ouma were great colleagues, and Peter Anderson kept me entertained with his wonderful sense of humor. It was humbling to teach students who were much more capable than I'd ever been, and I learned from the theses of people like Yannick Triebel. The late Konstantin Sofianos helped me adjust to the Cape. I'd also like to give a special thanks to Rentia Landman, the world's best HR person and someone who gave me support at a critical time, regarding both my career and my sanity.

The institution-positive approach taken by this book is in keeping with the generous support that it has received. Cape Town provided a Block Grant and teaching relief. I thank *English Literary History* for giving me permission to reprint material on Saul Bellow and Elizabeth Bishop, and *Twentieth-Century Literature* for permission to reprint material on Bishop and William S. Burroughs. *TCL*'s editors, Lee Zimmerman and Keith Dallas, were understanding when I told them that I was mugged at knifepoint—on campus—and the thieves made off with my contract for the Burroughs article, among other things. (I'm convinced that when one studies Burroughs, one's own life becomes more Burroughsian. Although this event was deeply traumatic, I've gained an odd comfort from imagining that I ran afoul of the Nova Mob.) Katherine Hazzard, Chris Westcott, and Alex Lewis provided sharp copyediting for these articles, and Lori Paximadis did a masterly job of copyediting the book manuscript. Micheal Sean Bolton, Christopher Breu, Marshall Brown, Oliver Harris, and Rob Johnson commented on the Burroughs material, and Nancy Grace has taught me about Beat Studies in general. Richard Flynn, Douglas Mao, Kirilka Stavreva, Kathleen Woodward, and Stephen Schryer improved the Bishop chapter. I'd like to thank Frances Ferguson for accepting the Bellow article at a key time when she was the editor of *ELH*. Eric Bennett gave helpful advice, and Omid Azadibougar provided hard-to-find materials for the Richard Wright chapter. I'm grateful to Timothy Brennan for comments on the project, and to him and the Said family for sharing the commencement speech that Edward Said wrote for Northfield Mount Hermon

School's 2002 graduation ceremony. Finally, I'd like to give a warm thanks to James McCoy, Meredith Stabel, Tegan Daly, Margaret Yapp, and the marketing team at the University of Iowa Press.

This book is dedicated to my parents, Allen and Courtney Strand. When I read Richard Wright's accounts of religion and impoverishment in his youth, I feel that I'm reading about my dad's midwestern Protestant upbringing in South Dakota. Like several of the writers discussed in the following chapters, Mom and Dad planned to move to Paris, where she would pursue her career as a painter, and he would liberate himself from his man-in-a-gray-flannel-suit job. Instead, Dad was drafted for a war that he opposed, and was in Saigon during the Tet Offensive. Their oldest son has often acted like a spoiled kid while the days of the American Century came to a close. Whatever success I've had is too little and too late, but I hope this book is meaningful for our changed times.

The Global Frontier

Introduction

·····························

For many Americans after World War II, the world was turned inside out: travel to foreign places became ever more convenient, while at the same time domestic interiors were flooded by touristic imagery. Travel was well on its way to becoming the world's largest industry, which led Dean MacCannell to argue that it constitutes our contemporary cultural sensibility; as he remarks in his classic *The Tourist: A New Theory of the Leisure Class* (1976), "everyday life is composed of souvenirs of life elsewhere."[1] Although scholars often focus on anticommunism as the primary ideological means by which elites garnered support for foreign policy initiatives, the appeal of world travel also persuaded the middle class to support Washington's global project. Christina Klein observes that after World War II, the "ordinary American tourist . . . came to be seen as an active figure in the economic integration of the world."[2] During President Truman's promotion of the Marshall Plan, the Economic Cooperation Administration encouraged tourism so as to infuse Europe with US dollars, while in the 1950s popular magazines touted Asia as a destination that was newly open to Americans.

However, there has been little scholarship that connects American literature to the explosion of global travel after World War II. American novelists, essayists, and poets shared our boundary-crossing, globalized era, and represented this mobility through their characters: Beat literature, such as that by Jack Kerouac and William S. Burroughs, was founded upon international travel; Saul Bellow's Augie March spends much of his time in Mexico and Europe, and *Henderson the Rain King* (1958) is set in Africa; Richard Wright and James Baldwin spent little time, if any, in the United States; Elizabeth Bishop, now considered America's premier midcentury poet, lived in Brazil. In contrast, the variety of terms that we have developed for midcentury literary culture—Cold War liberalism, containment culture, the indignant generation, fantasies of the new class, the discourse of the crisis of man—have a sense of nation-based insularity.[3] To be sure, the image of the 1950s as a period of suburban privacy and cultural normalcy has been discredited. Morris Dickstein revised our understanding the period in *Leopards in the Temple: The Transformation of American Fiction, 1945–1970* (2002), which, as its title suggests, argues for a merging of subversive 1950s literature (such as that of the Beats) with later countercultural energies.[4] More recently, Myka Tucker-Abramson locates the gestation of neoliberalism in writers' responses to New York–based urban renewal.[5] However, to use Alan Nadel's term, it is fair to say that the containment culture thesis still holds, insofar as midcentury writers were largely domestic creatures.

In so doing, American literature scholars have missed an engagement with postcolonial studies and the study of travel literature, which have been indissolubly linked since the publication of Edward Said's groundbreaking *Orientalism* (1978). In that work, Said criticized the self/other, master/slave, West/East binaries that served to legitimate colonialism. While *Orientalism* focused mainly on British and French texts, Said paid more attention to postwar American global dominance in *Culture and Imperialism* (1993), in which he has "a depressing sense that one has seen and read about current American policy formulations before. Each great metropolitan center that aspired to global dominance has said, and alas done, many of the same things."[6] But in cultural terms, the midcentury American metropolitan center was different from past centers: it said roughly the same things that Said was later to say in *Culture and Imperialism*. In *Cold War Orientalism: Asia in the Middlebrow Imagination, 1945–1961* (2003), Klein argues that American travel narratives had a cultural ethos that anticipated Said's critique of colonialism and Orientalism. Postwar writers did not narrate encounters with savagery, since they "eschewed the nostalgic search for the premodern and the authentic that has characterized so much Western travel writing about the non-West. Instead, they favored a head-on encounter with the modern."[7] American travel narratives "[were] infused with a structure of feeling that privileged precisely the values of interdependence, sympathy, and hybridity" that Said saw as potentially challenging Orientalism.[8]

However, there is a tension in the title of Klein's book, since "Orientalism" seems a misnomer unless the American Cold War ideology of interdependence and hybridity is actually a West/East binary in a renewed form. On the contrary, Klein gestures toward a "utopian impulse" in such writing that "suggested the potential for challenging the global arrangements of power that Washington pursued."[9] Even a novel like James Michener's *Hawaii* (1959), which is reviled by Asian American and Native Hawaiian scholars, comes off rather well in Klein's account. If postwar American travel narratives contested binaries and extolled cultural hybridity, then we need a different term than *Orientalist* to describe these narratives.

The book will use "frontier" as the central term for the cultural ethos of postwar American travel narratives. As Richard Slotkin observes, "the central mythological trope of American culture" is "the Myth of the Frontier," the terms and symbols of which dominated American culture in the 1950s and '60s.[10] At first, the use of this term for global travel might seem counterintuitive, since Slotkin's work associates the frontier with brutal violence. His magisterial trilogy *Regeneration through Violence* (1973), *The Fatal Environment* (1985), and *Gunfighter Nation* (1992) traces a line from the early Pequot Wars of Puritan settlers to the Vietnam War. White men constitute themselves as frontiersmen through a "face-to-face meeting with the Enemy," a bloody conflict with a savage Other. "It is this industrial and imperial version of the Frontier Myth whose categories still inform our political rhetoric of pioneering progress, world mission, and eternal strife with the forces of darkness and barbarism."[11]

Yet the term "frontier" also suggests new economic and technological developments that foster individual autonomy and material plentitude instead of violence. As Patricia Nelson Limerick points out, the term "frontier" has staying power because it continually revises itself: "[T]he American public has genuinely and completely accepted, ratified, and bought the notion that the American frontiering spirit, sometime in the last century, picked itself up and made a definitive relocation—from territorial expansion to technological and commercial expansion."[12] The concept of the frontier is an elastic one; while it lends itself to replicas of log cabins at Disneyland, it also suggests a more general ethos of independence, creative energy, and innovation, especially in the world of art, music, fashion, and commerce. Hence, "[T]he idea of the frontier and the pioneer have clearly become a kind of multicultural common property, a joint-stock company of the imagination."[13] This model of the frontier as "multicultural common property" is oriented toward creativity instead of violence, cultural syncretism instead of divisions. The phrase "joint-stock company of the imagination" suggests that pioneering can be generalizable across racial and gender positions, as in Limerick's anecdote about her conversations with tour groups and international scholars: "People from the Philippines, people from Senegal, people from Thailand, people with plenty of

reasons to resent the frontier and cowboy diplomacy inflicted on their nations
by our nation: many of them nonetheless grew up watching western movies
and yearning for life on the Old Frontier and the open range."[14]

To elucidate a frontier that involves commerce, technology, and imagination, we might deemphasize the twenty-sixth president of the US, Theodore
Roosevelt, in favor of the historian Frederick Jackson Turner. Turner's famous
essay "The Significance of the Frontier in American History" (1893) argued
that "the existence of an area of free land, its continuous recession, and the
advance of American settlement westward explain American development."[15]
Turner concluded that "now, four centuries from the discovery of America,
at the end of a hundred years of life under the Constitution, the frontier
has gone, and with its going has closed the first period of American history"
(60). For revisionist critics like Slotkin, Turner's thought is "nostalgic," since
his "key terms of value refer to an agrarian past"; for Slotkin as well as Amy
Kaplan, Theodore Roosevelt is the bête noire of aggressive, militaristic American expansion.[16] Theodore Roosevelt is a historical presence throughout the
landmark essay collection *Cultures of United States Imperialism* (1993), while
Turner is cited only twice.[17] Yet Turner's thought has had remarkable staying power, and we might explain this by turning to the context in which he
first presented the thesis, a meeting of the American Historical Association
in 1893.[18] This meeting took place in Chicago concurrently with the World's
Columbian Exposition, a social context that involves globalization in tandem
with professional autonomy. As Lee Benson notes in a thorough study of the
social context for the Frontier Thesis, Turner grew up during the "Communication Revolution," when the "international exchange of commodities and
services took place on a scale virtually unimaginable fifty years earlier," making for a "new global economy."[19] This new global economy accompanied the
growth of what has variously been termed the professional middle class, the
New Class, or the professional-managerial class—a stratum of professional
experts existing between the owners of capital and wage labor.[20] If Turner's
essay was inspired by this global communication revolution, then his famous
essay did not announce the end of the frontier, but rather its beginning.

Turner's own professional status helps to explain the rhetoric of the frontier essays, which often has precious little to do with the realities of wilderness survival. His signature essay celebrates "that masterful grasp of material
things, lacking in the artistic but powerful to effect great ends; that restless,
nervous energy; that dominant individualism, working for good and for evil,

and withal that buoyancy and exuberance which comes with freedom" (*FJT* 59). He ends "The West and American Ideals" (1914) with a long quotation from Tennyson's poem "Ulysses" (1842) to support his assertion that frontier life involved "self-confidence," "aspiration," and "creative genius" (*FJT* 155). I suggest that we can read the Frontier Thesis self-reflexively, as an assertion of professional creativity: Turner arguably turned the omnipresent simulacra of the log cabin and the wagon train into a narrative of middle-class self-affirmation, an ethos of individualism and empowerment. While he grew up in the "quasi-frontier atmosphere of Central Wisconsin," he had a middle-class background, as his father was a newspaper owner and editor.[21] Turner's primary milieu was not hunting, trapping, or farming, but rather the manipulation of the written word, which enabled an academic career that took him to the presidency of the American Historical Association and a professorship at Harvard. Numerous passages in his essays allegorize his own upward mobility, which was based on "creative and competitive individualism" (*FJT* 155). Indeed, for Turner the intellectual autonomy and stress on education that is characteristic of professionalism informs the world of agricultural labor itself. Writing in *The Atlantic Monthly* in 1903, Turner argues that "Even as he dwelt among the stumps of his newly-cut clearing, the pioneer had the creative vision of a new order of society. . . . He decreed that his children should enter into a heritage of education, comfort, and social welfare, and for this ideal he bore the scars of the wilderness" (*FJT* 95). Sitting among wood stumps, the pioneer dreams of upward mobility in a complex society, his children members of an emergent professional middle class.

One can therefore reverse the conventional understanding of Turner, orienting it from a nostalgic past to his active present: he did not provide middle-class Americans with a sepia-toned portrait of their frontier heritage, but rather enabled this middle class to think of its upward mobility in terms of frontier independence. Hence, when Turner redefined the pioneer as a professional in the early twentieth century, he was only making explicit what had been there all along.[22] "Pioneer Ideals and the State University" (1910) identifies the contemporary pioneer as a technocrat who will further industrial development and serve the state in an administrative and legal capacity. "How shall we conserve what was best in pioneer ideals?" Turner asks, before identifying the state university as the institution that will adjust such ideals to "the new requirements of American democracy" (*FJT* 112, 117). He argues that a "complex modern society" needs a class of "expert[s]" that will ameliorate conflict between labor and capital (114–15). Modeling what we might term a university-trained pioneer professional, Turner emphasizes that "science and society have not crystallized, but are still growing and need their pioneer trail-makers. . . . The test tube and the microscope are needed rather than ax and rifle in this new ideal of conquest" (117, 114).

In this view, the core tension in the Frontier Thesis is not the disappearance of free land but rather the professional's relationship to reformist government, and much of Turner's post-1893 career can be read as a struggle to reconcile the two models. As Richard Hofstadter notes, "Turner was among the earliest of modern American scholars to see how important the expert would become in the business of government."[23] Yet Turner was better at mythologizing upward mobility than explaining how middle-class professionalism could reform industrial society. Instead, he often imagined the frontier's literal extension through global space. "For nearly three centuries the dominant fact in American life has been expansion," Turner writes in 1896, arguing that the future holds "the extension of American influence to outlying islands and adjoining countries" (*FJT* 73–74). In 1914 he references Thomas H. Benton's dream of a "regenerated Orient": "Across the Pacific looms Asia, no longer a remote vision and a symbol of the unchanging, but borne as by mirage close to our shores and raising grave questions of the common destiny of the people of the ocean" (146).

It is fair to say that Turner never reconciled these competing visions of the pioneer professional—one oriented toward an ever-expanding global market, one oriented toward an activist state and social reform. His own faith in reform diminished during the Roaring Twenties, a period of political corruption and a sense of complacency bred of affluence. Instead of endorsing leftist politicians like Robert La Follette, a senator from his home state of Wisconsin who ran for the presidency in 1924, Turner oriented himself toward "the unrestrained individualism of the frontier past, an individualism free of all governmental interference."[24] A supporter and confidante of Herbert Hoover, Turner died in 1932, months before Franklin Delano Roosevelt took office and inaugurated the New Deal. According to biographer Ray Allen Billington, "the world of Frederick Jackson Turner died . . . when the Great Depression brought into focus the giant social upheaval that had been shaping for a generation. The new America that emerged was adjusted to a closed-space existence, its governmental philosophy was built on the belief that men must be protected from corporate exploitation now that escape to the West was no longer possible."[25] During the 1930s, the Frontier Thesis was deemed to be too individualistic for a more collectivist age of national solidarity and large-scale government intervention in the economy. This also affected the way in which American writers conceived of travel.

New Deal Tourism: The American Guide Series

The New Deal era involved a class-based nationalist politics, and at this time, even the American president made a systematic critique of the Frontier Thesis. As the historian Warren Susman notes, the image of Turner's pioneer was debated throughout the 1920s, with some valorizing an "extreme individualism, courage . . . [and] aloofness from social ties" that "might continue to withstand the onrush of standardization and conformity," and others attacking the pioneer ethos for opposing "high culture and social reform."[26] However, "only in the late 1920s did any systematic critique appear that questioned the truth and the efficacy of the Turner thesis itself. . . . [T]he Great Depression of 1929 stimulated thinking anew of the problems of [American] history."[27] In various speeches and publications, Franklin D. Roosevelt emphasized that a closed frontier necessitated coordinated state planning: "There is no safety valve in the form of a western prairie to which those thrown out of work by the Eastern economic machines can go for a new start."[28] The assessment is anachronistic where free land is concerned, since according to Turner, that safety valve had been shut off over four decades earlier. Roosevelt announced not the disappearance of free land but rather the advent of a modern welfare state, guided in part by reform-minded professionals.

The New Deal is still underappreciated by contemporary scholars in literary and cultural studies, even when their work attests to its value. In Michael Denning's magisterial survey of the 1930s, *The Cultural Front* (1996), a leftist militance informed a broad array of artistic productions in what he calls the "laboring" of American culture. *The Cultural Front* might be the best account we have of artists' relationship to New Deal reformism, yet Denning uses his terms for this cultural ethos—the Popular Front, the Cultural Front, the Age of the CIO (Congress of Industrial Organizations)—in such a way as to keep his radicalism safe from Roosevelt.[29] As Michael Szalay remarks, "Denning's desire to understand the Popular Front as a radical, working-class coalition depends on repressing the New Deal . . . [his] quick and often glib characterizations of New Deal liberalism are meant to dismiss from the start the very real possibility that numerous writers sympathetic to the left during the thirties saw the nascent welfare state in terms as utopian as they were ideological."[30] This belief in the possibility of the welfare state crossed racial lines, since even a critic like W. E. B. Du Bois eventually endorsed Roosevelt, as biographer David Levering Lewis points out. "Roosevelt's WPA had literally kept a million black people from starving to death, Du Bois calculated. . . . Whatever the president's mistakes and shortcomings, Du Bois reached a judgment he would hold to permanently that FDR was 'the only living man who can lead the United States on the path which will eventually abolish poverty.'"[31]

Contemporary American tourism, so overwhelmingly focused on getting away from it all, has its roots in the collectivist ethos of the New Deal era. As Michael Berkowitz argues in his essay "A 'New Deal' for Leisure," the growth of the twentieth-century American tourist industry is inseparable from government initiative. Berkowitz observes that instead of contracting during the 1930s, the travel industry expanded, as more American workers than ever enjoyed vacations. White-collar workers were the pacesetters in this development, since management theorists argued that intellectual labor, as opposed to manual labor, required a period of rest and relaxation; middle-class professionals would then be happier and more productive. Eventually blue-collar workers themselves employed this argument, leading to union demands for paid vacations as well as higher wages and benefits. "As the 1930s progressed, management's desire to secure industrial peace and labor's increasing militancy and consumerist ideology brought about a frenzied expansion of paid vacations to a majority of wage earners."[32] In this view, the taking of vacations was not merely relaxing but a "personal Keynesian stimulus" that would help the national economy to recover.[33] Even President Roosevelt played the role of a tourism promoter, taking his family on well-publicized vacations to national parks. In 1937, Roosevelt's government established the United States Travel Bureau, whose slogan became "Travel Strengthens America. It promotes the nation's health, wealth, and unity."

While paid vacations might at first seem very far from 1930s writers' concerns, Roosevelt made travel intensely relevant when he approved the Federal Arts Projects on September 12, 1935. A subsection of the Works Progress Administration (WPA), "Federal One" was comprised of four major projects devoted to writing, theater, music, and the visual arts. As Brian Dolinar emphasizes, "[t]he idea of creating a taxpayer-funded project to put unemployed writers back to work might seem like a far-fetched idea today, as politicians

call for reducing the size of 'big government,'" but even in the progressive
1930s, "the boldness of the undertaking... cannot be underestimated."[34] One
of the major endeavors of the Federal Writers' Project (FWP) was the American Guide Series, which created travel guides for each American state as well
as several major cities such as New York and San Francisco. Each volume of
the American Guide Series was divided into three sections: essays that described a state's history, culture, and economy, including an essay on literature; a description of the state's major cities; and specific tours—itineraries
that the tourist could pursue. The guides unabashedly sought to promote the
New Deal, as when the Tennessee state guide not only lavished attention upon
the Tennessee Valley Authority (TVA), but put one of the TVA dams on its
cover. Yet they were not merely government propaganda efforts or make-do
work for struggling writers. As the historian Jerrold Hirsch puts it, the guides
"develop[ed] a hopeful myth that mixed traditional American themes with
New Deal pluralism and reform."[35]

The Guides are absent from much scholarship on travel writing. For
example, Paul Fussell does not give any indication that they existed, although
he has appreciative words for Germany's Baedeker guides, which included
hugely successful English-language volumes. "What seems to make the Baedeker guides so clear an expression of the period [of modernist travel] is their
emphasis on seeing and learning, rather than, as in such successors as Fodor
and Fielding, on consuming."[36] Fussell is very concerned with this distinction
between travel and tourism, claiming that in contrast to the shallow tourist,
the traveler seeks knowledge and meaningful experience. In his introductions
to the selections in *Norton Book of Travel* (1987), he narrates the rise and fall
of travel writing, from its ascent during the Grand Tour of English aristo-
crats, to the golden age of modernist travel writing, to our own supposedly
narcissistic, image-oriented present. Although I will discuss Fussell's traveler/
tourist opposition in places, this opposition is not my book's central concern,
and I will often use the terms *traveler* and *tourist* interchangeably. Instead,
the central tension in *The Global Frontier* is between a commitment to state-
guided reform and progressive nationalism on one hand and the personal freedom of global travel and expatriate life on the other. Fussell's classic *Abroad:
British Literary Traveling Between the Wars* (1980) itself exemplifies this tension. The book has been criticized for its admiration for upper-crust white
males, but Fussell, an American critic, also takes part in a postwar tendency
to view government as a bureaucratic edifice that is antithetical to creativity

and self-expression, a view that crosses party lines (Fussell was a Democrat). In *Abroad*, Fussell uses the term "frontier" in its European sense—as a border between two countries—but his own sensibility is more akin to the American frontier. In *Abroad*, British writers try to escape state institutions for a free space of self-reinvention, even when these institutions are potentially capable of addressing social inequality. For example, Fussell makes a witty yet problematic criticism of passports, which involve "the numbers used in the modern world for personnel identification and coercion—social-security numbers, taxpayer numbers, driver-license numbers, license-plate numbers."[37] When the traveler returns from a holiday, his passage through immigration control is a moment of humiliation instead of triumph, "a reminder that he is merely the state's creature, one of his realm's replaceable parts."[38] But the state can also enable individuals; when one reads Fussell's book alongside the British public's support for the Beveridge Plan, which instituted their postwar welfare state, his criticism of "personnel identification and coercion" seems reductive.

Stimulated in part by the Great Recession of 2008, there has been a tide of excellent work on Federal One and the FWP, as well as the publication of forgotten or previously unpublished documents. Scott Borchert has made a convincing case for the literary merit of the Guides, "among the unlikeliest weapons in the improvised arsenal that the Roosevelt administration brought to bear upon the Depression": "These books sprawled. They hoarded and gossiped and sat you down for a lecture. They seemed to address multiple readers at once from multiple perspectives. . . . They guided tourists across the land but also deep into the national character, into a past that was assembled from the mythic and the prosaic, the factual and the farcical. The tours seemed less accessories for motorists than rambling day trips through the unsorted mind of the Republic."[39] Focusing in particular on the literature essays contained in the guidebooks, Wendy Griswold's *American Guides: The Federal Writers' Project and the Casting of American Culture* (2016) argues that the guides have had an overlooked influence on American literary culture. She uses the word "casting" in two senses: first, the guides encouraged Americans to think of each state as having its own unique culture. "[When] the Federal Writers' Project came along . . . states, not broader territories like the Midwest or New England, [became] the cultural units of regionalism. It was as if the federal government poured preexisting cultural differences into state-shaped molds, where they then hardened."[40] In addition to casting American literature into state molds, the guides introduced "a cast of heterogenous characters in the

nation's definition of its own culture . . . bringing women and minorities into
the nation's literary pantheon."[41] This second casting was not only related to
New Deal pluralism, but also the consequence of specific federal directives:
the guidebook essays that surveyed literature had to construct a literary tradition for each individual state, leading to the inclusion of a wide range of
women authors and more racial minorities. As Griswold puts it, "those who
looked into what the Guides had to say about this literature found women,
Native Americans, Hispanics, African Americans, theologians, cowboy poets,
explorers, proletarian novelists, the talented, the connected, the obscure—
a wildly diverse cast that, according to the federal government, made up the
ongoing production of 'Our Literature, from Sea to Shining Sea.'"[42] This aspect of the Guides not only anticipated the canon opening of the 1970s and
1980s, but may have influenced it: generations of students and researchers,
checking the guides out of libraries, were encouraged to think of American
literature in more capacious terms.

The Guides may have eventually changed the way Americans thought of
literature, but did they have an influence on literature at the time? FWP head
Henry Alsberg noted of a stigmatized genre, "The tour form is a difficult form;
it is like a sonnet; but, if you can learn it, you can be more interesting in the
description of a tour than in any novel."[43] Richard Wright was hired as an
FWP supervisor in 1935; reversing Alsberg's dictum, he turned the Guides'
tour form into poetry and novels (as well as his own travel books in the 1950s,
as I shall explain in a later chapter). His lengthy free verse poem "Transcontinental" (1936) is an example of how a Black leftist writer made creative use
of his FWP research. At first it might seem difficult to reconcile the poem's
vision of "collective farms" and "The Red Army . . . on the march" with the
Guides' nationalist affirmation.[44] Yet the poetic speaker of "Transcontinental" is not himself engaged in collective farming but rather going sightseeing,
viewing a panorama through the windshield as he floors the accelerator:

> The farms are a storm of green
> Past rivers past towns
> 50 60 70 80
> America America . . .
> Into Ohio Into the orchards of Michigan
> Over the rising and falling dunes of Indiana
> Across Illinois' glad fields of dancing corn

> Slowing Comrades Slowing again
> Slowing for the heart of proletarian America
> CHICAGO—100 MILES[45]

To borrow phrasing from Griswold, Wright pours international communism into the state-shaped molds of the American Guides. "Transcontinental" was inspired by the French communist Louis Aragon's "The Red Front" (1933), a poem of class-based militancy that takes the locomotive as its symbol of social change. Wright transforms the train into a car, and the Red Front into Popular Front Americana, imagining the novelist Mike Gold's account of a proletarian revolution selling "26 million copies," as well as a baseball game played by "Kenji Sumarira . . . Boris Petrovsky . . . Wing Sing . . . Eddie O'Brien."[46] Wright's automobile tour advances cultural pluralism while paying homage to a New Deal icon, Walt Whitman:

> Hop on the runningboard Pile in . . .
> Slowing Slowing for the sharecroppers
> Come on You Negroes Come on
> There's room
> Not in the back but front seat . . .
> Say You Red Men You Forgotten Men
> Come out from your tepees
> Show us Pocahontas . . . Tuck her in beside us[47]

In Nathaniel Mills's reading, "Transcontinental" celebrates the revolutionary agency of lumpenproletarians, members of an urban underclass who were denigrated in conventional Marxist thought as potentially reactionary thieves and idlers.[48] However, Wright's granting of agency to marginalized people does not rule out a reading of the poetic narrator's car as the FWP itself, which was remarkably diverse for the time period. As Jerre Mangione notes in his memoir *The Dream and the Deal* (1973), an invaluable eyewitness account of the FWP, 40 percent of the FWP's employees were women.[49] Not a conventional Washington bureaucrat, Alsberg was a Jewish socialist, as well as a closeted gay man, who had lived in Greenwich Village during the 1920s. He encouraged the New York FWP office to hire Claude McKay as well as Richard Bruce Nugent, thereby helping to support Black and queer writers after the system of private patronage had collapsed.[50] Contemporary scholars like Maryemma Graham and Thadious Davis have emphasized that the FWP was a far greater influence on African American writing than the earlier Harlem Renaissance.[51]

I am not claiming that the Guides were beyond criticism, since they could practice exclusions and indulge in stereotypes.[52] Black Americans comprised only 2 percent of the FWP's workforce, and Sterling Brown often became disenchanted with the bureaucratic demands of his job.[53] Nevertheless, I think we would err in writing off the FWP and its various activities, which included the compilation of slave narratives and folklore, as well as many travel-oriented books in addition to the guides themselves. The academic humanities are still influenced by a Foucaultian conception of the state that emphasizes control and normalization, while overlooking programs that can empower marginalized people. For example, while Wright's image in "Transcontinental" of Black and white leftists inviting Pocahontas onto their car might seem sheer fancy, it does register a sea change in the national government's relationship to Native Americans, in what has been called the Indian New Deal. In 1934, Congress passed the Indian Reorganization Act, which rejected assimilationist policies regarding tribes in favor of greater political autonomy. Roosevelt's alphabet soup of programs, including the WPA, built infrastructure as well as schools and hospitals on reservation lands. Put simply, whereas Theodore Roosevelt saw Native Americans primarily as antagonists, and Turner simply erased them from his imaginary frontier, Roosevelt sought to make Native Americans a part of his reimagined national community. In keeping with the FWP's mission to provide accurate representations of Native Americans in the Guides, Alsberg appointed the Native American writer and activist D'Arcy McNickle, author of the novel *The Surrounded* (1936), as editor of the "Indian and Archaeology" department. While the guidebook editors often resisted making Indigenous cultures a part of American modernity, "correct[ing] misperceptions . . . without actually transferring power to the communities themselves," Native American writers and communities found a voice in the state-level programs, especially that of Montana.[54] According to Mindy J. Morgan, "these state-sponsored projects illustrate how the wide scope of the FWP allowed for representations of tribal communities to emerge that sometimes challenged the uniform images of Native Americans presented by the national office. Individual fieldworkers were the primary authors of the material, and their collected texts reflected and stimulated discussions within the communities about their own history and concerns for future generations."[55]

One way of looking at this New Deal coalition is that various cultures of the modernist 1920s were able to coalesce around an activist state and a progressive nationalism in the following decade. The Great Depression's focus on social class accompanied cultural pluralism; economic and political integration did not entail cultural homogenization. This activist state and its legacy have been overlooked by participants in our still ongoing culture wars. For example, David Hollinger's *Postethnic America: Beyond Multiculturalism* (1996) is based on a contrast between two thinkers of the early twentieth century, Horace Kallen and Randolph Bourne. According to Hollinger, Kallen's multiculturalism insisted on the integrity of different cultural groups; Kallen thus opposed both white nationalism and the assimilative model of the melting pot. In contrast, Bourne, "multiculturalism's most illustrious precursor and prophet," went beyond multiculturalism by celebrating "dynamic mixing" instead of distinctive groups.[56] Hollinger extends this opposition to 1990s America, arguing that while contemporary multiculturalism has been important in countering white supremacist models of American society, the national ideal should be a more Bournean cosmopolitan model of voluntary affiliations. This postethnic perspective "appreciates multiple identities, pushes for communities of wide scope, recognizes the constructed character of ethno-racial groups, and accepts the formation of new groups as a part of the normal life of a democratic society."[57] While I endorse Hollinger's model of national solidarity and voluntary affiliations, he needs a stronger, class-oriented model of activist government, so that Americans are empowered to choose these affiliations. After all, in various leftist academic circles, *everyone* is against multiculturalism—for the philosopher Slavoj Žižek, it is the cultural logic of neoliberal capitalism, and for American studies scholars like Jodi Melamed and Nikhil Pal Singh, multiculturalism is white supremacy's strategy for defusing radical demands for democracy and racial justice.[58] Hollinger acknowledges that a white/Black binary still fissures the US, but gives the federal government an attenuated role in combating injustice. In the age of globalization, it might be easiest for a transnational elite to pursue a Bournean model of voluntary cultural affiliations.

If Roosevelt had managed to pass his Second Bill of Rights, we might now be closer to living in a genuinely progressive multicultural or even postethnic America. Unfortunately, the exigencies of World War II canceled out this earlier era of earnest, if halting, advances toward social justice. It was a military Keynesianism, stimulated by the world war and then the Korean War, that finally ended the Great Depression. During the president's self-described transformation from "Dr. New Deal" to "Dr. Win the War," the US military was segregated, and his Executive Order 9066 sent over 120,000 Japanese Americans to internment camps.[59] Nevertheless, I think there is a case to be made for Dr. New Deal, especially focusing on its evocation of FDR as a professional, one oriented toward the good health of the nation. As the historian James Kloppenberg relates, in his 1944 State of the Union Address, Roosevelt announced the Second Bill of Rights, which would ensure that every American had access to education, housing, a living wage, universal health care, and various forms of insurance. This American welfare state would rival any in Europe, and outdo the United Kingdom's Beveridge Plan. Facing an opposition comprised of Republicans and conservative Southern Democrats, Roosevelt's plan "was quickly branded 'socialist, fascist, and medieval,' an omnibus charge that indicted the Roosevelt administration for moving at once too fast, too slow, too far to the left, and too far to the right. Roosevelt had reason to act cautiously in 1944: charges of dictatorship and collectivism were fighting words."[60] Although Roosevelt himself may have thought that Federal One had served its purpose, it is worth noting that there were various plans to make the FWP a permanent institution; Wright, in particular, campaigned to convert the FWP into a "People's Art Project."[61] Reflecting on the ruins of the New Deal, Du Bois said it best: "None can say how far Franklin Roosevelt would have gone in reorganizing the economy of the nation if the work of the first eight years of his reign had continued and expanded. We might now live in a different world. But war intervened and once again, as so often in the past, ruined the future of mankind."[62]

The above quotation is from the last book Du Bois published in his lifetime, the novel *Worlds of Color* (1961). This was the concluding volume of his *Black Flame Trilogy*, a semi-autobiographical work of both fact and fantasy that centered on the academic Manuel Mansart. *Worlds of Color* constructs a myth about the New Deal, imagining that FDR was assassinated by a cabal of American financiers who "hated Franklin Roosevelt with perfect hatred. They cursed this crippled traitor to his class, who after refusing Hitler's blackmail, joined Communists to prevent American business from corralling the earth. These insane seekers for power swore by earth, heaven and hell to kill the God-damned meddler and wipe his memory from history."[63] Mansart is part of a "hard core of opposition" that includes "the socialists, the liberals, and the New Dealers," in a book that features an extended cameo appearance from (it is impossible to finish this sentence without an exclamation point) the WPA administrator and presidential advisor Harry Hopkins![64] But the president is murdered, which starts "the great march from the Revolution of Roosevelt to the counter-revolution of Truman."[65] I think it is fair to equate the narrator's view with that of the book's author, since Du Bois himself had run for the US Senate in 1950 as the candidate of the American Labor Party, promising to "restore the New Deal, and inaugurate the welfare state" in a campaign speech.[66] When he began his trilogy, Du Bois clearly had a lot of free time on his hands, but could not leave the country during a golden age of American tourism. Persecuted during the Red Scare, he was (as it were) the Man Without a Passport, with this key form of identification confiscated by the government for most of the 1950s. As such, he embodied what Doug Rossinow calls the "Second Progressive Era," a period lasting from 1924 to 1948, during which activists attempted to "push American politics to the left and bring incrementalist reformers along on the movement for social transformation."[67] While Du Bois stood fast against Senator Joseph McCarthy, younger writers revised or discarded their New Deal sensibilities, pursuing the freedoms of what I am calling the global frontier.

Postwar Travel and the Global Frontier

After World War II, American writer-travelers would see themselves in terms of a globalizing frontier instead of nation-centered New Deal solidarities. As Kloppenberg remarks: "'What? Me Sacrifice?' was the characteristic American response to calls for solidarity. Confidence in business and commitment to the superiority of the American way of life soared during the war and peaked at the war's end.... Americans were ready to celebrate, not ready to reform."[68] Meanwhile, the FWP's nation-centered initiatives morphed into imperial forms, providing a context for American literature that remains understudied. In the journal *Partisan Review*'s symposium on midcentury American culture, Norman Mailer observed that "a large proportion of writers, intellectuals, [and] critics . . . have moved their economic luggage from the WPA to the Luce chain."[69] Mailer's remark suggests that the American Guide Series became converted into the *Life* World Library, in keeping with the transition from Roosevelt's New Deal to *Time* and *Life* owner Henry Luce's American Century.

Luce's essay "The American Century," which appeared in the February 17, 1941, issue of *Life* magazine, might be read as a reformulation of the Frontier Thesis for the postwar era. Urging the United States to confront Hitler, Luce writes: "We start into this war with huge government debt, a vast bureaucracy and a whole generation of young people trained to look to the Government as the source of all life. The Party in power is the one which for long years has been most sympathetic to all manner of socialist doctrines and collectivist trends. The President of the United States has continually reached for more and more power."[70] Later in his essay, Luce says that FDR can become "the greatest rather than the last of American Presidents," but only if he abandons his ostensible commitment to national socialism in favor of "a vision of America as a world power which is authentically American," which involves the construction of a "vital international economy" and "an international moral order."[71] The young people who were inspired by the New Deal, which included FDR's brain trust of professional experts as well as Federal One's arts projects, are now to become pioneers of globalization: "America . . . will send out through the world its technical and artistic skills. Engineers, scientists, doctors, movie men, . . . builders of roads, teachers, educators."[72] To be sure, many of these professionals were not as ideologically doctrinaire as Luce and tried to retain progressive ideals, yet they often shared his sense that the US could serve as a beacon for the rest of the world.

This change in political outlooks was accompanied by a resurgence of what we might call Turner studies. As noted above, Turner was a labile thinker and there are diverse interpretations of his work, but I think his writings lend themselves best to a vision of national expansion accompanied by professional empowerment.[73] In 1956, the historian William Appleman Williams stressed that the Frontier Thesis had been central for several generations of intellectuals and policymakers: "[Turner's] statement of the idea . . . became the central, if not the only, thesis of Everyman's History of the United States. His personal influence touched Woodrow Wilson and perhaps Theodore Roosevelt, while his generalization guided subsequent generations of intellectuals and business men who became educational leaders, wielders of corporate power, government bureaucrats, and crusaders for the free world."[74] Here Williams describes a largely uninterrupted program of expansion, but it is important to reemphasize that this expansionist Frontier Thesis had been discredited in the 1930s.[75] For example, although Billington later became a propagandist for the frontier concept as well as Turner's biographer, his first book, *The Protestant Crusade* (1938), was a criticism of nativism and anti-Catholicism that did not cite Turner and only mentioned the frontier in passing, claiming "[it] had no effect on American behavioral patterns."[76] While a professor at Clark University, Billington served as the director of the Massachusetts office of the FWP, a productive unit that churned out several volumes in addition to the requisite state guide. The Massachusetts FWP became embroiled in scandal when *Massachusetts: A Guide to Its Places and People* (1937) was attacked by critics for its pro-labor viewpoint and, in particular, its discussion of the 1927 Sacco and Vanzetti trial, which had been a pivotal event for the American left.

Billington's postwar extolling of the frontier was stimulated by a market opportunity generated by American globalization. He was approached by another historian who suggested they coauthor a college textbook based on Turner's Western history course at Harvard. Synthesizing Turner's notes, course outlines, and essays into a panoramic narrative of development, Billington was the sole author of *Westward Expansion: The History of the American Frontier* (1949), which was longer than anything Turner himself had ever written. Although his book did not discredit the welfare state, Billington had become a full-bore American exceptionalist who believed the nation had transcended class conflict, as frontier individualism "blaze[d] the trails into the newer world of co-operative democracy that is the American future."[77] Even scholars who had reservations about Turner nevertheless contributed to his revival. In *Virgin Land* (1950), Henry Nash Smith claims that the Frontier Thesis "made it difficult for Americans to think of themselves as members of a world community because it has affirmed that the destiny of this country leads her away from Europe toward the agricultural interior of the continent."[78] But if we read the Frontier Thesis as an allegory of upward mobility and professional creativity, then *Virgin Land* is quite Turnerian in its establishment of a myth-and-symbol school that was its own American exceptionalist discourse. It is also important to consider the audience for books like *Westward Expansion* and *Virgin Land*. In the chapters that follow, I shall often discuss the Servicemen's Readjustment Act of 1944, or the "GI Bill of Rights," which can be considered a truncated form of the Second Bill of Rights—more a diminution of FDR's social vision than an extension of it. The GI Bill not only put students in Billington's and Smith's classes, but also enabled the boom in postwar tourism. The academic revival of Turner after World War II arguably helped to make the frontier the "central mythological trope" for college students as well as travelers in an era of American economic and technological expansion.[79] However, although the GI Bill primarily enabled white males, other Americans partook in this frontier mythology.

In the pages that follow, I do not argue that postwar writers thought in completely different terms than prior literary travelers. For example, European ways of conceiving of race and otherness persist in American narratives, and at times I will use "Orientalist" as a descriptor, in keeping with Said's seminal work. Nevertheless, *The Global Frontier* insists on a different governing term for the narratives' cultural ethos; instead of *Orientalism*'s stress on a "master-slave binary" and its variations—self/other, West/rest—the concept of the frontier foregrounds the tension between the nation-centered reformism of the 1930s and the more individualistic freedoms of the postwar era.[80] These freedoms involved transnational forms of identity formation that have been celebrated in more recent decades, especially since the end of the Cold War. The point here is not to construct an American exceptionalist account of midcentury travel, but rather to emphasize that we will not perceive the American exceptionalism if we automatically valorize the crossing of national boundaries and the cultural resistance of seemingly marginalized travelers. As Tony Tanner remarked in one of the first major surveys of postwar American fiction, *City of Words* (1971), writers had a "tendency . . . to posit society as a vast hostile mass. . . . All control is regarded as bad control; any authority is immediately interpreted as part of a malign authoritarianism stalking through the land seeking what further individual freedoms it may devour."[81] Yet the privilege of going abroad to escape such control was enabled precisely by global American authority. The ideology and itineraries of postwar writers overlapped with those of Williams's "wielders of corporate power, government bureaucrats, and crusaders for the free world," despite the writers' insistence that they contested the American mainstream.[82]

This complicity is revealed by the overlap of postwar creative writing with the tenets of modernization theory, an academic field that is informed by frontier mythology. As the historian Michael Latham explains, modernization theory was developed by midcentury social scientists who placed the United States "at the apex of their historical scale and then set about marking off the distance of less modern societies from that point."[83] At first it might seem counterintuitive to associate the nation-building project of modernization theory with the more individualistic ethos of the frontier. However, modernization theory partakes in postwar Turnerism insofar as theorists envisioned a globalized space for economic advancement and self-improvement, and valorized technocrats who would guide modernizing nations. In the view of the modernization theorists, the social conflicts of the 1930s had largely been resolved, allowing the US to serve as a beacon for poorer nations (including war-torn Western European countries). The Rooseveltian model of the

Democratic Party largely died with Henry Wallace's failed presidential run in 1948, and insofar as power elites sought to redesign developing countries in accordance with postwar America's newly triumphal capitalism, modernization theory was more a flight from the New Deal era than a fulfillment of it. Jonathan Nashel has even suggested that the American discourse of modernization-in-fast-forward was a packaged product, in keeping with the cars and Coca-Cola that flooded the Third World: "the modernization theory of the 1950s can be seen as America's entry into a market-style competition with the tenets of Marxism to win over their Southeast Asian consumers."[84] In keeping with this market-style professionalism, modernization theorists often drew on frontier imagery; the author of *The Passing of Traditional Society* (1958), Daniel Lerner, appealed to a wide audience with "The Grocer and the Chief" (1955), an essay in *Harper's Magazine* about a Turkish village—in effect, a frontier town—that is shown the way to capitalist modernity by a small entrepreneur who dreams big.[85] The author of *The Stages of Economic Growth* (1960), Walt Whitman Rostow, coined the term "New Frontier" while working as a speechwriter for the Kennedy campaign, and then joined the newly elected president as a key advisor.[86] As I will show, even the writing of Bishop and Wright overlapped with Rostow's thought, while Bellow and Kerouac can be related to one of the New Frontier's institutional offspring, the Peace Corps, which had a problematic relationship with consumerism and globalization despite its high ideals.

The best-known founder of postcolonial studies, Edward Said, was a steadfast opponent of ideologues like Rostow. Yet Said was also a paragon of American professional creativity and geographic mobility, and this book's more detailed analysis of postwar travelers will begin with him. In his study of literature's relationship to the discourse of modernization and development, Guy Reynolds notes that there are "very real differences between Said's Orientalism (as mapped onto classic European imperialist texts) and U.S. late modern readings of otherness. The subject here is not the classic colonial subject of postcolonial theory . . . [but] a self capable of transition between different social orders; a self responsive to and shaped by modern media; the self with a 'lifeway'; a consumerized self."[87] This is actually an excellent description of Said himself. As John Carlos Rowe observes, much of Said's "critical consciousness" was "deeply 'American,' just as he was himself not only a sometime scholar of American literature and culture but personally, existentially, and legally American."[88] "Existentially . . . American" is a striking characterization that suggests a reassessment of Said's persona, which is usually described in terms of marginalization and exile. As Rowe emphasizes, Said's cosmopolitanism, which Said contrasted with the rigid West/East binary of Orientalism, "has very strong roots both in the myth of American selfhood criticized effectively by the American myth critics and in American expatriates' careful cultivation of their 'otherness' abroad. . . . His role as a public intellectual cannot be understood without analyzing his affiliations with the Euro-American modernists, the New York intellectuals, [and] myths of the 'American Adam.'"[89] Some who knew Said well might insist that "American" was only one of his identities as a world traveler, and that he was primarily an Arab intellectual who felt most at home among his Arab contemporaries, but Rowe's relation of Said to midcentury American culture is worth pursuing.

Where Said's American identity is concerned, the first observation to make is that he did not experience the Great Depression, nor did he associate with intellectuals who could have conveyed the spirit of its leftist movements. This was true even of the English professor F. W. Dupee, Said's friend and colleague at Columbia University, although Dupee was a contrarian thinker who later opposed the Vietnam War. As Said remarks in the introduction to *Reflections on Exile*, "I discovered that the battles the New York intellectuals were still engaged in over Stalinism and Soviet Communism simply did not have much interest for me or for most of my generation, for whom the civil rights movement and the resistance against the U.S. war in Vietnam were much more important and formative."[90] For Said, Frances Stonor Saunders's *The Cultural Cold War* (1999) discredited these intellectuals with its revelations of CIA funding for anticommunist writers and journals, but the CIA's larger victory was to take part in blotting out the memory of progressive movements and institutions in which the New York intellectuals and *Partisan Review* only played a small part.[91] Said's biographer, Timothy Brennan, points out that "entering the United States at the height of the Cold War would color Said's feelings about the country for the rest of his life. . . . Said deeply distrusted the Cold War mentality all around him, the anti-Soviet paranoia, [and] the disregard for third-world realities."[92] Said was understandably perturbed by this Cold War mentality, but he seems unaware that it overwrote an earlier era in American political and social history. As Dickstein reminds us, "McCarthyism and militant anti-Communism were less a reaction to the Soviet threat abroad or disloyalty and espionage at home than a political wedge used by Republicans to fracture the New Deal coalition, in the same way that they would recapture power by demonizing liberalism in the 1980s."[93] This New Deal coalition is a major lacuna in Said's thought, and one might argue more generally that postcolonial studies does not pay enough attention to social class.[94]

Although the title of Said's memoir, *Out of Place* (1999), evokes cultural and political uprooting, his book also speaks to self-reinvention and upward mobility. One of his father's stories, "told and retold many times while I was growing up, was his narrative of coming to the United States . . . intended, in Horatio Alger fashion, to instruct and inform his listeners, who were mostly his children and wife."[95] Said's father earned American citizenship through military service in World War I, then set up a paint company in Cleveland after the war. As Said puts it, "return[ing] to Palestine in 1920 armed with U.S. citizenship, William A. Said (formerly Wadie Ibrahim) . . . turned sober pioneer, hardworking and successful businessman, and Protestant, a resident first of Jerusalem then of Cairo."[96] Said's pioneering father established a highly successful stationery business, and although he was based in Cairo and, later, in Beirut, he continued to feel a patriotic American sensibility: "He always averred that America was his country, and when we strenuously disagreed about Vietnam, he would fall back comfortably on 'My country, right or wrong.'"[97] Born in Jerusalem in 1935 and growing up in Cairo, Said inherited this American cultural identity. As Brennan states,

> His Americanness was . . . a cultural, not only a legal, status given his father's various quirks, which included turkey dinners at Thanksgiving and a taste for the American songbook. At the age of fourteen, he struck his Cairene cohort as more imposing for being American, and they were awed by his "American gadgets." This aura was still apparent on his visits home each summer while an undergraduate at Princeton. By then, Hoda [Guindi, a childhood friend] recalls, "he had become, to the rest of us left behind drearily continuing our schooling, an object of romance and envy as he was being 'educated abroad,' a phrase oft repeated in hushed, awestruck voices."[98]

The years described above would extend from 1949 to 1957, and the terms "turkey dinners" and "American gadgets" bring to mind David Potter's work of popular sociology, *People of Plenty* (1954), which claimed that the American national character is based on abundance.[99] While Potter's book might now be considered a Cold War period piece, based on the concept of an affluent middle class that no longer exists, the book does describe Said's class privilege.

As Said relates, "one of the main recreational rituals of my Cairo years was what my father called 'going for a drive.' . . . For more than three decades, he owned a series of black American cars, each bigger than its predecessors: a Ford, then a deluxe Plymouth sedan, then in 1948 an enormous Chrysler limousine."[100] In short, Said saw the US as a land of material plenitude and a space for professional autonomy. As Brennan observes, although he sought to free himself from his father's control, "he had internalized his father's upbeat take on American culture and certainly found success in the New World, like his father, as an improviser, experimenter, and self-inventor."[101]

To borrow Limerick's phrase, Said may even have yearned for life on the open range. Despite "railing against the homogenizing power of American film, newspapers, and comics," he was an avid moviegoer throughout his life.[102] As a youth in Cairo and the US, he enjoyed Western films starring Roy Rogers and Tom Mix as well as the *Lone Ranger* radio show, although his favorites were the Tarzan movies that starred Johnny Weissmuller. Said's essay on Tarzan, "Jungle Calling," might be read as his reflection on the Frontier Thesis. Said makes a sharp distinction between the films and the original novels by Edgar Rice Burroughs, which draw on a long history of white supremacist colonialism: "Burroughs was obviously influenced by *Robinson Crusoe*, Kipling's Mowgli, and Jack London. For the most part, the heroes of his Tarzan novels are always 'grey-eyed,' tall Anglo-Saxons. . . . Burroughs was a relentless Darwinian who believed that the white man would come out on top."[103] In terms of frontier models, Burroughs's aristocratic ideology might be roughly likened to that of Theodore Roosevelt (the young Burroughs tried to join Roosevelt's Rough Riders in 1898). In contrast, according to Said, Weissmuller's Tarzan is a jungle individualist whose "power and origins are almost totally obscure," although "of his wonderful strength and authority over the jungle there is no doubt. He has a special affinity for elephants, who frequently come to his aid en masse, something that does not occur in the novels." Although the movies could be racist, Tarzan battles white settlers as well as Black natives, and Said notes that Frantz Fanon was also a fan of the movies while a youth in Martinique.

In short, as with Turner's essays on the pioneer and frontier, "Jungle Calling" might be read in terms of autonomous professionalism. Said's essay functions as New Class allegory, since the jungle is a "system" to be mastered, with prestige and a certain wealth as a result (although Tarzan is supposedly "diverted from worldly success," his "powers" allow him to achieve "dignity and prestige").[104] Read in this way, the essay is akin to other pieces in *Reflections on Exile* such as the portrait of a literary mentor from his undergraduate days at Princeton, R. P. Blackmur. To borrow Brennan's phrase, Said seems drawn to "improviser[s], experimenter[s], and self-inventor[s]," creative professionals who empower themselves through institutions without ever becoming organization men. It is thus reasonable to relate Said's Tarzan to his own identity as a professional academic in America, especially when he defends the movies by saying, "before we throw Tarzan completely away as a useless degenerate without either social or aesthetic value, he ought to be given a chance as what in fact he is, an immigrant ... in permanent exile."[105] Although "Jungle Calling" celebrates the immigrant while Turner's "The Significance of the Frontier in American History" celebrates the pioneer, there is an overlap in terms of upwardly mobile professionalism and reinventing oneself through travel.

Taking this line of analysis on Said might change our view of his magnum opus *Orientalism*, which is often criticized for focusing on the British and French empires at the expense of the American one. Said does, in fact, discuss the US at length, devoting the last fifty pages of the book to the American adoption of European Orientalism. Perhaps it is most accurate to say not that *Orientalism* disregards America, but rather that *Orientalism* is itself a very *American* book. Most obviously, Said's identification of a sharp binary between Western and Eastern identities is enabled by his vantage point as an American academic. Commenting on nineteenth-century Orientalist discourse, "an area of concern defined by travelers, ... readers of novels and accounts of exotic adventure," Said claims that "every European, in what he could say about the Orient, was ... a racist, an imperialist, and almost totally ethnocentric."[106] While US imperialism did not start in 1945, one could argue that the writing of *Orientalism* was made possible by America's postwar displacement of the European powers, which in a sense museumized the British and French empires, allowing Said to scrutinize them and conclude that their representations constructed an imagined Orient.

But read through the lens of American studies, *Orientalism* is also exemplary of the paradigm in midcentury literary culture discussed above, namely an anticonformist and often antistatist individualism. In the concluding subchapter, "The Latest Phase," Said argues that the Orientalisms of Europe have congealed into an impoverished form in the US: "the Orient became, not a broad catholic issue as it had been for centuries in Europe, but an administrative one, a matter for policy."[107] Said's critical stance toward this watered-down, bureaucratic Orientalism is recognizable as the postwar discourse of the individual versus the organization, in which New Deal cultural solidarities and a commitment to progressive government were replaced by anxieties about social conformity and the discouragement of individual agency. In his description of America's Orientalism-as-administration, Said remarks that "there are grants and other rewards, there are organizations, there are hierarchies, there are institutes, centers, faculties, departments, all devoted to legitimizing and maintaining the authority of a handful of basic, basically unchanging ideas about Islam, the Orient, and the Arabs.... For every Orientalist, quite literally, there is a support system of staggering power.... This system now culminates in the very institutions of the state."[108] Criticizing Arab "native informants" who are guided by "European and American models," Said's own role as an intellectual is that of a super-professional who resists systematization by founding a system of his own, a field of professional expertise.[109] "I am not going to be falsely modest... [*Orientalism* is] quite nuanced and discriminating in what it says about different people, different periods, and different styles of Orientalism. Each of my analyses varies the picture, increases the difference and discriminations, separates authors and periods from each other."[110] This approach to postcolonial studies has empowered scholars around the world to criticize racism and stereotyping, yet it also seems fair to ask what Said's alternative political ideal for the US might be. *Orientalism*, as well as its 1994 afterword, is rather vague on this point, instead extolling what I would call a quintessentially American individualism: "*Orientalism*, and indeed all of my other work, has come in for disapproving attacks because of its 'residual' humanism, its theoretical inconsistencies, its insufficient, perhaps even sentimental, treatment of agency. I am glad that it has! *Orientalism* is a partisan book, not a theoretical machine. No one has convincingly shown that individual effort is not at some profoundly unteachable level both eccentric and, in Gerard Manley Hopkins's sense, original; this despite the existence of systems of thought, discourses, and hegemonies."[111] Although Said relates his eccentricity and originality to Hopkins's poetry, I would call his attitude Turnerian, insofar as Said located his professional freedom and creative self-making in travel.

The problem here is that this travel-oriented articulation of anticonformist selfhood was itself a postwar American privilege. As a professor at Columbia University—"the American university generally being for its academic staff and many of its students the last remaining utopia"—Said claims to occupy a culturally hybrid middle ground in New York City, which is "turbulent, unceasingly various, energetic, unsettling, resistant, and absorptive . . . what Paris was a hundred years ago."[112] It is important to remember that in the 1930s, New York City was also energetic and unsettling, yet the city helped to foster a progressive national culture as well as cross-class alliances that sometimes seem to have completely disappeared from American intellectual life, as writers and scholars pursue transnational articulations of selfhood. Late in his life, in a speech that he wrote for the 2002 graduation ceremony at his high school alma mater, Northfield Mount Hermon School, Said reflected on the vast cultural changes in America over a half century: "The Mount Hermon-Northfield that you graduates are leaving today is a vastly different and more complicated place than the one I came to fifty years ago as a homesick and disoriented fifteen year old from Cairo. You have cell phones, TVs, easy access to the entire world, and a far wider and more inclusive view not just of New England but also of very distant places like China and Australia."[113] As someone who was born in the Middle East and dreamed in Arabic, Said felt himself opposed to the Cold War mainstream for much of his life. But was there a possibility, as Hollinger might argue, that his immigrant identity could have been part of a progressive American nationalism? If so, then Said would be a Palestinian American first and foremost, and a more globalized form of identity would exist in a certain tension with his political ideals for the United States.

It is thus no accident that Klein finds that midcentury American writers anticipated Saidian notions of cultural hybridity and cosmopolitanism, since his own self-conception was related to this American context. The foregoing analysis is not meant to discredit Said as a spokesperson for Palestinian nationalism, and at various points in this book, I will cite him as a truth teller who made an important critique of American foreign policy. Part of this book's argument is that midcentury American travel narratives display an incipient neoliberalism, which is not true of Said's thought, since he was sympathetic toward socialist alternatives in the developing world.[114] Nevertheless, if we prioritize Said's American identity, then he and the literary travelers in the following chapters explore similar dilemmas. Writers like Burroughs and Bishop had good reason to expatriate themselves from postwar America because of their sexual identities, and for Wright, Paris offered a refuge from racial persecution that he faced even in relatively tolerant Greenwich Village. Yet this global travel was also a privilege, enabled by the power of the American dollar and an American passport. Contesting models of 1950s conformity,

Dickstein argues for "the essential continuity of the postwar decades"; in his view, literature highlights "the momentous social transformations—in the life of the middle class, for example, or in the position of blacks and women—that were taking place behind the conservative façade."[115] *The Global Frontier* argues that these "momentous social transformations" were most evident in travel narratives, which prefigured the cultural upheavals of later decades. Midcentury writers were convinced that self-realization could be achieved through travel, and pursued personal freedom and cultural enrichment outside their nation's borders. However, their privileges were enabled precisely by state power, and they were ultimately enabled by American corporate expansion instead of opposed to it. What's lost is the idea that they could play a role in state-based reform.

The first chapter discusses William Lederer and Eugene Burdick's bestseller *The Ugly American* (1958), which serves as a template for the rest of the book. Relating *The Ugly American* to conservative magazines such as *Reader's Digest*, for which Lederer worked as a writer and correspondent, I argue that the novel presages neoliberalism, since it argues that the New Deal had metastasized into a bureaucratic edifice that was counterproductive in the fight against communism in developing countries. This chapter also provides sometimes overlooked detail about the authors' careers; although a collaboration between an ex-Navy captain and CIA agent, and a Berkeley political science professor, might seem counterintuitive, their backgrounds made for a productive synergy, allowing us to directly relate Saunders's *The Cultural Cold War* to Mark McGurl's *The Program Era* (2009). Noting that Burdick's short story "Rest Camp on Maui" (1946) inspired Wallace Stegner to found a creative writing program at Stanford, I argue that *The Ugly American* is, in effect, a creative writing portfolio. Burdick's Hemingwayesque, GI Bill–supported workshop expertise influenced the form and style of *The Ugly American*, while Lederer's CIA activities enabled the authors to follow the workshop mantra "write what you know," narrating the suppression of anticolonial nationalist movements.[116] The final section relates this approach to Jack Kerouac's *On the Road* (1957), showing that Kerouac's countercultural style was generally in sync with the designs of American power elites instead of opposed to them. *The Ugly American* is a response to *On the Road* as well as to Graham Greene's *The Quiet American* (1955), countering Greene's jaundiced take on American culture and foreign influence with a Beat-influenced model of the postwar frontier spirit, which influenced the creation of the Peace Corps.

The next chapter relates postmodern fiction to postwar travel, focusing on William S. Burroughs to argue that his subversive ethos and fragmented style is related to the advance of American capitalism after World War II. Burroughs valorized a libertarian freedom that he associated with the Old West, and sought to recover this autonomy outside US borders. Accordingly, the protagonists of *Naked Lunch* (1959) creatively manipulate touristic imagery, acting as countercultural travel agents who disrupt organizational routine and fixed identities. Burroughs has gained respectability in the American literary academy largely through the claim that he anticipated French critical theory, in particular the écriture of Derrida and Barthes and the antistatism of Foucault. If so, he advanced American exceptionalism in a poststructuralist idiom, writing against nationalist movements that resisted the global marketplace. For example, *The Soft Machine* (1961) recodes the Guatemalan Revolution as the tale of a foreign adventurer's struggle against big government. While the permeability of national borders and intermixture of cultures has progressive aspects, Burroughs's work reminds us that an activist state is necessary to ensure social justice.

The third chapter argues that Bellow was less a rearguard defender of Eurocentrism than someone who was too global for his own good, endorsing transnational forms of identity formation that eventually came to undermine his own central position in Western literary culture. Backed by Franz Boas's protégé Melville J. Herskovits, Bellow began his professional career as a doctoral student in anthropology. He was profoundly influenced by the school of cultural relativism, which inspired him to make 1950s America itself an object of anthropological critique. However, he departed from Herskovits's New Deal–era concern for progressive alliances between Jewish and Black people, since the novel *Henderson the Rain King* (1958) imagines a renewal of personal identity outside the boundaries of the nation-state. Henderson's friend and colleague King Dahfu, a West African therapist and cosmopolitan intellectual, anticipates the postmodern anthropology of James Clifford, since the novel valorizes an intercultural syncretism. Although antiracist in intent, Bellow's vision of travel-fueled professional autonomy opposes nationalist resistance to imperialism and collective movements for social change. The chapter concludes by suggesting that Bellow's interest in globalized professional networks helps to explain his neoconservative turn in the 1970s, when he modeled a specifically Jewish American frontier buttressed by the United States and Israel.

Bishop has not only displaced Robert Lowell as America's premier mid-century poet, but also earned a reputation as a radical social critic due to her differential sexual identity. Combining Adrienne Rich's term for Bishop's poetic insight—the eye of the outsider—with Mary Louise Pratt's notion of *Imperial Eyes* (1992), this chapter argues that Bishop's feminist and queer identity was not in any way opposed to American globalization, but rather enabled by it. However, this is not to altogether discredit the political value of Bishop's poetry. We have not fully explored her literary career in Key West, Florida, which was a showpiece of the New Deal. Some of Bishop's most successful poems, such as "Florida" and "The Fish," were stimulated by government programs. Yet Bishop moved away from these social engagements during the postwar American Century. She bravely resisted the norms of Cold War containment culture and constructed her own transnational feminist literary network while living in Brazil in the 1950s and '60s. Yet Bishop also demonized Brazilian reformers, favored US investment and the control of inflation at the expense of populist initiatives, and befriended the Red-baiting, America-friendly politician Carlos Lacerda. Bishop's work suggests that we need to re-evaluate queer studies as well as feminism, since queerness can be reconciled with progressive government policies, and also accommodate itself to global inequality.

While Wright might simply be read as puncturing the illusions of white travelers, he was culturally labile in a way that lent itself to the freedoms of postwar globalization, which he struggled to reconcile with his convictions regarding social justice. It is important to note the middle-class elements in his background, which included a home that valued learning and upward mobility. Although scholars focus on the Communist Party, the New Deal and its arts programs were decisive for Wright, who serves as a model for the artist's productive relationship to the federal government. However, where *Native Son* is concerned, the transition from the 1940 novel to the 1951 film is also the transition from an antiracist progressive nationalism to postwar African American exceptionalism. Starring as Bigger Thomas, Wright experienced a touristic fantasy life as well as midlife crisis, and the Argentina-lensed film, which involved tax evasion in the Third World and puff pieces in *Ebony* magazine, functioned as an American imperial project. Although well-intentioned, Wright's exportation of the nation-unifying rhetoric of the New Deal to Ghana in his travel book *Black Power* (1954) aligns with the tenets of modernization theory. The chapter concludes by following Wright to the origin of the West's frontier in *Pagan Spain* (1956). To an extent Wright reproduces the Black Legend, which argued that relatively backward Spain had been punished by history for the atrocities of racism and colonialism. Wright draws on Max Weber to argue that Spain's saving remnant is a group of *"white Negroes,"* Spanish Protestants who have the discipline and rationality of Black Americans.[117] Although Wright thereby challenges racist stereotypes, his blurring of racial positions in relation to modernity is enabled by his own privilege as a globalized American writer and traveler.

For American writers, the price of incorporation into a privileged transnational class was not only forswearing communism, but also rejecting 1930s social commitments, which included a progressive nationalism and an interventionist state. My conclusion argues that contemporary literary scholars have inherited this legacy; often celebrating resistant identities, they forget that the state remains the terrain upon which progressive change must be effected, especially regarding social class. This point involves a reconsideration of literature's relationship to activist government, now that the global frontier of postwar travel appears to be closing.

Chapter One

. . . .

Ugly Americans

The Globalization of the Frontier
after World War II

T he *Ugly American* sold over four million copies and was turned into
a movie starring Marlon Brando in 1962. Giving an enduring term
to the English language, the book castigated the behavior of the
US's foreign service, which the authors argued was helping to lose the Cold
War. In 1959, the publisher took out an ad in the *New York Times* to announce
that presidential hopeful John F. Kennedy had mailed a copy to each US senator. As John Hellmann emphasizes, the book set the agenda for Kennedy's
campaign, which was based upon the slogan of the "New Frontier": "The Peace
Corps, the Alliance for Progress, the domestic emphasis on physical fitness . . .
every aspect of the New Frontier evoked the ideal found in *The Ugly American*."[1] *The Ugly American* directly inspired the Peace Corps, which Kennedy
created by executive order following his inauguration.

The Ugly American functions as an ideological template for the various
works of literature that follow, which might at first sound unlikely. Not only
is the work crude in its fictional techniques, but its endorsement of counterinsurgent warfare would seem to have little relationship to midcentury American writers. Yet its proleptical neoliberalism is similar to that of other writers
in the chapters ahead, especially Burroughs and Bishop; meanwhile, Bellow's
Henderson the Rain King has also been related to the Peace Corps. Richard
Wright himself endorsed the book in a letter to a friend: "Did you read *The
Ugly American*? It is badly written but a true novel and it makes you wonder
and wonder."[2]

This chapter approaches the *The Ugly American* as a travel-oriented fantasy
in which American professionals recover an imagined frontier independence
in the developing world, in the process making themselves what we would now

call culturally hybrid. However, even as Lederer and Burdick extol a transnational professional middle class, they also reveal the price that creative writers had to pay in order to join it. In *The Ugly American*, aspects of the progressive 1930s—national solidarity, cultural pluralism, a class of reform-minded experts—become transmuted into their anticommunist Cold War forms, which involved not only the suppression of progressive social alternatives abroad, but also the legacy of the New Deal at home.

The next section of the chapter explains that *The Ugly American* illuminates a general rightward shift in the institutions that enabled American creative writing, allowing us to connect two masterpieces of recent criticism, Saunders's *The Cultural Cold War* and McGurl's *The Program Era*. Burdick can get credit for inspiring the creation of Stanford's renowned creative writing program, since his story of World War II, "Rest Camp on Maui," deeply impressed Wallace Stegner. However, while McGurl stays focused on the "halls of mirror" of the MFA program (in which workshop participants often build the dynamics of the classroom into their novels), *The Ugly American* allows us to connect the Program Era to what CIA head James Angleton (quoting T. S. Eliot) called a "wilderness of mirrors."[3] In *The Ugly American*, Lederer and Burdick imagine exporting the creative writing workshop so as to fight anticolonial nationalism, a scenario that parallels the CIA's funding of overseas American writers as well as creative writing projects throughout Asia and Africa.

Although *The Ugly American* is often seen as a reply to Graham Greene's criticism of US imperialism, *The Quiet American*, the final section explains that Lederer and Burdick also responded to Jack Kerouac's *On the Road*. Kerouac's novel itself narrates a declension from 1930s social ideals; often seen as the epitome of anti-institutional transgression, *On the Road* is in fact deeply enabled by institutions. The protagonist Sal Paradise's imagination of the US is structured by the American Guide Series, while his auto-fueled adventures are financed by the GI Bill, replacing an earlier era of national solidarity with consumerist hyperindividualism. Lederer and Burdick found *On the Road*'s countercultural style useful not only for responding to Greene's portrait of American naivete, but also for making the activities of the CIA agent Edward Lansdale appealing to a general audience. As Reynolds observes, "the novel's fictionalization of U.S. involvement in Southeast Asia occupied a strange interzone where fact met fiction," and "embodied disjunctions in a quirky, hybrid form that brought together the real and the imagined."[4] The Peace Corps was born out of this postmodern frontier and worked to suppress anticolonial nationalism despite the high ideals of its participants, a tension that we shall also find in creative writers.

The Professional Middle Class Abroad

While Burdick had supported the Democrat Adlai Stevenson for president in 1956, and Lederer was an editor for *Reader's Digest* (which supported Eisenhower), these party affiliations did not keep the authors from coauthoring *The Ugly American* and its follow-up, *Sarkhan* (1965). Burdick did not make Du Bois's distinction between the revolution of Roosevelt and the counterrevolution of Truman. In his essay "The Democratic Party" for the June 1960 issue of *Holiday* magazine, he eulogized Truman for carrying on Roosevelt's legacy: "No one since [Andrew] Jackson was so marvelously attuned to politics . . . beneath his defiance and 'give 'em hell' surface, he had a masterly knowledge of what the Party wanted."[5] Instead of being concerned with the New Deal's unfinished attempt to confront social inequality, the authors shared a belief that postwar American government had become too bureaucratically cumbersome, and the American people too complacent, to effectively fight global communism. Although Burdick objected to Senator Joseph McCarthy's excesses, he had a similar worldview: "I'd rather be dead than Red," he told a crowd of UC Berkeley alumni in 1962.[6]

Born in 1918, Burdick came from a family that supported left-liberal causes; his parents named him "Eugene" after Eugene Debs. After serving in World War II as a Navy commander, he pursued graduate study in the social sciences at Stanford and then Oxford, earning his PhD with the dissertation "Syndicalism and Industrial Unionism in Britain until 1918" (1950). He then became a political science professor at UC Berkeley, where he worked until his premature death in 1965. The concerns in Burdick's fiction overlap with those of the counterculture and youth movements that surrounded him. His novel *Fail-Safe* (1962) imagines nuclear war with Russia; turned into a film in 1964, it has affinities with *Dr. Strangelove* (1964), albeit without the black humor. However, Burdick did not want the American public to be *too* political. In his essay for the collection *American Voting Behavior* (1959), he makes the following un-Debs-like observation: "Given the [public's] demonstrated low interest in domestic politics and the even lower interest in foreign affairs, one wonders . . . if in recent attempts to involve 'the public' more directly in international relations, the involvement is either possible or desirable. . . . Can popular participation mean anything less than 'intrusion of the masses' into politics?"⁷ Instead, Burdick endorsed the leadership of the "tough but humane professional," as Rupert Wilkinson notes in one of the few studies of Burdick's fiction: "Self-reliant and resourceful individualists, the heroes of these books are, nevertheless, geared to draw on highly-tuned supporting organizations as well as intensive training or experience."⁸

If the Pentagon had started its own version of the Federal Writers' Project, then it might have produced a writer like Lederer, who often criticized the establishment but supported its Cold War aims. Slightly older than Burdick, Lederer was born in 1912 to a doctor who fell on hard times; he weathered the Depression in the Navy and graduated from the US Naval Academy in 1936. When he became a junior officer, his first appointment was on a river gunboat patrolling China's Yangtze River, which began a long immersion in Asian politics. After World War II, he was a public information officer for the Navy, eventually serving as a special assistant to the commander of the Pacific Fleet, Admiral Felix Stump. From 1955 onward, he worked as an editor for *Reader's Digest*, and when he retired from the Navy in 1958, he became the magazine's correspondent for the Far East. Burdick's fiction features tough-minded, Hemingwayesque protagonists who demonstrate grace under pressure; Lederer's fiction is often comic, celebrating trickster figures who subvert the authority of stuffed shirts. For example, the unfortunately named Hymie O'Toole is the hero of "Hymie O'Toole Is Never Wrong," a short story that appeared in *Esquire* in 1951, and a book of stories about O'Toole's cousin, *Ensign O'Toole and Me* (1957), provided the basis for a short-lived TV series called *Ensign O'Toole*. While Lederer's stories lack the high-minded gravity of Burdick's, his characters are closer to the bloody business end of things where American foreign policy is concerned. His journalism and fiction drew material from his military career as well as from his involvement with the CIA (as I shall explain below, it is difficult to separate these things).

As Hellmann observes, *The Ugly American* functions as a jeremiad, castigating Americans for "abandoning [their] self-reliant individualism for bureaucratic conformity and hedonistic affluence . . . [and] turning their backs on the frontier."⁹ *The Ugly American* makes a criticism of mass society akin to that of David Riesman's *The Lonely Crowd* (1950), William H. Whyte's *The Organization Man* (1956), and C. Wright Mills's *White Collar* (1951). These

authors share a sense of organizational life's encroachment on personal freedom, which makes for overlaps in the thought of writers who might seem to
be radically opposed to each other. Mills, a contrarian thinker who influenced
the New Left, begins *White Collar* with a paean to the vanished frontier of
"small entrepreneurs"[10]: "Individual freedom seemed the principle of social
order. . . . A free man, not a man exploited, an independent man . . . here
confronted a continent and, grappling with it, turned it into a million commodities."[11] In Mills's view, these free men have been replaced by the "cheerful
robots" of America's postwar offices.[12] The title of Lederer's follow-up to *The
Ugly American, A Nation of Sheep* (1961), emphasizes this basic affinity.

Yet none of these writers simply advocated a recuperation of Protestant
thrift and masculine independence; instead, they tried to find alternative
models of individualism while acknowledging the realities of organizational
life and consumer society. Since Riesman eventually joined Lederer and Burdick in an advisory role for the Peace Corps, it would be helpful to comment
in detail on *The Lonely Crowd*. This book is often mistakenly read as valorizing the inner-direction of the nineteenth-century Protestant Ethic versus
the other-direction of the contemporary urban middle class. While Riesman
criticizes other-direction for excessive conformity and apolitical cynicism, he
also stresses that it has made the world a better place. As he emphasizes in
the 1961 preface: "No lover of toughness and invulnerability should forget
the gains made possible by the considerateness, sensitivity, and tolerance that
are among the positive qualities of other-direction."[13] Riesman then evalu-
ates other-direction positively in relation to what we now call globalization:
"There has been a general tendency, facilitated by education, by mobility, by
the mass media, toward an enlargement of the circles of empathy beyond
one's clan, beyond even one's class, sometimes beyond one's country as well."[14]
Riesman's recuperation of inner-direction involves the desirable third term of
"autonomy," a character type that combines the empathy of other-direction
with self-empowerment and free choice.[15] Riesman admits that the concept
of autonomy is obscure, but it can perhaps be summarized as taking a professional attitude toward recreation. Speculating that automation can free the
American middle class from alienating, other-directed work, Riesman argues
that in order to make full use of the resulting leisure time, consumers will
need the appropriate "skill and competence."[16] In fact, the middle class may
need to make use of "avocational counselors" such as "travel agents, hotel men,

[and] resort directors."[17] Autonomy, then, overcomes consumerist passivity by combining the virtues of inner-direction with a spirit of adventure and intercultural exchange.

In Lederer and Burdick's case, as well, it is important to understand the "frontier" in the Turnerian sense of self-realization and professional opportunities enabled by American expansion, and not merely in the sense of recovering individualism by roughing it in developing countries. To be sure, in the article "Salute to Deeds of Non-Ugly Americans" (1959), Lederer and Burdick valorized travelers who did "practical work with a no-nonsense application of elbow grease."[18] However, they chose an odd venue for this paean, since the essay in *Life* magazine is set within the cornucopia of the 1950s consumer marketplace, the text almost crowded out by advertisements for Hennessy cognac, Toastmaster cookware, the Studebaker Lark sedan, and the Schick 3 Speed razor. In particular, advertisements for American Tourister luggage and Argus cameras suggest that the non-ugly American world of strenuous frontier life is immediately available for the price of a plane ticket. In 1961, Burdick appeared in scuba-diving gear in an advertisement for Ballantine Ale, which called him "Undersea explorer... literary man... Ale man."[19] He owned a vacation home on the South Pacific island of Moʻorea (near Tahiti), and his personal favorite among his books was *The Blue of Capricorn* (1961), a collection of stories and essays in the vein of James A. Michener's follow-up to *Tales of the South Pacific* (1947), *Return to Paradise* (1951). As UC Berkeley's obituary for Burdick notes, he was "forever on the go—in Europe one day, New Zealand the next, the Philippines, Tahiti.... He was an avid hiker, a tennis addict; he had a Hemingway physique and posture.... He was linked with stage and screen celebrities, politicians and journalists, until the scholar in him was virtually submerged."[20] For his part, Lederer celebrated Pacific travel (and himself) in an article for the *Saturday Review*, "The Western Pacific." Encouraging "pioneers [and] real adventurers" to explore "the beauties and mysteries of the Far East," while dispensing advice on where to find the best deals (Hong Kong), Lederer recommends:[21] "You should spend at least two weeks in Hawaii. But once you spend two days there, you will come back.... Now it is my permanent residence."[22]

In Lederer and Burdick's work, postwar travel is oriented away from the American Guide Series and national solidarity toward confronting communism in the developing world, making for a general overlap of their novel with

Luce's recuperation of the Frontier Thesis in "The American Century." As they declare in their "Factual Epilogue" in *The Ugly American*'s most-quoted passage:

> We do not need the horde of 1,500,000 Americans—mostly amateurs— who are now working for the United States overseas. What we need is a small force of well-trained, well-chosen, hard-working, and dedicated professionals. . . . If we are not prepared to pay the human price, we had better retreat to our shores, build Fortress America, learn to live without international trade and communications, and accept the mediocrity, the low standard of living, and the loom of world communism which would accompany such a move. (*UA* 284)

As Klein notes, the figure of 1.5 million represents the total number of Americans abroad in places besides Canada and Mexico, not the number of people working for the American government.[23] In this view, the "dedicated professionals" might be considered a sort of anticommunist brain trust of global tourism, and *The Ugly American* stresses the professional credentials of the characters. For example, the farmer Tom Knox has a degree in animal and poultry husbandry from the State University of Iowa and has published a scholarly article in a journal called *The Iowa Poultryman*. Knox is thus best described not as a farmer but rather as an "egg expert" (*UA* 173). The Air Force colonel Edwin B. Hillandale is a member of a transnational class of specialists, "the only living Caucasian who is a graduate of the Chungking School of Occult Science" (177). When he arrives in Sarkhan, Hillandale exposes a sarcastic American diplomat as an incompetent social climber who "wanted to be a doctor, but . . . couldn't pass the entrance exams for medical school" (179). The ugly Americans thus seek to defeat conformist organization men, although they are organization men themselves.

If we emphasize the global travel that Lederer and Burdick pursued, then something comes in view that is usually not mentioned in criticism of *The Ugly American*: the 1955 Afro-Asian Conference in Bandung, Indonesia. At this conference, the leaders of decolonizing countries expressed views that were potentially threatening to American elites, endorsing nonalignment and national self-determination. I think it is this threat that makes *The Ugly American* skew rightward in its ideology, despite Burdick's admiration for Adlai Stevenson. Now read exclusively as a stand-alone novel, *The Ugly*

American was also disseminated to American readers in magazines that were reactionary in their politics, both internationally and domestically. It was serialized in the *Saturday Evening Post*, and Lederer's employer, *Reader's Digest*, included a lengthy excerpt in its Condensed Books edition for 1958. During the 1930s, both magazines had opposed New Deal programs and Popular Front organizations. In the early 1940s, *Reader's Digest* (much like Henry Luce) was concerned that the world war might give license to the president's socialist ambitions; in April 1945, the magazine printed a condensed version of Friedrich von Hayek's *The Road to Serfdom* (1944). As Klein explains, in the 1950s, "[*Reader's Digest*] found an easy harmony with the Eisenhower administration.... [It] promoted big business; opposed federal aid to education, highways, slum clearance, and urban renewal; gave weak support to the civil rights movement; fought Social Security and Medicare; and hammered away at federal waste and inefficiency, the mounting national debt, and uncontrolled spending. Overall, it favored less government and more private-sector problem solving."[24] This anti–welfare state position—a negation of Roosevelt's proposal for a Second Bill of Rights in 1944—was accompanied by a virulent anticommunism.

In this view, *The Ugly American*'s globalization of the frontier did not merely entail a confrontation with leftist nationalism abroad, but with the legacy of the New Deal at home. The novel codes an anti–big government perspective into an attack on the foreign policy bureaucracy, which the author portray as wasteful and inefficient. Living in Sarkhan (a Southeast Asian country that has the qualities of Laos as well as Vietnam), the ambassador Louis Sears sequesters himself inside a palatial home and attends cocktail parties attended largely by other foreigners. "The lawn of the [US] Embassy swept down . . . in a long, pure green, carefully trimmed wave" to "a wrought-iron fence," which constitutes a border between civilization and perceived savagery, "separate[ing] Embassy grounds from the confusion and noise of the road."[25] It is as if the authors had read Said's account of colonialism's "master-slave binary dialectic" and based their depiction of America's foreign service upon his critique.[26] Yet for Lederer and Burdick, it is specifically government bureaucracy and the waste of taxpayers' money that creates the neocolonial binary opposition.

The Ugly American takes its title from the story of Homer Atkins—as the authors would have it, ugly in appearance but beautiful in character—who sets up a small-scale business venture with a Southeast Asian native, which is the excerpt that was published in *Reader's Digest*. Atkins begins his career abroad as an advisor in Vietnam, facing a group of Vietnamese, French, and American officials: "The princes of bureaucracy were the same all over the world. They sat in their freshly pressed clothes . . . and asked engineers like Atkins silly questions" (*UA* 205). Atkins exemplifies the Turnerian slippage from pioneer to middle-class professional, since he is an engineer from Pittsburgh who "had spent his life making bids involving hundreds of millions of dollars and thousands of men (and his reputation)" (207). Atkins harangues the bureaucrats and denounces their pork-barrel projects: "You want big industry. . . . You want big T.V.A.'s scattered all over the countryside" (*UA* 208). The TVA was a centerpiece of the New Deal, considered one of its resounding successes and worthy of emulation; the progressive politician George W. Norris of Nebraska wanted big TVAs scattered all over the American countryside—eight, to be exact.[27] It became a famous worldwide symbol of activist government and even a tourist attraction. In 1937, the TVA received 110,000 American tourists as well as over six hundred foreign visitors, including politicians, intellectuals, and engineers from China and India.[28] However, from its inception the TVA faced powerful enemies, as the historian David Ekbladh observes: "A more activist state caused obvious discomfort among businesses. Utility companies were goaded by the specter of government-financed competition and regulation. . . . Traditional American anti-statism motivated other critics. All saw the TVA as an early symptom of metastasizing centralized planning."[29] During the 1950s, Eisenhower saw the TVA as one of the New Deal programs that fostered "creeping socialism."[30] This led to a paradoxical situation in which the Eisenhower administration extolled the TVA as a model of development for foreign countries, while opposing the agency domestically. TVA officials complained that it had been marked "For Export Only" and treated as "an asp in the bosom at home, a dove of peace abroad."[31] *The Ugly American* sought to make TVA an asp in the bosom abroad, as well. When the director of the United States Agency for International Development spoke at the opening of the TVA's new center for international visitors, he defended the agency, and American foreign aid in general, specifically from *The Ugly American*'s misrepresentations.[32]

In contrast to these wasteful public projects, Atkins will redeem American influence by establishing interracial relationships through private initiatives. Thwarted in Vietnam, Atkins gets himself transferred to the novel's fictional country of Sarkhan, where he goes into business with a local artisan, nicknamed Jeepo. Together, they design a water pump that will allow villagers to farm terraced crops more efficiently. When Atkins and Jeepo open a small warehouse, "[t]heir arguments, for some reason, caused the Sarkhanese workmen a great deal of pleasure . . . they were the only times that the Sarkhanese had ever seen one of their own kind arguing fairly and honestly, and with a chance of success, against a white man" (228). While this egalitarian relationship is in keeping with the novel's promotion of cultural exchange, it is also a middle-class fantasy of empowerment—as if Willy Loman's dilemma in *Death of a Salesman* (1949) could have been resolved if he had gone abroad. Initially referred to as "workmen" (228), the Sarkhanese factory employees transform into "engineer-salesmen," as Jeepo recruits them to sell the pump to the surrounding provinces. "[E]verything rested on the persuasiveness of the engineer-salesmen and the performance of the bicycle-powered pump" (229). The successful start-up of the "Jeepo-Atkins Company" concludes with an "improvised party [that] involved the entire village" (*UA* 230). This interracial egalitarianism obviously papers over the history of French colonialism, but it also elides class differences, since a magical upward mobility allows the entire village to join the ranks of middle-class professionalism.

The Ugly American is paradoxical in that while it celebrates "the sum of tiny things"—Americans' ability to enjoy local food or have conversations in foreign languages, which will win friends and influence people in Asia—it is also a prototypical model of globalization. In Hellmann's reading of the Atkins chapters, the novel sets a racially redemptive pastoralism in Southeast Asia, functioning as an expiation of white guilt in which Asians stand in for Indians. "[O]n this frontier . . . they would protect the dark man rather than destroy or enslave him, and improve rather than destroy his natural landscape."[33] However, *The Ugly American* might also be said to look ahead to late twentieth-century models of the global economy: "Over the entrance to the warehouse a small sign written in Sarkhanese said: 'The Jeepo-Atkins Company, Limited'" (*UA* 227). As incongruous or just plain weird as it might seem, the sign is worth pondering: if we relate it to frontier discourse, it is as if Chingachgook had started a business firm with Natty Bumppo, a construct that is hard to imagine in earlier writers like Conrad or Forster, or contemporaneous writers like Graham Greene. As the historian Daniel Immerwahr notes, "What is striking about these parables is how aggressively they reject the Jim Crow racism that was still the norm in U.S. society in the 1950s. At a time when interracial contact was still strictly controlled in many parts of the

country, we hear tell of whites sharing food, getting drunk, and making music
with Asians. It is surely relevant that Lederer's first marriage was to a Filipina,
a marriage that would have run afoul of the law in many states at the time of
The Ugly American's publication."[34] It is also important to note that *The Ugly
American* crosses racial lines by constructing an antigovernmental rhetoric;
the novel suggests that America's professional middle class is overburdened by
regulations in the same way that natives are oppressed by various bureaucracies, neocolonial and communist.

Immerwahr remarks that when he taught the novel at Northwestern University in the mid-2010s, his undergraduate students were entranced by it. It
is safe to say the inventors of "Hymie O'Toole" and "Edwin Hillandale[,] . . .
graduate of the Chungking School of Occult Science" would not have lasted
for five minutes on Twitter, but I think *The Ugly American* has a perverse
cultural endurance because it speaks our contemporary language of neoliberal selfhood. For example, Joseph Buttinger castigated *The Ugly American*
in "Fact and Fiction on Foreign Aid: A Critique of *The Ugly American*," a
1959 review for *Dissent*, the socialist magazine founded by Irving Howe.
Buttinger argues that, from being "dam-building maniacs," American experts effectively plan small-scale as well as large-scale projects, and develop
beneficial programs for education, health, infrastructure, and agriculture.[35]
Unfortunately, Buttinger exemplifies Howe's famous remark on the welfare
state: "It seems easier, if not more intelligent, to die for the Stars and Stripes,
or the Proletarian Fatherland, than for unemployment insurance and social
security. There are fewer subrational loyalties, and perhaps no encompassing
mystique, for the welfare state to exploit."[36] In the New Deal era, the welfare
state *had* actually drawn on such cultural energies, but no more, certainly in
this case: over half the length of the novel itself, Buttinger's fifty-one pages
of dense type are not merely boring but mind-numbing, only readable when
he discusses the absurdities of *The Ugly American*. Moreover, he bypasses the
issue of Vietnamese national self-determination, in a way that contrasts with
the stance which 1930s writers had taken on events like the Spanish Civil War:
"Some recurrent prophecies of disaster notwithstanding, there is in Vietnam
no 'rising tide of anti-Americanism.' The Communist party, although in control in North Vietnam, has not become a 'strong contender for power' in the
South, but has rather lost all hope of a victory."[37] This from a magazine called
Dissent! One can see why a new generation of leftists might see Buttinger as an
antagonist, although this would eventually lead to a congruence of left-wing

and right-wing attacks upon the welfare state.[38] As McGurl notes, "the politics of the sixties were, in retrospect, more complex than a simple rejection of the capitalist status quo: it was after all the regulatory bureaucracies of the still-hegemonic liberal welfare state that were often identified as the problem for sixties radicals."[39] In the following two sections, I will explain how *The Ugly American* illuminates a rightward shift in the institutions that supported creative writing, which opposed progressive nationalisms in the Third World and made the liberal welfare state seem like an enemy instead of a friend.

Cold War Creative Writing

"What must it have sounded like when an agent approached New York publishers with the idea [for *The Ugly American*]?" Immerwahr asks, speculating about the sales pitch for the unlikely bestseller: "'It's a novel set in faraway fictional country [in] a region few people in the United States care about. . . . Mainly, it's a stitched together series of vignettes about problems in the State Department. Oh, and there are two authors—a known recipe for successful fiction—a naval officer and a political scientist.'"[40] But to give credit where due, Burdick and Lederer were extremely successful writers of popular fiction, and met at a Bread Loaf Writer's Conference in the late 1940s. Immerwahr notes that in an interview, "Lederer oddly denied that [CIA agent Edward] Lansdale was the basis for [the fictional] Hillandale: 'Bullshit, the character's about *me*!,' he exclaimed."[41] Although facetious, Lederer's declaration suggests the novel's element of self-referentiality, or what McGurl calls the "autopoetic process" by which creative writers draw on personal experience for their fiction.[42] In reflexive fashion, this experience often includes the institutional context in which that fiction was produced. In a way, the novel *is* about Lederer and Burdick, and their autopoetics open the possibility of connecting the institutions and networks of postwar writing to those of espionage.

The Program Era has inspired a generation of scholars to set postwar American literature within the context of institutions. Although creative writing programs are often stigmatized for producing assembly-line fiction, McGurl shows that the university has fostered a highly successful system for producing creativity, "when the modernist imperative to 'make it new' was institutionalized as another form of original research sponsored by the booming, science-oriented universities of the Cold War era."[43] To demonstrate the institutionality of postwar fiction, McGurl analyzes a short story by Burdick, whose "Rest

Camp on Maui" appeared in *Harper's Magazine* in 1946. At the time, Burdick was a veteran on the GI Bill studying at Stanford, where he took a class with the famed novelist Wallace Stegner. "Maui" impressed Stegner so deeply that it inspired him to found a creative writing workshop on the West Coast that would rival the University of Iowa's in prestige.

"Rest Camp on Maui" concerns a group of Marines in the Pacific War, who are interviewed by a magazine journalist who visits them in their tent. Although the journalist is shallow and prying, Burdick-as-narrator enters the heads of the Marines to narrate their traumatic wartime experiences, focusing on the relationship between a Jewish lieutenant and a Jewish private: the lieutenant resists the anti-Semitism of his colleagues, and the private resists the condescension of the magazine journalist. For McGurl, there is nothing so remarkable about the short story itself, which, as he observes, ends up producing the same story of interethnic male bonding that the journalist would have. McGurl uses "Maui" to illustrate that while "the literature of this period would remain obsessed by individuals ... its true originality ... is to be found at the level of its patron institutions, whose presence is everywhere visible in the texts as a kind of watermark."[44] Burdick's short story about the GIs reproduces the Stanford-based institution in which he wrote the short story; following the injunction to "write what you know," creative writers tended to allegorize their MFA workshops.[45] For McGurl, the university stepped in after World War II to both buffer and facilitate the writer's relationship to the market, offering an institutional context in which imaginative writing could be done. In short, the university funds literary creativity as a form of research and development. Burdick's later career exemplifies this connection between university-sponsored fiction and academic knowledge production; although he went on to become a political science professor at UC Berkeley, he continued to write novels that melded Cold War political imperatives with self-reflexive literary professionalism.

However, although the story registers its classroom context in the university, "Rest Camp on Maui" has a global context: it is set on an imperial possession that would become a US state in 1959, and the title "rest camp" prefigures Hawaii's postwar role as a holiday paradise. This allows us to reverse focus: instead of setting the GI Bill within the Program Era, we could set the Program Era within the larger story of the GI Bill and American expansion. In the opening pages of his book, McGurl suggests precisely this global dimension of the Program Era when he makes a surprising equation between the MFA program and tourism. "Since reading novels and being on vacation are so often aligned in popular practice, we might well suspect a deep link between the two. Isn't the printed matter of the novel put back on the shelf in a sense the 'souvenir' of the quasi-touristic imaginary experiences that were had inside it?"[46] For McGurl, the "self-tourism of creative writing" makes it a part of the larger "experience economy," which goes beyond Marx's concept of commodity fetishization by "trad[ing] more and more in purely symbolic, notionally 'immaterial' goods."[47] Countering charges that MFA programs produce literary organization men who all write alike, McGurl convincingly argues that the university has produced diversity—not just the technomodernism of Thomas Pynchon and the lower-middle-class modernism of Raymond Carver, but also the high cultural pluralism of writers like Toni Morrison and Philip Roth, which has made for a "diverse aesthetic democracy."[48]

I think McGurl is right about university-based creative writing's enabling of diverse voices, but his narrative of the postwar MFA program's ascent seems inseparable from a larger narrative of neoliberal capitalism, in which star writers "contribute a certain form of prestige to the university's overall portfolio of cultural capital . . . testify[ing] to the institution's systematic hospitality to the excellence of individual self-expression."[49] This model of literary production favors creative self-making over more collectivist ways of writing self and nation. As McGurl observes in a brief footnote, "the example set by the Federal Writers' Project and other New Deal initiatives along that line was no doubt instrumental in establishing the legitimacy of its own form of institutional support for artistic production."[50] *The Program Era* can be read as narrating the shift from the national solidarity of the New Deal to a more individualistic postwar ethos. The book begins by discussing the metafiction of *Lolita* (1955), and this turn to a Russian émigré whose politics were akin to those of Ayn Rand has the effect of skewing McGurl's book rightward. If we equate novels with tourism, then Nabokov may well have consulted the American guides that were available to him at Cornell University or in local libraries, but they are not mentioned in *Lolita*. Instead, Humbert Humbert uses the American Automobile Association's guides as well as, in a weird time lag, Baedeker's *The United States, with an excursion into Mexico* (1899).[51] We might contrast his cross-country jaunt at the beginning of *Lolita*'s book 2 with John Steinbeck's remark in the roughly contemporaneous *Travels with Charley in Search of America* (1962): "If there had been room in Rocinante [his truck] I would have packed the W.P.A. Guides to the States, all forty-eight volumes of them. .... The complete set comprises the most comprehensive account of the United States ever got together, and nothing since has ever approached it. It was compiled during the depression by the best writers in America . . . But these books were detested by Mr. Roosevelt's opposition."[52] As Benjamin Mangrum has shown, the supposedly apolitical Nabokov can be considered part of the opposition to Roosevelt's legacy.[53]

If we shift focus from *Lolita* to its competitor on the bestseller lists during late 1958, *The Ugly American*, we get an argument for connecting the Program Era with the Cultural Cold War. Diverging from McGurl, Eric Bennett, himself an Iowa MFA, argues that workshops emphasize small-scale personal experience and a limited range of literary models, discouraging novels of ideas that imagine alternatives to the status quo. Bennett also reveals that the Farfield Foundation, a CIA front, donated money to Iowa's program, although he admits it is hard to connect this with literary production.[54] In assessing the CIA's influence, it might be better to set Iowa in the wider constellation of American writing that Lederer and Burdick inhabited. Saunders has shown that CIA funding influenced the editorial content of postwar little magazines in the US and Europe, in terms of the journal's ideological perspective, and which specific writers were supported. Meanwhile, as the journalist Fred Landis observed in 1988, "[*Reader's*] *Digest* is the world's most widely circulated magazine; it is also the most ignored by intellectuals and journalists."[55] The CIA enjoyed a much higher influence here, since the magazine "enjoyed an intimate relationship with the agency perhaps unmatched by any other major American communications giant, with the exception of Time-Life."[56] Founded in the 1920s, the magazine began by excerpting and condensing material from other sources, but eventually generated its own research and articles, which were often related to US espionage. Landis provides an example: "The *Reader's Digest* seems to have a great interest in copper mines in socialist countries"; when Salvador Allende led a socialist government in Chile, the *Digest* had a reporter study industrial accidents in Chilean copper mines, and soon after, "the CIA organized the copper workers to go on strike against the workers' government, a classic example of psychological warfare."[57]

With McGurl's approach in mind, we might call *The Ugly American* a middlebrow modernism that applies the workshop dictum "write what you know" to the experience of CIA skullduggery.[58] As Klein notes, Lederer and Burdick "organize the novel as a kind of dossier, full of resumes, State Department cables, letters from foreign service recruits, and transcripts of interviews."[59] But

The Ugly American's short stories might also be likened to the Hemingway-influenced work that would make up the portfolio for an MFA degree.

Indeed, the story "Nine Friends" narrates an effort to export the Program Era to Asia so as to fight communism. Like several of the Ugly Americans, Father Finian, a Catholic priest from Massachusetts, is a professional writer whose published articles include "The New Deal and Catholic Social Theory." Paralleling the fictional Hillandale's inspiration by Lansdale, Finian was inspired in part by Thomas A. Dooley, an expatriate physician who enjoyed celebrity status in the 1950s. Dooley took part in relocating Vietnamese Catholics to the south of the country after the French defeat at Dien Bien Phu in 1954, writing about the experience in his bestselling *Deliver Us from Evil* (1956), a book that not only introduced Americans to the anticommunist cause in Southeast Asia but also to Vietnam. Dooley received extensive editorial and marketing advice from Lederer, who helped to create Dooley's rebellious yet well-meaning narrative persona. In this view, the character of "Dooley" in *Deliver Us from Evil* was a kind of dry run for the array of think-outside-the-box anticommunists in Lederer's *The Ugly American*. After Dooley's death, it was revealed that he had been a CIA employee and that many of the events in *Deliver Us from Evil* were fabricated. But *Deliver Us from Evil*, which was serialized in *Reader's Digest*, was a propaganda effort from the start. Many critics have speculated that the Lederer-Dooley endeavor was precisely intended to engineer support for Cold War policies in the region.

Given Dooley's CIA connection, it is unsurprising that the fictional Finian in *The Ugly American* comes off as a covert operative as well as Catholic priest. However, Finian's activity in Burma also suggests the workshop context of Burdick's "Rest Camp on Maui" and the Bread Loaf Writers' Conference, as well as the contemporaneous emergence of MFA programs at Stanford and Iowa. As Bennett observes in *Workshops of Empire* (2015), "the first generation of soldier writers" took Hemingway as their model: "Hemingway was *the* influence in writing workshops full of demobilized G.I.s."[60] This was not merely due to Hemingway's masculine persona but to his writing style, which lent itself to classroom instruction. "A great challenge for the creative writing classroom is how to regulate an activity . . . whose premise is the validity and importance of subjective accounts of experience," Bennett observes. "On what grounds does a teacher correct student choices?"[61] Hemingway provided an answer with workshop-friendly formal methods: "One classmate can point to metaphors drawn from a reality too distant from the characters' worldview.

Another can strike out those adverbs."[62] Accompanying these formal methods was a reactionary view of Hemingway that suited the anticommunist liberal consensus. Southern Agrarians turned postwar New Critics, as well as reformed Marxists, could agree that while historical and economic conditions might vary, "people are people" and "universals endure."[63]

The Ugly American constructs a globalized Hemingway who lends himself to expression by Asian intellectuals. In addition to his tough persona, Finian takes a stylistic minimalism from Hemingway, which enables communication in a foreign land: "Finian had also learned the language. He had chewed into it like a cold chisel driven into granite. . . . Leaf, tree, water, big, little, walk, hop, jump, down, sideways, lizard, river . . . he was astonished at how few were the essential words of a language. . . . He wanted complex needs to be put in simple sentences" (*UA* 49). Finian fights communism in Burma by forming a small group (the "nine friends" of the story's title) that doubles as an anticommunist cell and writing workshop. In a series of meetings in the forest, Finian sets the agenda ("why do Burmans believe what the Communists say?" [56]), then goes silent as the young Burmese debate the question amongst themselves. Eventually Finian produces a report on the discussions:

1. We desired a community in which choice of life and religion existed.
3. . . . [W]e had to demonstrate to the people that the Communists had no interest in them, but were interested only in power. . . .
4. . . . [W]e had to make ourselves experts in persuasion.
5. We had to persuade in terms of events which are known to Burmans.
6. We had to persuade in words which would be understood by everyone.
7. Complex ideas had to be put dramatically and powerfully. (*UA* 59–60)

Finian's students thus learn some of creative writing's mantras, including "write what you know" and "show don't tell." Armed with a "ditto machine" brought from the US, Finian and his protégés found a journal, *The Communist Farmer*, which excerpts and abridges work by writers like Marx and Lenin, in keeping with the modus operandi of *Reader's Digest* (*UA* 60). The goal is to reveal to Burmese peasants the contempt in which they supposedly are held by communist intellectuals, in "a classic psywar misinformation campaign."[64] The quasi-literary nature of the whole enterprise, and its basis in classrooms and Bread Loaf conferences, is pointed up by Finian's request to the American Commissary for pens, to be distributed "as prizes to the natives who did the best job in distributing their newspaper" (*UA* 70). With the usual bureaucratic hypocrisy, the ambassador, who lives large at taxpayers' expense, objects that "[he] couldn't allow individuals to use commissary items to support private business" (70). *The Ugly American* not only makes the point that creative entrepreneurs are more adept at fighting Asian communism than state bureaucracies, but that this is the very basis for differentiating freedom from tyranny.

Highlighting the element of creative writing makes sense of the many absurdities that Buttinger notes in his *Dissent* review, in which he discusses *The Communist Farmer* at length. "Was it distributed free and if so, where did Finian get the money to supply himself with paper, to house his 'machine' and to support himself and his busy crew? ... Questions of this nature are never entertained by Lederer and Burdick, who also ignore the 'fact' that hardly more than thirty per cent of these northern Burmese peasants would be able to read."[65] With some exasperation, Buttinger goes on to observe that we are never told if the journal runs genuine work by communists like Mao Zedong, or articles ascribed to communists that are actually ghostwritten by Finian and his students. The story's absurdities remain absurd, but are more comprehensible when one recognizes that "Nine Friends" emerges from a crossroads that includes US espionage in the Third World, CIA involvement with magazines ranging from *Partisan Review* to *Reader's Digest*, and creative writing classes that retain traces of their gestation in Quonset huts. Covert funds that were exposed a decade later by *Ramparts*, and explored in more detail by Saunders at the end of the century, are hidden in plain sight—only the CIA could have paid for Finian's enterprise, but this intelligence agency blends into the foliage in what was, for most American readers, an exotic locale.

To return to McGurl's model of creative writing pedagogy, although the Burmese student-writers learn to write what they know, and show instead of tell, one can't say that they find their voices, since the entire project aims to rob Burma of national self-determination. Instead of creating an aesthetic democracy, Finian and the Ugly Americans deter democracy, in accordance with other elements of US foreign policy.[66] Albeit crudely, Lederer and Burdick represent what the CIA was actually up to at the time in developing countries. As Juliana Spahr observes, "The list of journals that the CIA either seems to have in some way been behind the inception of (either directly established or the journal was created out of the social milieus that were formed because of CIA-funded reading rooms or other cultural organizations), significantly supported, or manipulated in some way is long and international."[67] Spahr's list indicates that at the time of *The Ugly American*'s publication, the CIA was moving from a focus on Europe (where it supported journals like *Encounter* and *The Paris Review*) to Asia and Africa (where it backed journals like Indonesia's *Konfrontasi* and Uganda's *Transition*).

It is beyond this chapter's scope to assess whether CIA backing compromised Asian or African writers. What can be said is that the CIA attempted to counter the influence of the "the novelists' international," which is Denning's term for an international network of modernist writers who were broadly associated with socialism but departed from Soviet-mandated realism.[68] Wright had been one of the foremost figures of this network in the 1930s and early 1940s, drawing inspiration from authors as varied as Gorky, Joyce, Proust, and Malraux, while writing masterpieces of progressive fiction. Despite its rich insights, I think that *Workshops of Empire* underplays the significance of this earlier time period. Focused on Paul Engle, who wrote doctrinaire leftist poetry in the mid-1930s, Bennett overlooks the variety of workshops—from the FWP, to Wright's South Side Writers' Group, to the union-supported writing groups described in Denning's *Cultural Front*—which offered writers the opportunity to "coordinate the personal with the national or international."[69] These workshops often looked to international models for inspiration, from Moscow to Malraux's Paris, so as to strengthen American democracy; in contrast, postwar America saw itself as a model for everyone else to follow, a drive underwritten by CIA influence and money.

As I shall explore in more detail in the final chapter, Wright himself followed this exceptionalist trend. A certain mythology has grown up around his account of the Bandung Conference, *The Color Curtain* (1956), which Vijay Prashad calls a foundational document of Afro-Asian solidarity.[70] Yet the CIA-backed Congress for Cultural Freedom financed Wright's visit to Indonesia. In addition to visiting Bandung for the international conference, he socialized with various writers and critics in Jakarta who also had CIA ties.[71] Contrary to some accounts, the conference itself was not entirely ignored by the American press; the May 2, 1955, issue of *Life* magazine gives a wide overview of the meeting, complete with photographs and short biographies of all the major participants. While *Life* is happy to report that the participants often disagreed with each other, thus forestalling any united front against American control, *The Color Curtain* is often more frankly

Orientalist. Wright denounces the legacy of Western colonialism, but his description of Chinese premier Zhou Enlai, who "had no little experience in organizing mystic-minded peasants . . . [and] would be content for a while to snuggle as close as possible to this gummy mass and watch and wait," does not give anticolonial nationalism much ideological breathing room.[72] Although "Nine Friends" might seem exaggerated, Finian's role was assumed by various American writer-travelers who may have been contrarian critics of their own government at times, but were nevertheless stridently anticommunist in a way that lessened Third World countries' self-determination.

On the Road in the New Frontier:
From the GI Bill to the Peace Corps

Kennedy saw himself as a patron of the arts, but his New Frontier would be different from the New Deal. As Borchert observes, the post-Sputnik era saw unprecedented federal support for universities, which created new opportunities for writers but also came with restricted political parameters: "Writers who might once have worked for the FWP were now more likely to enjoy federal support, if they did at all, in this roundabout way: as academics. Others found succor in the funds that sloshed between government agencies, private foundations, and CIA front organizations, as certain little magazines and writing workshops enlisted—wittingly and unwittingly—in the Cold War. Such an atmosphere would have made the memory of a bona fide government cultural project such as the WPA's Federal #1—initiated, staffed, and run by the state—seem like a shocking aberration from a misguided time."[73] Borchert's remark serves as an excellent thesis statement for an analysis of On the Road: still often read as a novel of personal freedom and cultural subversion, the novel is also a meditation upon the institutions that enable creative writing. As such, it shows how certain elements of the counterculture merged with Ugly American discourse.

After founding his creative writing program at Stanford, Stegner commented: "The young writer who in the twenties headed for Greenwich Village and who in the thirties took out by boxcar to bum his way through a hundred odd jobs to fame now heads for some graduate school of English to study with some professional writer."[74] The relative stability of graduate school might seem far removed from the Beat ethos, which for many critics, involved "the street as a viable alternative to the university."[75] But as Nancy Grace points out, the majority of the Beats "enjoyed what only about five percent of the American population from the 1930s through 1950 could afford: a college education of at least several terms."[76] Kerouac himself attended Columbia University on a football scholarship, and continued his association with campus life after dropping out. In part 2 of *On the Road*, the protagonist Sal Paradise effuses: "What I wanted was to take one more magnificent trip to the West Coast and get back in time for the spring semester in school. And what a trip it turned out to be!... I drew my GI check and gave Dean eighteen dollars to mail to his wife; she was waiting for him to come home and she was broke."[77] The passage indicates the essential link between freewheeling travel on one hand, and regular GI checks and university semesters on the other.

In fact, *On the Road* is just a narration of the transition from the FWP, to the GI Bill, to CIA-sponsored literary initiatives. Kerouac was born in 1922 into a conservative family in Massachusetts, of French Canadian background. It does not seem likely that his family would have appreciated the FWP's *Massachusetts: A Guide to Its Places and People*, since his father detested Roosevelt and the New Deal.[78] Nevertheless, Kerouac grew up with FDR's Fireside Chats on the radio, and enrolled at Columbia when the Guides were being released to great public acclaim. Many critics have noted that despite *On the Road*'s reputation for spontaneity—Kerouac taped together a long scroll and wrote the first draft continuously, aided by coffee and speed—his novel had prior versions. But it is also important to note that Kerouac's experience of travel in the late 1940s and early '50s, upon which the novel was based, was itself mediated by research and guidebooks. *On the Road* is a pre–Interstate Highway System novel; these freeways, signed into law by Eisenhower, were only begun in 1956. In the late 1940s, one would need to do a certain amount of homework to travel across the country, and like the novel's author, Sal has the characteristics of a high-achieving student: "I'd been poring over maps of the United States in Paterson for months, even reading books about the pioneers and savoring names like Platte and Cimarron and so on" (*OTR* 11). It was in this interim period—between the late 1930s, and the late 1950s—that the American Guide Series was relevant for actual travel (since then, they have mostly been used for research).

I suspect that Kerouac actually turned to the guides to write his novel; not only that, but he would have made a stellar FWP researcher and writer himself, had he been born earlier. Wearing his learning on his sleeve as he hitchhikes through the northeast, Sal informs us that he is traveling through "the same wilderness Ben Franklin plodded in the oxcart days when he was postmaster, the same as it was when George Washington was a wild-buck Indian-fighter, when Daniel Boone told stories by Pennsylvania lamps and promised to find the Gap, when Bradford built his road" (95). In keeping with the Guides' state-based approach to American culture, Sal meets characters like "Mississippi Gene" and "Montana Slim" (24), while the novel's hero Dean Moriarty has "a real Oklahoma accent" (4). The third chapter offers us a condensed guide to Nebraska—its history, economy, topography—followed by Sal's claim that as he rode on a truck while drinking alcohol, he "took a big swig in the wild, lyrical, drizzling air of Nebraska" (22). According to Griswold, the American Guides invented the idea that for writers of literature, Nebraska had a special lyrical quality to its air that was unique to the state.

Another way that the FWP influenced *On the Road* is through its folklore programs. Although Kerouac's interest in jazz and Zen Buddhism has drawn more attention, he was also a fan of Black folk singers such as Huddie Ledbetter ("Lead Belly"), as well as deeply inspired by poems such as Carl Sandburg's 1936 masterwork *The People, Yes*, which tried to achieve a kind of collective American folk voice. The Guides took part in this effort to record American folklore; director Alsberg continually pestered his state directors to put folklore in the guidebooks, and on one occasion, was rebuffed when the New Jersey director "airily asserted that there wasn't any."[79] For his part, Kerouac insisted that the northeast had folklore, having Sal encounter the "Ghost of the Susquehanna," a "shriveled little old man" who haunts the back roads of Pennsylvania (*OTR* 94). More importantly, Kerouac turns his Beat colleagues into folkloric characters. The FWP's folklore director, Benjamin Botkin, thought that the study of folklore should emphasize "the continual creative response of various American subcultures to their world."[80] In an early article called "Lore of the Lizzie Label," Botkin gave scholarly attention to signs that college students attached to their Model T's (the precursors of today's bumper stickers). As Hirsch explains, "by referring to literate college students as a folk group and the printed material they created as lore, Botkin knew he was pushing far beyond his contemporaries' understanding of these terms."[81] Botkin's *A Treasury of American Folklore* (1944) was a bestselling testament to this FWP initiative. *On the Road*'s representation of the Beat coterie—Neal Cassady as Dean; Allen Ginsberg as Carlo Marx; William S. Burroughs as Old Bull Lee—seems congruent with this revisionist approach to American folklore. Kerouac makes a self-conscious attempt to rewrite his "current friends," all of them "intellectuals," as folkloric legends: "Carlo Marx and his nutty surrealist low-voiced serious staring talk, Old Bull Lee and his critical anti-everything drawl" (9).

One of the foundational texts of the American counterculture is thus intimately linked to New Deal government programs and what Hirsch calls their "democratic romantic nationalism."[82] However, although *On the Road* retains the imprint of the federal guidebooks, Kerouac was hardly a spokesperson for progressive causes in his own day; he cheered on Joseph McCarthy (while smoking marijuana) during the HUAC hearings. As Dickstein reminds us, in the 1950s, "patriotism and anti-Communism became ways of discrediting liberalism and breaking up the electoral majority once enjoyed by the New Deal."[83] In ideological terms, we would be more likely to associate *On the Road* with a libertarian frontier than with a welfare state that flirted with socialism. The historian Thomas Frank has argued persuasively that Beat literature was a precursor of neoliberal capitalism. Frank observes that the Beats' cultural resistance was enabled by the latest advances in consumer technology: "That frenzied sensibility of pure experience, life on the edge, immediate gratification, and total freedom from moral restraint, which the Beats first propounded back in those heady days when suddenly everyone could have their own TV and powerful V-8, has stuck with us through all the intervening years and become something of a permanent American style."[84] In Frank's account, corporate America caught up to the Beats rather quickly. *The Conquest of Cool* (1997) argues that the paradigm of 1950s advertising, which emphasized science and rationalism, gave way to marketing strategies that encouraged consumers to think of themselves as rebels: indeed, management gurus and advertisers anticipated the cultural ferment of the later 1960s. As Frank emphasizes in his article "Why Johnny Can't Dissent," the Beats and their descendants hold "that the paramount ailment of our society is conformity, a malady that has variously been described as over-organization, bureaucracy, homogeneity"; however, this idea has become "capitalist orthodoxy, its hunger for transgression upon transgression now perfectly suited to an economic-cultural regime that runs on ever-faster cyclings of the new."[85] For Frank, this mindset has toxic consequences for the welfare state: if everyone is a rebel, the sometimes humdrum but vital programs of a national government are overlooked or discredited.

Yet Frank's argument points up a rich irony where *On the Road* is concerned: although the book is often celebrated as a resistance of early Cold

War norms, Sal's unfettered individualism is enabled by the Cold War state, specifically the GI Bill. As Joseph Darda observes: "The GI Bill gave white working-class men a foothold in a growing middle class, functioning as a form of white affirmative action, a GI 'bill of whites,' that would worsen racial and gender imbalances in income and wealth."[86] Just so, although he seems the epitome of countercultural deviance, Sal is a professional in training, "going to school on the GI Bill of Rights" (*OTR* 99). "Moloch! Moloch! ... demonic industries! spectral nations! invincible madhouses! granite cocks! monstrous bombs!," Ginsberg rails in the seminal poem *Howl*, attacking the convergence of industrialism and war that would later be dubbed the military-industrial complex.[87] Pace Ginsberg, one helpful thing that Moloch does for Sal is pay for his travels. "Sav[ing] about fifty dollars from old veteran benefits" enables Sal's first trip to the West Coast (*OTR* 10); a succession of GI checks funds a follow-up trip across the country (117, 141, 161); "GI education checks" enable a brief relocation to Denver (163); finally, when he concludes his travels with a trip to Mexico, one of Sal's friends imagines "sign[ing] up for GI Bill in Mexico City College" (234). Not only are the Beats' road trips funded by the US government, but veteran's benefits are most likely a part of the money-changing ritual in the border city of Nuevo Laredo, Mexico, when "[they] saw great stacks of pesos on a table and learned that eight of them made an American buck" (250). A government program thus enables the vision of Mexico as "one vast Bohemian camp" (275).

On the Road allows us to emphasize the distinction between FDR's Second Bill of Rights, which would have created a more ecumenical welfare state, and the GI Bill, which streamlined middle-class white privilege. *On the Road* narrates an escape from the New Deal–era solidarities described in the introduction, almost to the point of parody. If we figure Wright's poem "Transcontinental" and *On the Road* as automobiles, "Transcontinental" is continually picking people up, becoming ever more diverse in terms of race and gender, while *On the Road* takes on passengers for short intervals before kicking them off. For example, Sal briefly works as a cotton picker in California in an episode that recalls *The Grapes of Wrath* (1939) as well as Carlos Bulosan's *America Is in the Heart* (1946), but when he receives money from his aunt, he quickly leaves a Mexican community, as well as his young lover, behind. Desperately ill in Mexico City, Sal realizes "what a rat [Dean] was" when Dean abandons him to return to the States, but this seems like karmic comeuppance for what Sal himself has done for the entire novel (*OTR* 276). For Dean's part, while his Oklahoma accent recalls the progressive regionalism of the 1930s, he is also "a sideburned hero of the snowy West," the embodiment of the frontier that Roosevelt criticized (4). Dean evokes both of these time periods: a delinquent from a broken home, he might have benefited from New Deal social policies in an earlier day, but at midcentury he enjoys auto-fueled abandon as one of the people of plenty. A remarkable hallucination that Sal has while driving through Mexico is an encapsulation of the argument of *The Global Frontier*:

> But now the bouncing was no longer unpleasant; it was the most pleas-ant and graceful billowy trip in the world, as over a blue sea, and Dean's face was suffused with an unnatural glow that was like gold. . . . In that moment, too, he looked so exactly like Franklin Delano Roosevelt— some delusion in my flaming eyes and floating brain—that I drew up in my seat and gasped with amazement. . . . The mere thought of looking out the window at Mexico . . . was like recoiling from some gloriously riddled glittering treasure-box that you're afraid to look at because of your eyes, they bend inward, the riches and treasures are too much to take all at once. (259)

The scene might be read as a general commentary on postwar American writers, who once exhibited commitments to virtuous New Deal institutions and progressive sensibilities but later betrayed these commitments as their professional privileges, their transnational ambitions, and their globalized personae took hold. I sometimes wonder if the entire novel can be read as a lament for the national solidarity of the Great Depression of Kerouac's late childhood and early youth. Jason Spangler reads *On the Road* in this way when he calls Kerouac "a child of the 1930s" whose "work serves as a memory bank and moral conscience for victims of Depression trauma."[88] Even so, the book does not have the subversive value that people still ascribe to it. Although Kerouac was sometimes criticized by high-minded Cold War tastemakers in journals like *Encounter* and *Partisan Review*, his own writing was often published in these same Cold War liberal journals. Sal's account of his brief stay in the Mexican community in California was published in the *Paris Review*, and "A Billowy Trip in the World," which centers on a visit to a Mexi-can brothel, appeared in the annual *New Directions*. This latter story, which serves as the climax to the novel, is set in Ciudad Victoria (called Gregoria by Kerouac), the capital of the state of Tamaulipas. The Beats experience a "por-nographic hasheesh daydream" by having sex with Mexican teenagers while blasting Pérez Prado records (265), so that "all the city of Gregoria could hear the good times" (261).[89] In my view, the term "sexual liberation" has always been problematic and even oxymoronic, but in this passage, the Beats definitely come across as agents of sexual imperialism, exploiters instead of liberators. While *On the Road*'s interest in poor nonwhite cultures might depart from the middle-class mores of the time, this interest nevertheless seems a CIA-endorsed form of cultural hybridity that can fairly be connected with American global dominance.[90]

If one views Kerouac and the Beats in this way, it is not surprising that an anticommunist political science professor at UC Berkeley would take an interest in them. Burdick was teaching at UC Berkeley at the same time that Kerouac and the poet Gary Snyder bonded over a shared interest in art and Eastern religions. This relationship was memorialized in Kerouac's *The Dharma Bums*, which was published in October 1958, the same month as the book version of *The Ugly American*. In contrast to his mentor Stegner, who thought the California counterculture was "the quintessence of individualism run amok," Burdick was fascinated by their energies, even as he specifically resisted New Left politics.[91] In 1959, Burdick wrote a brief journal article, "The Politics of the Beat Generation," in which he noted: "The hipster believes that the organization and institutions of our society have, beneath their confection-like facade, killing and senseless muscles."[92] This was the anxiety that Burdick had himself recently expressed in *The Ugly American*, and would later express in novels like *Fail-Safe* and *The 480* (1965).[93] Although Burdick does not see the Beats becoming a mass movement, he claims that "their *potential* would seem to be growing."[94]

I think that Lederer and Burdick found countercultural attitudes useful in their attempt to overwrite national liberation movements in developing countries, and make overseas adventure seem more exciting than fighting for social change in the US. In particular, *The Ugly American*'s stories about Edwin Hillandale respond to American youth culture, although they were directly inspired by Lederer's friend, the military advisor and CIA agent Edward G. Lansdale. Max Boot's recent biography describes Lansdale as a "laid-back advertising man from California [who] became a guerrilla-warfare guru, covert-action specialist, and one of the most unconventional generals in the nation's history.... [His] yin-yang approach, of hunting down guerrillas and terrorists while trying to attract the support of the uncommitted, is the basis of modern 'population-centric' counterinsurgency doctrine."[95] Lansdale's career began in the Philippines, where he helped to suppress the Huk Rebellion, a peasant movement that opposed the landed oligarchy. Although Lansdale's activities are still classified, he did brag about one bloody propaganda trick, when he captured a Philippine nationalist insurgent, punctured two holes in his neck, and drained his blood, then left his corpse on a rural trail in hopes that this supposed victim of a rural vampire would terrify the insurgents and their sympathizers.[96] Lansdale also played an advisory role to Ramon Magsaysay, who appeared on *Time* magazine's cover in November 1951 and won a landslide presidential vote in 1953 with extensive CIA support.

Flushed with success from his Philippine adventure, Lansdale then transferred to Vietnam. In addition to fomenting discord in North Vietnam, Lansdale sought to do for South Vietnam's leader Ngo Dinh Diem what he had done for Magsaysay, making him the embodiment of the American Century in Asia.[97] Here there is an overlap with Graham Greene's novel *The Quiet American* (1955), which criticizes this imperial fantasy. In *The Quiet American*, the supposedly naïve and innocent Alden Pyle, who is actually a CIA operative, comes to Vietnam looking for an alternative to both a dying French colonialism and an insurgent native communism, an America-friendly "Third Force."[98] Pyle supplies a local mercenary, General Thé, with US-manufactured plastic, which Thé uses for bombings that will be blamed on the communists. After a deadly explosion in a crowded square, the novel's protagonist, an English journalist named Thomas Fowler, helps the communists assassinate Pyle. According to Boot, Greene did not base his character Pyle on Lansdale, but *The Quiet American* became associated with the Lansdale legend. Lansdale himself served as an advisor on the 1958 film version of *The Quiet American*, which (much to Greene's chagrin) rewrote Pyle as the hero and Fowler as a conniving dupe of the communists.

We might see the tension between *The Quiet American* and *The Ugly American* not only as a battle over Lansdale's public image, but also as a battle between rival writer-spies, as American imperial influence replaced the dying British and French empires. As Robert Stone observes in an introduction to *The Quiet American*, "[Greene's] family was of the professional middle class, the backbone of the British Empire in its last years. If not a ruling class, it was certainly an administrative cadre and a self-conscious elite.... It was Greene's fortune ... to witness the rise of American influence in the world. The sense of imperial mission left him sentimental and proprietary about what we still call today the Third World."[99] Greene's brother worked in Malaysia conducting psychological warfare against communist insurgents, and Greene himself operated as a spy in Vietnam for MI6, since Britain was trying to find its own version of Ngo Dinh Diem or the fictional General Thé.[100] Meanwhile, Lederer also did intelligence work in Asia and may have considered himself the equal of Lansdale, as Robert Dean relates:

> An admirer of Lansdale, Lederer also saw himself as one of the adventurous imperial operatives defending American interests in Southeast Asia. Admiral Felix Stump, commander of the Pacific fleet, had given Lederer a variety of political assignments in the region, including the loan of the captain's services to Allen Dulles of the CIA "in connection with [a] special project" in Indochina. Lederer once boasted to a friend that his tasks involved "some of the blinkingest cloak and dagger stuff."[101]

One can therefore imagine Lederer taking Greene's representation of American naivete and vulgarity quite personally. Greene not only makes Pyle ineffectual, but also an embodiment of a plasticized mass culture that contrasts with British sophistication (the novel begins with an epigraph from Byron, and Fowler is able to trade quotes from Pascal with the French chief of police). As for Pyle, "he looked more than ever out of place: he should have stayed at home," a judgment that Fowler applies to Americans in general: "I was tired of the whole pack of them with their private stores of Coca-Cola and their portable hospitals and their too wide cars."[102] Fowler thus defeats a vulgar consumerism in addition to a pernicious foreign influence. In fact, Greene sometimes undermines his critique by making Pyle such a naïf, since it's hard to see how he can be innocent and a scheming manipulator at the same time (in an especially low blow, Pyle is still a virgin!). *The Quiet American*'s criticism of American impotence and ineptitude came out at a particularly stressful time for Lederer, when he was making a failed bid to work at MIT as a foreign policy strategist:

> Lederer believed that his experience made him an expert in counterinsurgency, psychological warfare, and "nation building." *The Ugly American* was a mass-market expression of Lederer's thwarted ambition to join the ranks of counterinsurgency defense intellectuals at CIA-sponsored think tanks like MIT's Center for International Studies (CENIS) to help in "developing a system of mass producing a crowd of 'poor men's Lansdales.'"[103]

In light of Bennett's *Workshops of Empire*, we might call Lederer the reverse of Iowa's Paul Engle: whereas Engle was a failed poet who became a top-notch administrator and supporter of new talent, Lederer was a frustrated would-be administrator who became a bestselling novelist. In any case, Lederer's team-up with Burdick provides more evidence that "Rest Camp on Maui" leads us toward US foreign policy and not just the dynamics of the MFA workshop.

As we have seen, to an extent Lederer and Burdick grant *The Quiet American*'s charge of incompetence, except they specifically target the US foreign service bureaucracy. Meanwhile, in order to upstage the supercilious Greene and redeem American creativity and cultural savvy, *The Ugly American* turns not only to Hemingway but also to the Beats. In a scathing criticism of *The Ugly American*'s reimagination of the American West in a Third World context, Richard Drinnon argues that "[Edwin Hillandale, the fictional version of Lansdale] was a sort of twentieth-century reincarnation of Johnny Appleseed, warning folks in the backcountry against modern merciless savages [i.e., communists] and handing out the seeds and saplings of American democracy."[104] The novel indeed rewrites this traditional frontier mythology, but its fictional version of Lansdale also draws on countercultural energies so as to depart from Pyle's shrink-wrapped insularity. In "The Six-Foot Swami from Savannah," Hillandale uses his certification from the Chungking School of Occult Science to bond with Sarkhanese officials, including the prime minister, who "himself has a Ph.D. in Occult Science" (*UA* 181). These passages have been likened to Rudyard Kipling's *Kim* (1901), but I think they also respond to the Beats' growing interest in Eastern religions coupled with the novel's continual emphasis on expert professionalism.

The Ugly American anticipates and globalizes Frank's argument about the Beats—that is, that the Beats anticipated neoliberalism and inspired Madison Avenue advertising agencies. Hillandale draws on countercultural energies to defeat leftist nationalism, while also coming off as a CIA-backed ad man. The character is initially introduced to us through Magsaysay, who himself appears as a character in the novel, telling an American ambassador to keep his personnel "out of the cocktail circuit, away from bureaucrats": "The Rag-Time Kid—Colonel Hillandale. He can do anything" (*UA* 108). The story that follows, "The Ragtime Kid," downplays Hillandale's military status, telling us that he "was sent to Manila as liaison officer to something or other" and that his middle initial stands for "Barnum" (*UA* 110). He "embrace[s] everything Filipino . . . even attend[ing] the University in his spare hours to study Tagalog," so that he becomes "Manila's own private character" (110). To support Magsaysay's presidential campaign in an unfriendly province, Hillandale rides

into the town square on a red motorcycle with "The Ragtime Kid" painted on
its gas tank. What follows is a G-rated version of the Beats' visit to Gregoria;
playing "favorite Filipino tunes in a loud and merry way" on his harmonica,
Hillandale gets "three hundred Filipinos standing in a tightly packed circle
singing their heads off" (112). In the presidential election that follows, Magsaysay handily wins the province. But the real-life Lansdale never mastered
Tagalog or owned a motorcycle.[105] Instead, Hillandale's small carnival reads
like one of the many spontaneous parties in *On the Road*, or a benign version
of Marlon Brando's film *The Wild One* (1953), through a tourism-oriented
image of Philippine culture. The episode looks ahead to white male fantasies,
arguably found in both the Peace Corps and in *Lonely Planet* guidebooks, of
being a rock star in the Third World.

In a word, Hillandale is a Cold Warrior but also an anti-Pyle, drawing on
countercultural energies to make fighting communism seem cool and fun. The
novel did the trick, since many young people signed up for the Peace Corps
after reading it. It would be unfair to call these recruits "poor men's Lans-
dales"; as Elizabeth Cobbs Hoffman has emphasized, many young Americans
were motivated by genuine idealism, and they often did good in developing
countries.[106] Nevertheless, part of their mission was to maneuver decolonizing
movements in accordance with American interests. There is even an overlap
between the Peace Corps and the New Frontier of modernization theory,
since Rostow's *The Stages of Economic Growth* (subtitled *A Non-Communist
Manifesto*) was required reading for the first trainees.[107]

From the Beat perspective, this might seem like cynical co-optation, especially since the Beats themselves were not welcome in the new organization.
A *New York Times* article claimed that "Peace Corps applicants are tested
with a thoroughness known only to generations of white mice: misfits, beats,
soapbox rebels and introverted malcontents are spotted and rejected with
surprising skill."[108] As Molly Geidel points out, "the Peace Corps drew on
the same desires and identifications that were becoming dominant in white
youth culture and attempted to reroute those desires and identifications into
their own narratives . . . expelling beatniks because of the beats' sustained
forays into homosexuality and risky racial fantasy."[109] But we might ask how
risky the Beats really were. As I have suggested above, although they often
saw themselves as traveling beyond the clampdown of state authority, their
privileges were enabled precisely by state power. As we will see in the next
chapter, as cartoonish as the character of Hillandale may seem, he is akin to

other transnational picaros such as Burroughs's A. J. in *Naked Lunch* as well as various subversive tourists from the later cut-up trilogy (the Subliminal Kid in *Nova Express* conducts a one-man psywar akin to Finian's crew in "Nine Friends"). Arguing that Bellow's *Henderson the Rain King* "embrace[s] the creative imagination of man as the antidote to the bureaucrat's bookkeeping," Merve Emre perceives an incongruity in the novel being assigned to Peace Corps trainees.[110] "Bellow . . . was roped into an institutional process of which he was critical: an act of institutional training on the part of the Peace Corps book committee that encouraged readerly identification, all the while occluding the novel's critical edge."[111] But if we read Henderson as an Ugly American-style anticommunist professional, the book's inclusion on the Peace Corps syllabus is understandable. This observation about Bellow also holds for feminist and queer writers whom Emre sees as vaguely oppositional to mainstream Cold War norms. In June 1956, Bishop wrote to her fellow poet Robert Lowell, "I read *The Quiet American* expecting to be made mad, but it's just rather silly, or else poor Hemingway."[112] Bishop's remark not only functions as a pithy summary of *The Ugly American*'s response to Greene, but also indicates her own problematic relationship to Third World nationalism, since she was close friends with a Lansdale-like personage, the Brazilian politician and media gadfly Carlos Lacerda. Although we would not usually put Bishop, or Wright, in the same sentence as Allen Dulles, these writers indirectly partook in the suppression of anti-imperial nationalist resistance, as we shall see in the following chapters.

Chapter Two

. . . .

The Last Frontier

William S. Burroughs's Early Work
and International Tourism

William S. Burroughs's image as a subversive avant-garde writer, uncompromisingly contesting all forms of social control, has shown remarkable staying power. Over sixty years after the publication of *Naked Lunch* (1959), many critics would agree with Timothy S. Murphy that Burroughs's literary career is based upon a resistance to "the totalitarian system of modern capitalism and its ideological tool, the state."[1] It follows that Burroughs urges us to contest capitalist globalization, since his "oppositional art . . . challenge[s] the standardized consciousness imposed by multinational corporate enterprise."[2] Burroughs's radical thought also has important lessons for the developing world. Oliver Harris claims that Burroughs received a "political education" during his travel in South America, which makes for a meaningful link between *The Yage Letters* (1963) and Che Guevara's tale of the road, *The Motorcycle Diaries* (1995).[3] Brian Edwards likens Burroughs to Frantz Fanon, arguing that his "sympathetic attitude toward Maghrebi independence" was complicated by a concern for just forms of postcolonial government: "the problem (as Fanon also sensed within the Algerian revolution) is whether that which will follow revolution will replicate the established order."[4]

This chapter begins by putting Burroughs's postmodern art in the context of international tourism, which in the late 1940s and the 1950s was dominated by American money. Although he favored an off-the-beaten-track itinerary, Burroughs shared in the mobility and buying power of the postwar American middle class, and valorized destinations such as Mexico, where a "single man lives high . . . for $100 per month"; Ecuador, where supposedly "2 ex-soldiers" traveling with $2,000 "[n]ow own large banana plantation, hacienda, live like kings"; and Tangier, where one can "have a room in best district for 50¢ per day."[5] My purpose here is not simply to denounce Burroughs for "playing the imperialist Ugly American abroad, able to buy what and whoever he wants with his 'Yankee dollar.'"[6] In keeping with the analysis of *The Ugly American* in the previous chapter, I think that our evaluation of the liberatory power of Burroughs's early work relates to how we evaluate a national government as an agent of progressive change. According to Edwards, although Burroughs may have flirted with "American Orientalism," *Naked Lunch* ultimately "refuses the narrative coherence or the authorial stability that the pure American voice usually delivers. . . . The breakdown of smooth rendering of speech is connected with Burroughs's antinational project and thus resists globalization, which relies on coherent difference and on the maintenance of nation-states."[7] But it is not clear that we should celebrate Burroughs for his power to resist state control.

Burroughs valorized the libertarian freedom that he associated with the vanished frontier of the American West, and sought to recover this autonomy outside America's borders. Accordingly, his fragmented narratives are not only influenced by Tristan Tzara and the avant-garde of Paris, but by his status as a kind of subversive travel agent. Burroughs has gained respectability in the American literary academy in large part through his work's anticipation of various concepts in French social theory, and his emphasis on cultural intermixture can even be said to anticipate postcolonial notions of hybridity. But it is necessary to emphasize that his work creatively engages with the global marketplace, which is portrayed as a space of creative freedom. Although Burroughs often subjects America's mainstream culture to withering satire, his narratives are enabled by what one might call "touristic écriture."

The problem with critics' largely unqualified endorsement of Burroughs is that they tend to use a unitary model of domination, with government and the capitalist economy collapsed into a single form of social control. As Brennan and other postcolonial theorists have argued persuasively, a strong national government may be the only way that an exploited populace in the South can resist the wealthy North.[8] Yet Burroughs's 1950s and '60s fiction portrays governments and national liberation movements in the Third World as oppressive forces that place arbitrary limits upon personal freedom. Hence, his vision of creative individualism is only liberating for certain people, as it was articulated in a specifically middle-class idiom, that of the libertarian frontier.

Burroughs's postwar remodeling of this frontier relegates important public issues, most importantly the contestation of social inequality, to the logic of the marketplace. *Naked Lunch*'s model of erotic freedom in the periphery of the world system involves the concept of a (frequently underage) sexual labor force. Meanwhile, *The Soft Machine*'s central chapter, "The Mayan Caper," recodes the anti-imperial Guatemalan revolution as the tale of a heroic individual's struggle against big government.

The final section of the chapter argues that Burroughs anticipates a later era of creative, boundary-crossing professionals who do not owe allegiance to any larger social collectivity such as the nation-state. Observing that Burroughs makes an ideological accommodation with global capitalism does not, in itself, discredit him. In fact, when critics insist that his work functions as a "'blueprint' for identifying and resisting the immanent control mechanisms of global capital," the thrust of their social critique is misdirected, since global capitalism is not *necessarily* an evil, given its technological cornucopia and its encouragement of cultural syncretism.[9] Rather, the ultimate problem with Burroughsian ideology is that it attacks bureaucracy in toto while overlooking the role that a state can play in ameliorating social inequality. The neoliberal hyperindividualism of Burroughs's art assaults "country talk" and "party talk" without offering an alternative vision of shared values and political action.[10]

"Liv[ing] in Proper Style":
Burroughs and International Tourism

Numerous critics link Burroughs's fiction to flight, which becomes the trope for a free subjectivity. For Robin Lydenberg, "the cut-up text suggests the possibility of flight, of continual evolution and change," while Tanner notes that Burroughs's own term for his fragmented technique was "sky writing."[11] In her famous essay on *Naked Lunch*, Mary McCarthy suggests that Burroughsian flight may be more literal.

Last summer at the International Writers' Conference in Edinburgh, I said I thought the national novel, like the nation-state, was dying and that a new kind of novel, based on statelessness, was beginning to be written. This novel had a high, aerial point of view and a plot of perpetual motion. Two experiences, that of exile and that of jet-propelled mass tourism, provided the subject matter for a new kind of story. There

is no novel, yet, that I know of, about mass tourism, but somebody will
certainly write it.[12]

It is significant that McCarthy herself doesn't make the connection between
Naked Lunch and what might be called tourist literature. Instead she refers
to Burroughs's life in Tangier as exile, which is in keeping with his link to an
older modernist tradition of escaping the repression of middlebrow America
for a less restricted, culturally richer life abroad. Likewise, when we depict
Burroughs specifically as an individual who crossed borders, we are likely to
call him an explorer or a traveler instead of a tourist. Fussell makes useful
definitions of these opposed terms: "All three make journeys, but the explorer
seeks the undiscovered, the traveler that which has been discovered by the
mind working in history, the tourist that which has been discovered by en-
trepreneurship and prepared for him by the arts of mass publicity."[13] He adds
that tourism's emphasis on leisure and play contrasts with the work and physical hardship involved in travel, a word which derives from *tripalium*, a Latin
word for a torture instrument.

   In his explicit foray into the genre of travel writing, "In Search of Yage"
(composed in 1953 and comprising most of 1963's *The Yage Letters*, published
with Allen Ginsberg), Burroughs casts himself not merely as a traveler who en-
dures insects and sickness, but as a New World explorer, searching the South
American jungle for a little-known hallucinogen. However, Burroughs did
eventually find his yage, and it is worth looking closely at the vision that not
only concludes his account, but also serves as the centerpiece to *Naked Lunch*
in a chapter entitled simply "The Market." For Ginsberg, the yage experience
revealed that "we are all one Great Being," leading him to assault "A Material-
istic consciousness [which] is attempting to preserve itself from Dissolution by
restriction & persecution of Experience of the Transcendental."[14] Burroughs,
in contrast, emphasizes precisely the material, as a vision of "incredible journeys through deserts and jungles and mountains" ends not in mystical tran-
scendence but rather in the "Composite City where all human potentials are
spread out in a vast silent market"; "crowded cafe[s]" and "unthinkable trades"
surround the traveler who gets "blackout drunk."[15] Instead of falling under
a specific generic rubric of travel writing, "In Search of Yage" itself traces a
route from the exploration of the unknown to the plenum of tourism, where
all forms of experience are available through the marketplace.

   I suggest that the vision of an unfettered free market which concludes

Burroughs's narrative represented precisely what he sought in his journey beyond US borders. Critics generally discuss Burroughs's travel in romantic terms, emphasizing his role as a persecuted addict of opium and its derivatives, and more recently, as a pioneering explorer of queer desire; they have minimized his scathing critique of a welfare state that placed limitations on the total freedom to buy and sell. In various letters to Ginsberg and Kerouac in the late 1940s and early '50s, Burroughs emphasized that the United States was not merely overrestrictive and conformist, but "a Socialistic police state similar to England, and not too different from Russia" (*L* 57). He finishes off this 1949 letter to Ginsberg by declaring "Believe me socialism and communism are synonymous, and both unmitigated evil, and the Welfare State is a Trojan Horse" (58). In 1950 he asked Kerouac, "What ever happened to our glorious Frontier heritage of minding ones [sic] own business? The Frontiersman has shrunk to a wretched, interfering Liberal bureaucrat." Burroughs then goes on to attack Ginsberg, stressing their friend's absorption into a "snivelling, mealy-mouthed tyranny of bureaucrats, social workers, psychiatrists and Union officials" (61). Kerouac did justice to this ideological disposition in his memorable portrait of Burroughs as "Old Bull Lee" in *On the Road*, which stresses Lee's nostalgia for the vanished American frontier. "Bull had a sentimental streak about the old days in America, especially 1910, when you could get morphine in a drugstore without prescription and Chinese smoked opium in their evening windows and the country was wild and brawling and free, with abundance and any kind of freedom for everyone. His chief hate was Washington bureaucracy; second to that, liberals; then cops."[16] Although Lee/Burroughs claims the frontier was alive and well after 1890, he nevertheless endorses Frederick Jackson Turner's vision, which valorizes "dominant individualism" and "that buoyancy and exuberance which comes with freedom" (*FJT* 59), traits which produce an "antipathy to control, and particularly to any direct control" (53). As I discussed in the previous chapter, *On the Road* contains a residual New Dealism in its approach to American geography and history, and its use of folklore. In contrast, Burroughs was a lifelong libertarian who was opposed to activist government; as he remarked of his days at Harvard, when he was irritated by discussions of communism and the "Russian experiment": "I don't want to hear about the fucking masses and I never did."[17]

Rob Johnson has elucidated Burroughs's commitment to frontier libertarianism, which involved a brief life as a conventional farmer in South Texas (a project which accompanied his more well-known East Texas farm, which grew marijuana and opium and served as an entertainment venue for other Beats). "Burroughs saw the farmer as the embodiment of American free enterprise and rugged individualism. . . . Although [his] views on the 'control machine' would later brand him as a member of the counterculture, it is important to know that Burroughs's views on farming were mainstream Republican ones."[18] Burroughs was a fan of the pundit Westbrook Pegler, a print-based predecessor of later white male conservatives on radio and TV such as Rush Limbaugh.[19] Yet Johnson misses an opportunity to show how these views influenced Burroughs's fiction; instead, he goes in the opposite direction, stating that Burroughs's post-Texas intellectual development was oriented toward a quasi-socialistic, communal ideal. Where *Naked Lunch* is concerned, the claim involves putting an enormous amount of weight upon a single passage, that which follows the Talking Asshole routine: "Bureaus cannot live without a host, being true parasitic organisms. (A cooperative on the other hand *can* live without the state. That is the road to follow. The building up of independent units to meet needs of the people who participate in the functioning of the unit. A bureau operates on opposite principle of inventing needs to justify its existence.)"[20] The passage has no clear program for such a cooperative, which might refer to an association of like-minded professionals instead of an anticapitalist society, and it explicitly identifies the *state*, not capitalism, as the major embodiment of humanity's bureaucratic enemy. Something of this critical confusion finds its way into Johnson's otherwise excellent book, as he indicates that Burroughs's endorsement of communes in the 1980s was prefigured by his early profit-sharing plans in South Texas. "When he made a profit, Burroughs says in a letter to Allen Ginsberg, he shared it with the workers, a cooperative business practice that would have made the local farmers suspicious of him and even angry."[21] But this practice is only mentioned in Burroughs's May 1, 1950 letter to Ginsberg, and it is not clear whether it was a nice idea that was never put into practice, or whether it merely involved transactions with business partners such as Kells Elvins. Certainly profit-sharing did *not* involve the Mexican laborers who did the real work, as Johnson makes patent elsewhere: "it was thus all too easy for men like Kells and Burroughs to act the part of landed gentry, complete with dark-skinned workers doing all of the real labor at slave wages."[22] The enforcement of a minimum-wage law is one way in which a state can meet the needs of the people.

Burroughs's sale of his farms did not involve leaving his frontier ideology behind, but rather globalizing this ideology through international travel. If "the tourist is best defined as a fantasist equipped temporarily with unaccustomed

power," as Fussell would have it, then the global power of the dollar enabled
Burroughs to imagine an endless marketplace, unrestricted by state control
or corporate homogenization.[23] While he was not a conventional tourist—
in contemporary terms, Burroughs's wallet-conscious itinerary is more akin
to that of a *Lonely Planet* guidebook—he nevertheless shared in the buying
power of the American middle class. The grandson of the famous inventor of
the adding machine, he never inherited a fortune, but his parents gave him a
monthly allowance of $200. A "tidy sum in those days," according to biogra-
pher Ted Morgan, the money went even farther in less-developed countries.[24]
As Burroughs wrote to Kerouac in 1949, "I am so disgusted with conditions I
may leave the U.S.A. altogether, and remove myself and family to S. America
or Africa. Some place where a man can get something for his money, and live
in proper style" (*L* 27).

Accordingly, Burroughs relocated the frontier from the American West to
the Third World. A 1951 letter to Ginsberg begins by attacking stifling corporate bureaucracy, claiming that because a company "is depersonalized and
guided by no other principle than profit," it "thereby surrenders all claim to
ethical consideration": "A company takes great pains not to be an individual.
A company never trusts anybody with anything. Therefore a company is fair
game, and personally I would not hesitate to defraud a company if I could"
(*L* 79). Importantly, Burroughs attacks organizational conformity and not
capitalism per se, as he goes on to argue that Latin America can allow one to
recover entrepreneurial autonomy, exhorting Ginsberg to become a tycoon in
Mexico.

> One thing I am sure of. If you want to give yourself a chance to get rich
> and live in a style that the U.S. has not seen since 1914, "Go South of
> the Rio Grande, young man." Almost any business is good down here,
> since markets are unlimited. This country down here (I mean the whole
> of Mexico and points south) is about where the U.S. was in 1880 or so. I
> know of any number of business deals here in Mexico D. F. that would
> make any man rich who applied himself over a period of say 10 years. Per-
> sonally I have decided on farming and ranching . . . you live like a king on
> a ranch while you are making the $. Hunting and fishing, and a hacienda
> full of servants for about nothing a year in expenses. (78)

To be sure, Burroughs never followed through on this moneymaking
scheme, which blends the frontier ideal of independent land ownership with
a neocolonial fantasy in which he commands the labor of faceless darker-

skinned minions. In biographical terms, his autonomy was based not on the strenuous effort of business ownership but rather on the creative usage of leisure time. As he told Kerouac, Mexico was "very cheap. A single man could live good for $2 per day in Mexico City liquor included. $1 per day anywhere else in Mexico. Fabulous whore houses and restaurants. A large foreign colony. Cock fights, bull-fights, every conceivable diversion" (53). In fact Mexico made him regret his heroin addiction, as it kept him indoors when there was limitless freedom outdoors. "There is more to miss in Mexico than in the States because here *no limits are imposed on experience*" (71; my emphasis). In letters to Ginsberg, he warned his friend away from vacation destinations which would place limitations on such experience. "Like I say, do not feel like a trek across Europe at great personal expense to Vienna. *Not* particularly cheap, very crowded in the Summer and boys very much an unknown quantity. DON'T GO TO ISTANBUL. I have it from those who been there, *nowhere*. Expensive, much police surveillance—they don't like any foreigners, you need a permit for everything" (363–64). In contrast, Burroughs idealized the comparative lack of social control in Mexico, where "a man can walk the streets without being molested by some insolent cop swollen with the unwarranted authority bestowed upon him by our stupid and hysterical law-making bodies. Here a cop is on the level of a street-car conductor. He knows his place and stays there" (57). But Burroughs's utopia turned out to be Tangier, a "hub of unregulated free enterprise" that became a "capital of permissiveness" after World War II.[25] In *Queer* (which was written in 1952 but not published until 1985), the narrator describes Mexico City as a "terminal of space-time travel, a waiting room where you grab a quick drink while you wait for your train. That is why I can stand to be in Mexico City or New York. You are not stuck there; by the fact of being there at all, you are travelling."[26] In this view, Tangier was the ultimate space-time terminal, a space of radical freedom where one moved "outside any social context," as Morgan explains: "Tangier was as much an imaginative construct as a geographical location . . . a place where everyone could act out his most extreme fantasies."[27]

Global travel thus allowed Burroughs to experience the stateless "perpetual motion" that McCarthy described in her famous essay, and I argue that international tourism and the power of the dollar enabled his postmodern art.[28] Initially Burroughs represented tourism in strictly mimetic fashion, as *Junkie* (1953) depicts a man's search for commodities (specifically morphine and its derivatives) that were not readily available in the United States. As noted above, "In Search of Yage" is a more complex travel narrative, tracing an arc from the exploration of the New World to the pleasures of an unregulated market. In a literary sense, Burroughs became Burroughs when he did not merely represent tourism, but rather used global mobility itself as the basis for a new kind of cultural production.

International Travel and Artistic Form: Burroughs's "Touristic Écriture"

Burroughs has gained respectability in the American literary academy largely through his work's anticipation of various forms of French critical theory. Lydenberg's *Word Cultures* (1987) made a direct equation between Burroughs and forms of écriture that she associates with Derrida and Barthes. A decade later, Murphy discussed Burroughs primarily in relation to Deleuze and Guattari in *Wising Up the Marks* (1997), while Harris has dubbed him "the Lacanian Real of American literature."[29] To be sure, these scholars have different emphases; Murphy, for example, is severe with Lydenberg, arguing that "if we are going to get Burroughs's books off the shelf and back onto the streets," we must contest formalist approaches, since Lydenberg's deconstructionism "enclose[s] antagonism within capitalist production and its handmaiden, abstract representation or textuality."[30] Yet Murphy's assessments of Burroughs's significance often have a decidedly Lydenbergian feel to them; both critics tend to see liberatory potential in certain avant-garde artistic concepts, especially the notion that Burroughs explodes conventional notions of authorship and of subjectivity more generally. For example, Lydenberg states that Burroughsian form "creates the possibility of a broader cosmic journey that extends across all texts, all cultural codes, all identities," while Murphy claims that Burroughs sought (and, late in his career, found) "an escape route from the linked control systems of capital, subjectivity, and language."[31] In part, my objection to these perspectives is a philosophical one, based upon Seán Burke's insight that "it is to the very romantic tradition against which theory aligns itself that the Death of the Author [argument] belongs."[32] More importantly, the concept of Burroughs going on a cosmic journey outside capital and subjectivity makes us miss the opportunity to relate his narratives to social developments such as American political and economic influence and the enormous increase in middle-class global mobility after World War II. Indeed, perhaps the strongest criticism that one could make of contemporary Burroughs criticism is that it risks the reproduction of American exceptionalism in a poststructuralist idiom.

Burroughs's trangressive artistic form needs to be reassessed in view of its relation to global history and, more specifically, the marketplace of tourism. Dean MacCannell's celebrated study *The Tourist* might be a good starting point for this task, especially since it draws on Saussurean semiotics and has appealed to Paris-influenced literary theorists. MacCannell makes a case for the much-derided tourist, who has a "positive vision of the world . . . search[ing] the entire world for things that are worth seeing, doing, decrying, preserving, experiencing."[33] *The Tourist* is one of the seminal texts to explore an ostensibly post-Marxist experience economy, in which the "value of such things as programs, trips, . . . sights, [and] spectacles . . . is not determined by the amount of labor required for their production" (23). Instead, "their value is a function of the quality and quantity of *experience* they promise," making for "an immense accumulation of reflexive experiences which synthesize fiction and reality into a vast symbolism, a modern world" (23). MacCannell's book is especially notable for breaking down the distinction between the authentic and the ersatz, which structures the traditional opposition between the cultured traveler and the shallow tourist. Drawing on MacCannell, Jonathan Culler calls tourists the "unsung armies of semiotics . . . [who are] interested in everything as a sign of itself, an instance of a typical culture practice: a Frenchman is an example of a Frenchman, a restaurant in the Quartier Latin is an example of a Latin Quarter restaurant, signifying 'Latin Quarter Restaurantness.'"[34] Culler goes on to criticize Fussell as well as Daniel Boorstin, the author of *The Image: A Guide to Pseudo-Events in America* (1962), both of whom have an elitist self-confidence that the genuine travelers of the past can be distinguished from the mere tourists of today.

However, if tourists are the "unsung armies of semiotics," what is their cause? Often misread as valorizing the nomad suggested by its title, *The Tourist* is on a search for solidarity, orienting itself toward the collective. Although his semiotic approach erodes the traditional distinction between the authentic and the ersatz, MacCannell values society's collective agreement to pursue such distinctions, to "conserve a solidarity at the level of the total society, a collective agreement that reality and truth exist somewhere in society, and that we ought to be trying to find them and refine them" (*T* 155). *The Tourist* has a strong moral agenda that might be linked to Cold War liberalism and the sidelining of progressive alternatives. Although his work has an interdisciplinary appeal, MacCannell's PhD is in sociology, and he employs sociological theory that was put to consensus-oriented purposes after World War II, when the field searched for equilibrium and deemphasized the social conflict of the 1930s. Drawing on Emile Durkheim, MacCannell represents the world as a moral whole, united by a touristic collective consciousness. While the labor market becomes ever more differentiated and fragmented, tourism can reintegrate society through a "solidarity" based in leisure time: "The consensus about the structure of the modern world achieved through tourism and mass leisure is the strongest and broadest consensus known to history" (139). Middle-class tourists have a "transcendent consciousness," forming a collective agreement about which of the world's sights are worth seeing, and thus conducting a global exchange of what MacCannell calls "the gift of shared notice" (13, 193).

The Tourist's concern with social solidarity explains what might otherwise seem quite puzzling in a book lauded for its demotic approach to the experience economy. To put it in the terms of postwar French theory—specifically, Derridean deconstruction—MacCannell makes a sharp criticism of the tourist who has no concern for "reality and truth," but rather engages in what we might call semiotic free play (T 155). MacCannell notes that the tourist can manipulate time and space, using amateur photography to make himself the great sight, instead of the landmark (147); he has the freedom to get things wrong, to creatively rearrange the historical data surrounding a given attraction (139). MacCannell criticizes such touristic practice in moralistic terms that are analogous to the denunciation of writing that Derrida claims to find in Saussure.

> The version of "the truth" contained in these examples, the basis of touristic certainty, is adapted to a type of society in which social relationships are arbitrary, fleeting and weightless, in which growth and development takes the form of an interplay of differentiations. Within this manifold, the individual is liberated to assemble and destroy realities by manipulating sociocultural elements according to the free play of his imagination. This is the worst feature of modernity and, at the same time, the grounds of our greatest hope: perhaps we can individually or collectively put together the "right combination" of elements and make it through to a better world or a higher stage of civilization. (140–41)

The problem with identifying "the free play of [individual] imagination" as "the worst feature of modernity" is that MacCannell does not clearly identify an alternative—that is, a sense of social responsibility for his postwar leisure class. This globetrotting class may agree on which sights are worth seeing, but how will this consensus lead to a "better world"? *The Tourist* seems influenced by a kind of residual New Dealism—the nation-centered, reform-oriented model of 1930s travel described in my introduction, which the book registers as an almost ghostlike presence, while its author tries to relocate Rooseveltian national cohesion to the globalized itineraries of postwar tourism. As with Fussell's work, *The Tourist* could have benefited from paying attention to the American Guide Series, but instead devotes much of a chapter to Baedeker's guide to Paris from the year 1900 (*T* 57–76). In a new preface to the 2013 edition of *The Tourist*, MacCannell notes that international tourism has increased exponentially, accompanying a global development in which "economic inequality between nations fell while inequality within nations rapidly grew to historically unprecedented levels" (xvi). MacCannell continues to be appreciative of tourists, yet this transcendent consciousness of money and leisure seems perfectly homologous with the contemporary status quo of global capitalism and social inequality.

Burroughs's proleptical poststructuralism was based on his experience of international travel, which offered new possibilities for creative individualism. In keeping with his frontier ideology, which emphasized total freedom from the collectivity and the state, Burroughs cheerfully defied conventional sign systems; he had no interest in supporting MacCannell's desired "consensus about the structure of the modern world achieved through tourism and mass leisure" (*T* 139). To use Saussurean terms, Burroughs did not seek to codify a holistic touristic langue but rather valorized parole, that realm of unpredictable individual performance that Saussure claimed was not in the purview of linguistics.[35] "What are you *thinking*?" asks the "squirming American tourist" in *Naked Lunch*'s "Atrophied Preface," which mocks the sedate routine of the frequent flyer (*NL* 209):

> Why all this waste paper getting The People from one place to another? Perhaps to spare The Reader stress of sudden space shifts and to keep him Gentle? And so a ticket is bought, a taxi called, a plane boarded. We are allowed a glimpse into the warm peach-lined cave as She (the airline hostess, of course) leans over us to murmur of chewing gum, dramamine, even nembutal. (197)

In contrast with this conventional routine, Burroughs emphasizes unfettered global mobility. "I am not American Express," he insists, opposing himself to the conventional business travel agency. "If one of my people is seen in New

York walking around in citizen clothes and next sentence Timbuktu putting down lad talk on a gazelle-eyed youth, we may assume that he (the party
non-resident of Timbuktu) transported himself there by the usual methods
of communication" (198). Of course "the usual methods of communication"
may simply refer to planes, taxis and hotel rooms, out of which his characters
construct their deviant itineraries. But we might also read "communication"
as *writing*, specifically Burroughs's own manipulation of sociocultural fragments. In fact, the "Atrophied Preface" often becomes a literary equivalent of
snapshots and souvenirs—a slide-show for his fellow Beats, as it were. "Now
I, William Seward, will unlock my word horde" (208) he declares, his "horde"
of word-images contrasting with the typical tourist's passive "hoard" of col-
lectibles, safely enclosed in a handbag or suitcase:

> This book spill off the page in all directions, kaleidoscope of vistas, med-
> ley of tunes and street noises, farts and riot yips and the slamming steel
> shutters of commerce, screams of pain and pathos and screams plain
> pathic, copulating cats and outraged squawk of the displaced bull head,
> prophetic mutterings of *brujo* in nutmeg trance, snapping necks and
> screaming mandrakes, sigh of orgasm, heroin silent as dawn in the thirsty
> cells, Radio Cairo screaming like a berserk tobacco auction, and flutes of
> Ramadan fanning the sick junky like a gentle lush worker in the grey sub-
> way dawn feeling with delicate fingers for the green folding crackle. (208)

It would not have been possible to produce this hybrid amalgamation of
signifiers before "international mass tourism produces in the minds of the
tourists juxtapositions of elements from historically separated cultures"
(*T* 27). Here my analysis of the market-oriented juxtapositions of the "Atrophied Preface" has an affinity with Michael Clune's study of the cut-up trilogy. Drawing a parallel between Heideggerian phenomenology and Friedrich
Hayek's model of the price system, in which economic growth is enabled by
discrete individual judgments made in concrete, everyday contexts instead of
by centralized state planning, Clune shows that Burroughs's cut-ups are artistic works in which "the price system plays a basic role in framing individual
knowledge and perception."[36] Clune's analysis accords with Burroughs's own
assessment of his work; as the latter stated in "My Purpose Is to Write for
the Space Age," a 1984 *New York Times* essay that amounted to a summa-
tion of his career, "Space travel involves time travel, seeing the dimension of
time from outside time, as a landscape spread out before the observer, where a

number of things are going on simultaneously—as in the Djemalfnaa in Marrakech: Gnaoua drummers, snake charmers, trick bicycle riders. The image of a vast market occurs repeatedly in [my] later work."[37] For Clune, a "vast market" provides the economic logic of Burroughs's early avant-garde practice, as well. Unfortunately, Clune's admitted fascination for the "alien, impossible light" in the "virtual space of the cut-ups" forecloses a more thorough investigation into their sociohistorical context.[38] Insofar as Clune argues that Burroughs undoes oppositions such as "collective/individual" and takes us beyond a "Cartesian model of the individual subject," his analysis reproduces the conventional assertion that Burroughsian artistic form is so radical and innovative that it cannot possibly be linked to a specific ideological interest.[39]

On the contrary, the goal of Burroughs's radical semiotics is not to destroy the illusion of unified selfhood, but to free the self from a uniform text or cultural code and enable this self's creative manipulation of dominant codes. To use Roland Barthes's terms from *Mythologies* (1957), if the touristic signifiers of the "Atrophied Preface" are liberated from the control of Nation, State, and Official Culture, they nonetheless remain radically decontextualized, shorn of their history and amalgamated within Burroughs's countercultural itinerary.[40] The narrator is thus empowered insofar as he can order disparate locations and cultural artifacts within a series of commas. In fact, Burroughs often delights in this omnipotence: "I, William Seward, captain of this lushed up hash-head subway, will quell the Loch Ness monster with rotenone and cowboy the white whale. I will reduce Satan to Automatic Obedience, and sublimate subsidiary fiends. I will banish the candiru [a predatory South American fish] from your swimming pools" (*NL* 205). The phrase "white whale" is abstracted from the intricacies of Melville's novel and made to signify a radically individualistic credo, that of "I, William Seward," who makes a series of boasts: that he will domesticate the Loch Ness monster, the legend of which is enabled by tourists' (and hoaxers') handheld cameras; that he will pacify Hell and make it safe for a sightseeing tour. The passage expresses a fantasy of omnipotence, based on the tourist's historically unique ability to fragment culture and rearrange it, just as if he were manipulating a "kaleidoscope" (207).

One might say that the cut-up trilogy turns *Naked Lunch*'s manipulation of sociocultural elements into a professional specialty. On the most basic level, the practice of cutting up involved taking scissors to a newspaper or magazine and rearranging the fragments in new combinations. For Lydenberg, this puts Burroughs in an avant-garde lineage that extends from the surrealist Tristan

Tzara through Derrida. However, Burroughs emphasized that the practice does not enable an escape from centered subjectivity, but rather foregrounds the insight and expertise of the cutter. "People say to me, 'Oh, this is all very good, but you got it by cutting up.' I say that has nothing to do with it, how I got it. What is any writing but a cut-up? Somebody has to program the machine; somebody has to *do* the cutting up. Remember that I first made selections. Out of hundreds of possible sentences that I might have used, I chose one."[41] The comment validates Timothy Melley's evaluation of Burroughs in *Empire of Conspiracy* (2000), a book that cogently analyzes the way in which many postmodern American novelists do not deconstruct the notion of "extraordinary individual autonomy," but rather seek precisely to preserve this integral selfhood.[42]

In Burroughs's case, the passage from the reportorial realism of *Junkie* to the fragmentation of the cut-ups involved the liberation of the self through international travel, which unfettered creativity and enabled the construction of a potentially unlimited oeuvre. As Burroughs explained to the *Paris Review* in 1965, "For exercise, when I make a trip, such as from Tangier to Gibraltar, I will record this in three columns in a notebook I always take with me. One column will contain simply an account of the trip, what happened. I arrived at the air terminal, what was said by the clerks, what I overheard on the plane, what hotel I checked into. The next column presents my memories; that is, what I was thinking of at the time, the memories that were activated by my encounters; and the third column, which I call my reading column, gives quotations from any book that I take with me. I have practically a whole novel alone on my trips to Gibraltar."[43] Here, cutting up involves creatively rearranging the three columns—travel narrative, personal memories, and literary quotations—into new combinations. Burroughs's practice of touristic écriture is based upon a kind of empowered marginality, the middle-class traveler's freedom to cross national borders and rearrange cultural fragments.

"The Mayan Control Machine": Frontier Individualism, the Nation-State Form, and Third World Revolutionary Movements

What relationship does Burroughs's work bear to what Edwards calls "American Orientalism"? Although Melley terms the postmodern recuperation of integral selfhood "agency panic," Burroughs's narratives certainly do not display the anxiety that so many critics have located in white identity formation during the High Cold War period; indeed, in the "Atrophied Preface," *Naked Lunch* announces itself as generating anxiety.[44] For Edwards, Burroughs's mindset is thus fundamentally postcolonial instead of imperial, and he discusses *Naked Lunch* much as one would discuss the work of Homi Bhabha, which famously valorizes the "Third Space of enunciation," a position of liminality where "symbols of culture have no primordial unity or fixity."[45]

I think Edwards is correct to locate prototypes of such postcolonial models of identity in *Naked Lunch*. Later, Burroughs commented, "I have always seen my own work in the light of the picaresque—a series of adventures and misadventures, horrific and comic, encountered by an antihero," and *Naked Lunch*'s characters may indeed be described as picaros of the global economic system.[46] None of them manipulates the sociocultural kaleidoscope of the "Atrophied Preface" more exuberantly than A. J., the embodiment of Burroughs's yage-inspired vision of a "Composite City where all human potentials are spread out in a vast silent market."[47] Interzone promotes not only the chaotic intermixture of cultures, as the "Opening Bars of East St. Louis Toodleoo" play over "[m]inarets, palms, mountains, jungle," but also the breakdown of racial boundaries: "The blood and substance of many races, Negro, Polynesian, Mountain Mongol, Desert Nomad, Polyglot Near East, Indian—races as yet unconceived and unborn, combinations not yet realized pass through your body" (*NL* 96). In contrast to the images of suburban racial homogeneity promoted by America's mainstream media, the identity of *Naked Lunch*'s protagonist is combinatorial, heterogenous. A. J. "had at one time come on like an English gentleman," although "he is actually of obscure Near East extraction. … His English accent waned with the British Empire, and after World War II he became an American by Act of Congress" (132–33). Although his US citizenship and his reputation as an international playboy suggest an Americanized James Bond, rather than directly advancing the interests of Washington, DC's power elite, A. J. turns the international marketplace of tourism into a space of cultural resistance. Within ten pages he appears at Interzone's US embassy, Cincinnati's Anti-Fluoride Society meeting, the New York Metropolitan Opera, the Chez Robert restaurant (presumably in Paris), Venice, and a New York nightclub (133–41). Targeting tourist attractions and sites of commodified leisure, A. J. disrupts them by mingling elements from disparate locales: on the opening night of the Metropolitan Opera, his introduction of a semi-mythical aphrodisiac from Colombia, the Xiucutil grasshopper, leads to an orgy; at Venice's Piazza San Marco he traumatizes conventional tourists with a cutlass, a "huge reproduction of a Greek urn topped by a gold statue of a boy with an erection" which spurts champagne, and a gigantic barge, "a monstrous construction in gilt and pink and blue with sails of purple velvet" (137).

Nevertheless, hybridity can have different ideological articulations, and in Burroughs's case, the "Third Space" is an American West—as fantasized by the middle class—rearticulated in global terms. Although one might be tempted to cite Guy Debord and call A. J. a super-powered Situationist, *Naked Lunch* does not focus on wage labor, nor does it suggest capitalism is unjust because it involves the unequal distribution of material abundance.[48] Rather, the narrative is enabled by Debord's famous insight that "the spectacle is *capital* accumulated to the point where it becomes image."[49] *Naked Lunch* formulates a middle-class ideal that is missing from Debord's traditional Marxist model of the capitalist spectacle and the proletarian worker, as the novel insists on the creative individual's capacity to fragment and recombine images.

Burroughs supports cultural intermixture and the breakdown of hierarchies as long as the result is a specifically American vision of idealized individual autonomy. For a striking example of such creative individualism, I would point to Dr. Benway, *Naked Lunch*'s model of the free professional, trading his services on the global marketplace and dissolving national borders in the process. While Benway has been described by generations of critics as an embodiment of George Orwell's Big Brother, he is clearly an anti-bureaucrat.[50] Interzone's nationalist Party Leader doesn't want to enlist Benway's services because he "[m]ight do almost anything.... Turn a massacre into a sex orgy" (*NL* 112). Similarly, in an operating-room scene Benway makes a comical defense of professional autonomy against organizational control, or what might be called medical deskilling. The nurse asks him if a tool should be sterilized, to which Benway responds, "Very likely but there's no time.... You young squirts couldn't lance a pimple without an electronic vibrating scalpel with automatic drain and suture.... Soon we'll be operating by remote control on patients we never see.... We'll be nothing but button pushers. All the skill is going out of surgery.... All the know-how and make-do.... Did I ever tell you about the time I performed an appendectomy with a rusty sardine can?" (55). Kicked out of the country of Annexia after a bloody fight involving an operating table and a baboon, Benway turns Freeland's bureaucratic order into chaos, escapes Freeland to become a ship's doctor for the entrepreneur Hassan O'Leary, and finally ends up taking a position with Interzone's nebulous organization Islam, Inc., which, significantly, is run by A. J.

In short, I think that critics have misread *Naked Lunch*'s introduction of Benway as a "manipulator and coordinator of symbol systems, an expert on all phases of interrogation, brainwashing and control" (*NL* 20). The passage refers to Benway's amoral autonomy, not his service to the state, and indeed Benway uses his manipulation of symbol systems to disrupt state planning. As Morgan points out, *Naked Lunch*'s Freeland Republic functions as a carica-ture of the "cradle-to-grave welfare state" Burroughs despised so mightily.[51] It would therefore be redundant to argue, citing Foucault, that the inmates form a reverse discourse when they escape the Reconditioning Center and ram-page over the globe, since the counter-discourse is precisely Benway's. While Culler's conventional tourists function as the "unsung armies of semiotics," converting "cities, landscapes and cultures" into sign systems, Benway engi-neers a system of counter-tourism that dissolves this orderly world[52]:

> By plane, car, horse, camel, elephant, tractor, bicycle and steam roller, on
> foot, skis, sled, crutch and pogo-stick the tourists storm the frontiers,
> demanding with inflexible authority asylum from the "unspeakable con-
> ditions obtaining in Freeland," the Chamber of Commerce striving in
> vain to stem the debacle: "Please to be restful. It is only a few crazies who
> have from the crazy place out broken." (*NL* 41–42)

If this passage presents difficulties of interpretation—since the "crazies" are now located in "all nations," where exactly is "asylum" located?—it is because Benway has dissolved all national collectivities into a permanent revolution of forms, a postmodern frontier in which "Rock and Roll adolescent hoodlums . . . shit on the floor of the United Nations and wipe their ass with treaties, pacts, alliances" (41).

This vision of unregulated fluidity and heterogeneity is very far removed from the imperial power/knowledge formations that critics such as Said and Pratt have identified in European travel literature. Thus, one might plausibly argue that Burroughs's "focus on disruptive codes" not only erodes Oriental-ist binaries, but also subverts the master narrative of Henry Luce's "Ameri-can century."[53] In Edwards's view, if the mainstream media tended to view Tangier and Morocco more generally as a degenerate, lawless space of Cold War intrigue, Burroughs "queers the American media's queering of Tangier by producing an antidote to the 'pure voice' of America: a series of broken sig-nals imagined as illegible doodles that suggest a future community that might oppose the global culture of control associated with McCarthyist America as global force."⁵⁴ But it is difficult to locate such a "future community" in Burroughs's early work. As we have seen, Burroughs enjoyed what might be called an unregulated market of experience in the periphery of the world system, and his narratives extol a creative professionalism enabled by this free global space.

In this view, while Burroughs's frontier libertarianism involved a critique of American foreign policy, his work nevertheless represents a globalized form of middle-class privilege, which entails a stake in the extension of the market system. Limerick has called attention to this aspect of frontier ideology, pointing to the way pioneers in the Old West tended to blame recalcitrant nature, hostile Indians, and especially the federal government for their hardships. "In effect, Westerners centralized their resentments much more effectively than the federal government centralized its powers."⁵⁵ For Limerick, this makes the frontier an "empire of innocence," as pioneers thereby disavowed the rapaciousness of their own economic activity. Burroughs's postmodern frontier works in a similar fashion. His stateless, perfectly mobile human being, whom in *The Soft Machine* he dubbed a "naked astronaut," serves as a trope for a globalized empire of innocence, wherein the middle-class traveler is not only blameless regarding the world's ills but actively oppressed by conspiratorial forces.⁵⁶ For Burroughs, these oppressive forces include Third World nationalist movements and governments, which threaten to limit the traveler's ideal freedom. In short, if Burroughs's travel literature undermines the Orientalist binaries of civilization/savagery and adult/child, it accommodates American power by depoliticizing important political issues and transferring them to the logic of the global marketplace.

Indeed, in Burroughs's libertarian world, neocolonial children often behave like adults. Greg Mullins argues that during Burroughs's stay in North Africa, sex came to replace drugs as the major experience that took one beyond the boundaries of conventional selfhood. "The promiscuous mixing occasioned by sexual tourism became, for Burroughs, a metaphor for understanding Tangier as a space where national, religious, and cultural interests could be blurred and where unrestrained and proliferating desire could supplant bounded identities and ideologies."⁵⁷ Mullins's model of hybridity accords with my own reading of Burroughs's work, but I would stress that such touristic desire was based on what we might call a globalized class privilege. For example, the political parties that sought to incorporate Tangier within the Moroccan nation in the 1950s were harsh critics of the absolute license enjoyed by tourists. In

Pratt's terms, while Burroughs may have resisted the homogenizing "imperial eyes" of colonialism through a vision of sexual intermixture, Interzone was nevertheless a "contact zone," a social space where "cultures meet, clash, and grapple with each other, often in highly asymmetrical relations of domination and subordination."[58] Such a perspective on Third World tourism does not entail the uncritical valorization of nationalist movements; as Said observes, they are capable of their own "despotisms" and "ungenerous ideologies."[59] Nevertheless, the Moroccan nationalists remind us that the global market was not free for everyone, and in some cases involved highly asymmetrical social relationships.

Burroughs does not critique such asymmetry, instead reserving his sharpest satire for officials and agents of the law who would place limits on the tourist's desire. In *Naked Lunch*, the Party Leader is one of the book's few characters who is not only clownish, but evil, in part because he wants to restrain sex tourism. Midway through the book, he and the other members of the Nationalist Party drink "cigars, [and] scotch" on a balcony. Looking down at Interzone's Market, the Party Leader says that what his country needs is "Ordinary men and women going about their ordinary everyday tasks" (110), which is, of course, immediately shown up as a conformity-inducing demand. A "street boy" climbs over the railing, but instead of expelling the boy, the Party Leader attempts to reason with him about his trade. "What do you think about the French . . . the Colonial bastard who is sucking your live corpuscles?" he asks, to which the boy responds, "Look mister. It cost two hundred francs to suck my corpuscle. Haven't lowered my rates since the year of the rindpest when all the tourists died, even the Scandinavians." The boy's work is clear: he is a prostitute who services tourists, one of whom is an American.

> "Uhuh. . . . Well I got a date with a high-type American client. A real classy fellah."
> P. L.: "Don't you know it's shameful to peddle your ass to the alien unbelieving pricks?"
> "Well that's a point of view. Have fun."
> P. L.: "Likewise." Exit boy. "They're hopeless I tell you. Hopeless." (112)

The passage is fascinating because it is the only time in the book where we get anything like a national or "native" perspective on the activities of tourists in Interzone. Yet the perspective is undermined before it's even articulated, as Burroughs begins the passage by describing the Party Leader as a "successful gangster in drag" (110). The nationalist agitator comes off as corrupt and hypocritical, a square who tries to impose his "point of view" on a hip free-thinker who advises the uptight bureaucrat to "Have fun."

This pivotal scene upsets a model of Burroughs as a defier of oppressive social orders, and reveals that Burroughs could himself impose such an order on others. If we pay careful attention to the sociohistorical context of his fiction, narratives of resistance against all forms of domination start to appear equivocal—not committed to the direct extension of Western territorial control, but rather to the global extension of a free-market ideology. It is easy enough for contemporary readers to be amused by the dissolution of the Freeland Republic, that culturally homogenous nation in the industrial core of the world system, but Burroughs took the same oppositional stance toward governments in the periphery. In my view, Burroughs's attitude toward revolution has little in common with Fanon's concern for a national "collective consciousness" based on "enlightened and coherent praxis."[60] On the contrary, when Burroughs narrated a revolt against oppression in a Third World country, he made the figure of resistance a heroic tourist who is enabled by technology such as the instant camera and tape recorder. In a sense, he advances a hyperindividualistic version of modernization theory, oriented toward nation-smashing instead of nation-building.

For example, *The Soft Machine*'s central chapter, "The Mayan Caper," recodes a Central American revolution as a lone individual's battle against a unified system of control. In 1944 Guatemala contested neoimperialism when the first successful revolution in the country's history overthrew the dictator Jorge Ubico. After several years of factional conflict, the minister of war, Jacobo Arbenz Guzmán, won the presidency with 65 percent of the popular vote. Arbenz's land reforms drew hostility from institutions such as the American corporation United Fruit, which dominated Guatemala's infrastructure and owned almost half its land while enjoying a virtually tax-free status. Predictably, United Fruit began to push for US intervention against a "communist" regime, which included a mass-media campaign as well as lobbying in Washington, DC. Arbenz successfully resisted a counterrevolution engineered by the CIA in 1954, but lost the support of the army when he attempted to turn Mayan workers and peasants into a militia; he was then ousted in a coup that installed a new dictator. As the historian Walter LaFeber concludes, "Guatemala had fully returned to the system. Its industrial and agricultural diversification stopped. The coffee oligarchy and UFCO were reestablished" (125).

This social history of Central American revolution informs *The Soft Machine*, whose protagonist is under assignment by a TV program to deliver a spectacular tale of adventure. He travels to Mexico to study the ancient Mayans, who "lived in what is now Yucatan, British Honduras, and Guatemala" (*SM* 86). According to Burroughs, the ancient Mayan empire was the ultimate totalitarian society, where subjectivity was molded by the power/knowledge system of a small caste of priests. As he stated in an interview, "[They] possessed one of the most precise and hermetic control calendars ever used on this planet, a calendar that in effect controlled what the populace did thought and felt on any given day."[61] Having achieved expert knowledge about the ancient Mayans, the narrator then has an operation in which his body is split in half and combined with that of a contemporary Mayan worker. Although he claims that he thereby becomes a "composite being," "thoughts and memories of the young Mayan drifting through [his] brain" (*SM* 90), what results is not so much a transcultural self as an empowered tourist who uses his hybrid qualities for subterfuge. The narrator pays a "time guide" to have himself transported backward in history (91), where he works in the cornfields of ancient Maya, evading telepathic surveillance by "turn[ing] on the thoughts of a half-witted young Indian" (94).

It is hard not to see an allusion to CIA skullduggery in the narrator's strategic adoption of a Mayan persona, implying that Burroughs has rewritten the ostensibly communist Arbenz government as a pre-Columbian totalitarian regime. However, if the story has elements of a Cold War allegory, it is not one that is directly equivalent to the interests of Washington, DC; in fact Burroughs equated the Mayan empire not with Second or Third World socialist governments, but rather with the "police organization" of the media mogul Luce.[62] Instead, the vision of freedom in "The Mayan Caper" is based on Burroughs's conception of the global marketplace as a liminal space where the Western traveler can evade bureaucratic control—that is, Burroughs is radical in the sense of being more right-wing than anyone. The protagonist's autonomy includes the creative use of consumer gadgetry, since he goes back in time equipped with a "small tape recorder," a "transistor radio concealed in a clay pot" (91), and a "camera gun" that can mix images with "radio static" (97)—devices that do not make him too much different from any traveling journalist or tourist, but do make him almost superhuman in the context of ancient Maya. In a parody of Fordist bureaucracy, the priests themselves do not know how their "control system" really works: "I undoubtedly knew more about it than they did as a result of my intensive training and studies—The technicians who had devised the control system had died out" (95). Burroughs's criticism of this regime is not so much that it enforced a rigid social hierarchy, but rather that it snuffed out individual creativity.

Accordingly, the ensuing rebellion does not involve group action on the part of the oppressed peasants, but rather the manipulation of the dominant symbol system by a resistant individual. The protagonist's "disguise as a mental defective" allows him to carry on an affair with a priest (94), which gives him access to the calendars and codices which control the field workers. He then disrupts the routines of the agricultural society with "sound and image track rebellion" that parallels the rampage of Benway's Rock and Roll adolescent hoodlums (96).

> Inexorably as the machine had controlled thought feeling and sensory impressions of the workers, the machine now gave the order to dismantle itself and kill the priests—I had the satisfaction of seeing the overseer pegged out in the field, his intestines perforated with hot planting sticks and crammed with corn—I broke out my camera gun and rushed the temple—This weapon takes and vibrates images to radio static—You see the priests *were* nothing but word and image, an old film rolling on and on with dead actors—Priests and temple guards went up in silver smoke as I blasted my way into the control room and burned the codices— Earthquake tremors under my feet I got out of there fast, blocks of limestone raining all around me—A great weight fell from the sky, winds of the earth whipping palm trees to the ground—Tidal waves rolled over the Mayan control calendar. (97)

If this sounds like *Raiders of the Lost Ark* (1981), George Lucas's film is also an homage to the adventure serials of the 1930s and '40s, into which Burroughs has arguably spliced himself. Despite the conclusion's demotic reference to liberated workers, the hero of "The Mayan Caper" is finally a lone frontiersman with his equipment belt.

The narrative thus displaces American power only to reinscribe it, erasing Guatemalan politics and history. For Mayan peasants and workers of the 1950s, the notion that the state is inherently panoptic and controlling is simply false. But Burroughs collapses the distinction between a US-supported dictator and a democratically elected nationalist who is willing to arm peasants in order to fight against a CIA-funded insurrection. "The Mayan Caper" flattens

out the complexities of the struggle between United Fruit, the American government, and the Guatemalan government, fusing these institutions into a
single system of control that is defeated by a heroic individualist. Burroughs's
world-systemic hybrid resists incorporation into any larger collectivity or dia-
chronic national narrative, but his subversive freedom is actually based upon
the global power of the US economy, as his Mayan identity and his ticket to
the past are bought with a "brief case of bank notes" provided by the evening
news (91). Hence, the TV message that follows the narrator's trip, which is
intended to disrupt the complacency of the Cold War audience, has no political content. Instead of jarring viewers into an awareness of how their buying
patterns are connected to larger social and political forces, the message promotes a libertarian freedom that is impossible to distinguish from a self-help
slogan. "I am here to tell you what I saw—And to tell you how such time trips
are made—It is a precise operation—It is difficult—It is dangerous—It is the
new frontier and only the adventurous need apply—But it belongs to *anyone*
who has the courage and know-how to enter—It belongs to *you*" (85; author's
emphasis).

Critics who argue that Burroughs's tongue is firmly in his cheek here must
consider that *Nova Express* bases its apparently earnest vision of global rebellion upon the same market-oriented, hyperindividualist model. The first
chapter's use of the loaded term "adolescent gooks" does not lead to insight
into the dynamics of imperialism and the history of a particular developing
country such as Vietnam.[63] Rather, *Nova Express*'s central episode of resistance involves the Subliminal Kid "t[aking] over bars cafes and juke boxes
of the world cities," projecting film and sound at "arbitrary intervals" so that
"nobody knew whether he was in a Western movie in Hongkong or The
Aztec Empire in Ancient Rome or Suburban America" (155–56). The result
is the same kind of chaotic free play stimulated by Benway in the Freeland
Republic and by the tourist-adventurer in Ancient Maya: "The People-City
pulsed in a vast orgasm and no one knew what was film and what was not and
performed all kinda sex acts on every street corner" (157). While Lydenberg's
deconstructive reading argues that *Nova Express* envisions "a new time and
a new space, a morning beyond the boundaries of the city, the body, and the
page," in my view the novel's climax bears out Fernand Braudel's assertion that
"Each time decentering occurs, a recentering takes place."[64] The only difference between the Nova Mob's scheme to turn Earth people into "Paralyzed
Orgasm Addicts" (159) and the protagonist Hassan i Sabbah's liberation of

his followers in sexual immersion tanks (164–65) is that the former paradigm involves bureaucratic control and standardization, while the latter privileges the creative imagination of a free individual. In both cases, all of Earth's culture is turned into manipulable fragments. From this perspective, what at first looked like resistance—of colonial cultural hierarchies, of state control and national homogeneity—now looks like accommodation, a globalized form of American exceptionalism that gives the marketplace the power to transcend social inequality and class conflict.

Globalizing Burroughs:
The Marketplace and Social Justice

What is the legacy of Burroughs's early avant-garde work? Surely he has stimulated an enormous amount of creativity, but such creativity seems to mesh with capitalism instead of resist it. As Loren Glass observes, "Burroughs owes his success to the structural transformations of capitalism in the contemporary era, . . . and his aesthetic innovations actually helped contribute to those transformations as they have been articulated in the global culture industry, which is increasingly friendly to radical aesthetic experimentation."[65] In this view, Burroughs was not a critic of capitalism *per se* but rather of its 1950s articulation. Many Burroughs critics persist in viewing global capitalism as an imposer of "standardized consciousness," but as David Harvey emphasized in his classic *The Condition of Postmodernity* (1990), this is not at all what capitalism looks like today. From a globalized perspective, Burroughs's fiction can be read precisely as advocating a shift in regimes of accumulation: from "Fordism," which involved standardized mass production and a certain cultural homogeneity, to the decentered and fluid model that Harvey terms "flexible accumulation," which is based upon "difference, ephemerality, spectacle, fashion, and the commodification of cultural forms."[66] Given the contemporary plethora of niche markets and lifestyle choices, especially since the rise of the Internet, it is only slightly hyperbolic to assert that mainstream culture is no longer the Bland New World of Fordism, but rather has come to resemble the playful world of Interzone. In this view, the creative self-expression that Burroughs discovered on the margins of the 1950s tourist industry has since become the dominant ethos of economic globalization.

For critics who call upon Burroughs to help us resist the ostensible control mechanisms of global capital, to make the above point is necessarily to discredit him. But I would object to the terms of the debate, which presuppose that economic globalization is an unmitigated evil, and assume that consumer culture is bad without fully explaining why it is bad. One can make a positive evaluation of this consumer culture, as Fredric Jameson does in *Postmodernism, or, The Cultural Logic of Late Capitalism* (1991). "As far as taste is concerned (and as readers of the preceding chapters will have become aware), culturally I write as a relatively enthusiastic consumer of postmodernism, at least of some parts of it: I like the architecture and a lot of the newer visual work, in particular the newer photography. The music is not bad to listen to, or the poetry to read."[67] To be sure, Jameson distinguishes mere taste from the more important critical tasks of analysis (that investigates "the historical conditions of possibility of specific forms") and evaluation (that "interrogate[s] the quality of social life itself by way of the text or individual work of art").[68] Yet his statement "food and fashion have also greatly improved, as has the life world generally" strikes me as evaluative.[69] The paean to the postmodern consumer economy contrasts with his earlier "remind[er] . . . that this whole global, yet American, postmodern culture is the internal and superstructural expression of a whole new wave of American military and economic domination throughout the world: in this sense, as throughout class history, the underside of culture is blood, torture, death, and terror."[70]

It seems to me that to discuss the legacy of Burroughs's early work is precisely to explore Jameson's sociological aporia. Burroughs was hardly squeamish about avant-garde art's imbrication in the marketplace; as he told the *Paris Review* in 1965, "I see no reason why the artistic world can't absolutely merge with Madison Avenue. Pop art is a move in that direction. Why can't we have advertisements with beautiful words and beautiful images?"[71] In this view, Burroughs's much-criticized 1994 television advertisement for the Nike Air Max 2 was neither a sellout, nor a covert gesture of subversion. If the advertisement lacks the revolutionary gloss of *Nova Express*'s opening chapter, its images of vigorous male athletes (accompanied by Burroughs speaking from a laptop computer) retain the emphasis on a multiracial, globalized force of youth. Nike's emphasis on self-empowerment even recalls the protagonist's exhortations in "The Mayan Caper." To merge the cut-up trilogy with marketing campaigns for tennis shoes might seem crass, but a disparaging view holds Burroughs to high standards that he often disregarded. As he reminded us in 1983,

The past 40 years has seen a worldwide revolution without precedent owing to the mass media. . . . Tremendous progress has been made in leading ordinary people to confront these issues which now crop up in soap operas. Gay and junky are household words. Believe me, they were not household words 40 years ago.[72]

Pace Jameson and Burroughs, I would prefer to remain agnostic about whether America's life world has improved or simply become very different. If one identifies greater self-expression and cultural diversity with progress, then Burroughs certainly made a major contribution. However, accompanying this change has been a vast increase in social inequality, which is at its highest level since the years preceding the Great Depression. How can it be that our world is getting so much better and so much worse? Jameson, I think, does not fully answer this question, perhaps because of the limitations of Marx's two-class model of capitalist society. But if we consider that one of the major productive engines of late capitalism and postmodern culture is a globalizing professional-managerial class, then we can better explain the concurrent improvement and debasement of our life world. MacCannell was right to identify not the proletariat (i.e., wage laborers), but rather the salaried middle class as the world's revolutionary class, which was transforming the globe through its creative energy, mobility, and technology. Unfortunately, while *The Tourist* imagined a Durkheimian collective consciousness emerging from this global mobility—a "gift of shared notice," exchanged during leisure time, that would overcome the fragmentation of the division of labor—what has happened is just the opposite (*T* 193). In the US, an empowered segment of this middle class, trading its services on the global market, has sought to secede from its fellows, which parallels trends in other nation-states.

In a word, one of our major social problems in the twenty-first century is not too much state control but rather the *antistatist* ideology of many global elites, who envision negative liberty in a stateless cosmopolitan space. In this view, the pernicious aspect of capitalism's new global frontier is symbolized by Nike's logo of a flying man, which, while it obviously refers to the athleticism of the basketball star Michael Jordan, also serves as a visual representation of the global picaros in Burroughs's four major novels of the 1950s and '60s. Burroughs can justifiably be accused with contributing to a neoliberal ideology that has relegated the state to the role of a mere enabler of multinational enterprise. In a recent appraisal of Burroughs as well as other Beats, Steven Belletto remarks that *Naked Lunch* "leaves readers with a kind of spontaneity that rebukes or evades not just the political systems in Interzone, but *any* political or social order associated with the state."[73] But a government must protect workers from exploitation, or children from the sexual depredations of tourists, or peasants from the machinations of a corporation such as United Fruit. Burroughs's vision of "complete freedom" on the "last frontier" gives no positive role to government, or indeed to any social bond that transcends the workings of the global market. As he stated in his 1969 manifesto *The Job*, "To travel in space you must leave the old verbal garbage behind: God talk, country talk, mother talk, love talk, party talk" (7). As the concept of postmodern literature itself recedes into history, country talk, far from being verbal garbage, is a language that we need to relearn.

Chapter Three

To Jerusalem and Back with Huckleberry Finn

Saul Bellow's Postwar Revisions
of Jewish American Identity

Saul Bellow's *The Adventures of Augie March* (1953) was hailed by critics as the first novel to place a specifically Jewish voice within the American mainstream. Later in his career Bellow became an exemplar of the white literary establishment, marking himself as a culture warrior with the challenge, "Who is the Tolstoy of the Zulus? The Proust of the Papuans? I'd be glad to read them."[1] For many critics, Bellow's whitening of Jewish culture demands critique, as his work is perceived as extolling a "liberal humanism" and "history of progressive historical Enlightenment" that excludes Black voices, which has led to the lessening of his reputation.[2] A review of the first volume of Zachary Leader's monumental two-volume biography mentioned that "many people under the age of 50 have barely heard of Bellow," America's most decorated novelist and the 1976 Nobel Prize winner for literature.[3] This chapter shall argue that Bellow was less a rearguard defender of Eurocentrism than someone who was perhaps too global for his own good, endorsing transnational forms of identity formation that eventually came to undermine his own central position in Western literary culture. Yet a study of Bellow's early life and oeuvre reveals an alternative way of relating Jewish American identity to literature, driven not by globalization but rather by progressive movements and state institutions like the FWP, an alternative that our culture as a whole has forgotten.

The first section of the chapter makes a case for Bellow's New Deal-era progressivism. It is well-known that he was an adherent of Leon Trotsky, in the manner of many Jewish intellectuals associated with the *Partisan Review*. But Bellow's leftism also involved an endorsement of Roosevelt's reform projects, especially the FWP, which enabled his writing career. Perhaps inspired

by the example of the FWP's star employee, Richard Wright, Bellow wrote
two lengthy works of antiracist fiction, one of them a novel that would have
been published in 1942, had the press's editor not been drafted. This early
progressive Bellow has been covered over by the World War II–era Bellow
who explored psychological interiority in *Dangling Man* (1944). When he did
return to a broader social canvas, it was in the context of globalization, with
the exuberant titular picaro of *Augie March* embodying the postwar explosion
of American tourism.

The bulk of the chapter will analyze *Henderson the Rain King* (1959), a novel
that maps Bellow's early interest in antiracist cultural anthropology onto the
postwar mythology of the frontier. The cultural relativism of Jewish American
anthropologists like Franz Boas and Melville J. Herskovits encouraged Bellow
to de-hierarchize the world's cultures, giving *Henderson* a strongly egalitarian
tone when compared to its predecessor, Joseph Conrad's *Heart of Darkness*
(1899). Yet Bellow did not straightforwardly endorse Herskovits's model of a
racially progressive and culturally pluralist America. Rather, for Bellow the
appeal of cultural relativism was the way it enabled an attack upon mainstream mores at the height of the Cold War. The novel is as much a record of a
journey west—Bellow composed the novel in Nevada, on a flight from social
routine as well as his first family—as it is a meditation on Herskovits's research
in African cultures.

Bellow attempts to redeem the frontier by transforming a history of violence and exploitation into a story of liberated professional creativity. Instead
of constituting postwar Jewish American identity through the anxious fear of
a racial other, *Henderson the Rain King* functions as a highly self-conscious reworking of Leslie Fiedler's essay "Come Back to the Raft Ag'in, Huck Honey!"
(1948), as Bellow professionalizes Fiedler's model of a homoerotic interracial
companionship. The character of King Dahfu, a therapist and cosmopolitan
intellectual, makes *Henderson the Rain King* prescient with respect to recent
anthropological theory, as the novel valorizes an intercultural syncretism.
Commenting on the anthropological figure of the "native informant," James
Clifford remarks that "[a] great many of these interlocutors, complex individuals routinely made to speak for 'cultural' knowledge, turn out to have their
own 'ethnographic' proclivities and interesting histories of travel. . . . [They]
have seldom been homebodies."[4] Bellow constructs a kind of Jewish American exceptionalism in which his protagonist atones for the sins of the past by
becoming a doctor in the Third World, working alongside other members of
the postcolonial "educated classes."[5]

However, while Bellow attempts to retain a Jewish American social conscience regarding racism, his earlier progressive commitments now emphasize individual freedom, as well as Cold War anticommunism. Toni Morrison argues that *Henderson*'s conclusion functions as an exercise in Africanist othering, but the book's personification of cosmopolitanism, a "Persian" orphan, is better understood as an elision of Iranian nationalism (*H* 335). The final section of the chapter comments on Bellow's engagement with Israel, suggesting that travel to Israel influenced his rightward political turn later in life. Perhaps ironically, Bellow transferred his 1930s sense of social solidarity to Jerusalem, but instead of an interracial progressivism, he ended up discrediting both Palestinians and African Americans for their supposed dependence on welfare. Instead of discrediting Bellow, I argue that we need to question the transnational turn itself, and recover his early commitment to an integrated national community.

Bellow's 1930s Travel:
The South Side and the American South

A short story by Bellow, "Looking for Mr. Green," helps to illuminate his ideological passage from the 1930s to the early Cold War. Although it was published in 1951 in the Jewish American journal *Commentary*, "Looking for Mr. Green" is set during the Great Depression, when a government relief worker, Mr. Grebe, goes to Chicago's South Side to deliver a welfare check to the African American man of the title. "[Grebe] searched for names and numbers among the writings and scribbles on the walls. He saw WHOODY-DOODY GO TO JESUS, and zigzags, caricatures, sexual scrawls, and curses. So the sealed rooms of pyramids were also decorated, and the caves of human dawn."[6] In keeping with the representation of the trip as akin to a journey into Conrad's heart of darkness, Grebe meets an Italian grocer who rants: "[Black people] stabbed and stole, they did every crime and abomination you ever heard of, men and men, women and women, parents and children, worse than the animals" (100). Finally Grebe is almost assaulted by a naked Black woman, who says "maybe I is, and maybe I ain't" when asked if she is Mrs. Green, but who nevertheless takes the check (108). This gives Grebe a feeling of elation—"[Green] *could* be found!" he exults—although the Kafkaesque mood of the story makes what he was looking for ambiguous (109).

Despite the implicit criticism of the grocer, the story arguably displays a racism that runs throughout Bellow's oeuvre. Yet it is only fair to point out that Richard Wright, in *Native Son* and the posthumously published 1930s novel *Lawd Today!* (1963), also took a sharply critical view of South Side life. Another view of the story is that while Grebe might seem to carry out the most mundane tasks of a welfare state bureaucracy, his job enables interracial connections and a potential sense of solidarity. Grebe delivers a welfare check to Winston Field, a Black war veteran whose name suggests that mainstay of twentieth-century Chicago capitalism, Marshall Field's department stores. Field could be one of the contemporaneously written *Augie March*'s eccentrics, enthusing about a plan to stimulate Black business and create millionaires through investment organized by mail-order subscription. Field's plan might owe more to Charles Ponzi than to W. E. B. Du Bois's program for Black business in *Dusk of Dawn* (1940), but in the 1930s setting, what binds him to Grebe is a shared investment in progressive government. "Oh, it's d' Government man," Field says when he sees Grebe, and insists on showing documentation such as his Social Security card and naval discharge: "'It's not your check, it's a government check and you got no business to hand it over until everything is proved.' He loved the ceremony of it, and Grebe made no more objections" (101). Field redeems the Black Belt for Grebe, who muses that "it wasn't desolation that [the South Side] made you feel, but rather a faltering of organization that set free a huge energy, an escaped, unattached, unregulated power" (103–104). The sense of optimism and potential contrasts with Bellow's later attacks on Chicago's slums, supposedly created by an overindulgent welfare state.

Bellow spent the 1930s thinking about, and agitating for, a better form of social organization, which makes him akin to Black writer-activists like Wright and Ralph Ellison. Greif observes that "Green is the one color name that is also by common agreement a 'Jewish name,'" which suggests that "the mysterious figure Bellow's Gentile Grebe is pursuing is also a Jew—or, say, a trace of the Jewish inside a story about blacks written by a Jew in a Jewish publication interested in blacks."[7] Greif's analysis enables us to read the story allegorically, as the narration of a shift from Bellow's 1930s sensibility, which would have offered more capacious racial and class alliances, to a politically restrictive 1950s world. In this view, Mr. Green is Bellow himself, an earlier literary persona who has become opaque by midcentury, when the Red Scare discouraged progressive commitments.

In his student days in the 1930s, Bellow had these passionate leftist commitments. According to biographer James Atlas, at the University of Chicago,

Bellow and his friend Isaac Rosenfeld "were known as Zinoviev and Kamenev, after the two disaffected Bolsheviks who had briefly shared power with Stalin." Rosenfeld and Bellow collaborated on a Yiddish parody of T. S. Eliot's "The Love Song of J. Alfred Prufrock" (1915). According to Ruth Wisse, it was with this brief poem that "American Jewish letters gave notice of its independence from Anglo-American modernism."[8] If so, the American Jewish voice contested the politics as well as the anti-Semitism of Eliot:

> La mir gehen gich, durch gesselach vos drehen sich
> Wie di bord bei dem Rov....
> In zimmer vo die weiber sehnen
> Redt men fun Karl Marx und Lenin.
>
> Let's go, quick, through alleys that twist and tangle
> like the Rabbi's beard....
> In the room the wives and women
> talk about Karl Marx and Lenin.[9]

But in the 1930s, the most important communist for Jewish intellectuals was Trotsky, whom Bellow idolized in part because of his learnedness: "How could I forget that Trotsky had created the Red Army, that he had read French novels at the front while defeating Denikin [Anton Denikin, leader of the anti-Bolshevik Imperial Russian Army]?"[10] At the University of Chicago and at Northwestern, where he received his bachelor's degree, Bellow contributed to progressive student newspapers, including an attack on Burroughs's favorite anti–New Deal journalist, Westbrook Pegler. In his senior year, he organized dishwashers and chambermaids for the CIO, an experience that was later fictionalized in the thirteenth chapter of *Augie March*.

While Bellow's Trotskyist intellectualism might seem completely opposed to the American mainstream, it could be reconciled with the social programs and nationalist ethos of the New Deal. As with Wright (who, I shall argue, was a creation of the FWP and not the Communist Party), the state enabled Bellow's writing career. His wife, Anita Goshkin, had been a campus radical and union organizer while at the University of Chicago, and after leaving graduate school, she distributed welfare checks for the Chicago Relief Administration. This raises the possibility that "Looking for Mr. Green" recounts a story told to Bellow by his wife, adding gender variability to the story's progressive racial affiliations. Anita encouraged Saul to visit the WPA office, at which point he became a member of the FWP, whose Illinois branch was run by an English professor at his alma mater of Northwestern, John T. Frederick. This position was not only a financial boon but also a source of legitimation: an FWP brochure listed Bellow as "a beginning writer with promise," although his only publications had been in the college papers. In addition to working on the Illinois state travel guide, Bellow was assigned to write biographies of midwestern authors like Sherwood Anderson, experiences that were to inform the topos and characters of *Augie March*. Bellow later claimed: "We adored the Project, all of us.... With no grand illusions about Roosevelt and Harry Hopkins, I believe they behaved decently and imaginatively."[11] As Atlas emphasizes, although Bellow cited radical manifestos that denounced the New Deal as a mere stopgap, "in reality, he was comfortable with—even comforted by—Roosevelt's benign paternalism."[12] Bellow's essay "In the Days of Mr. Roosevelt," published in 1983 in *Esquire*, provides a lyrical account of listening to one of FDR's Fireside Chats, broadcast over car radios, while walking down the street. "You felt joined to these unknown drivers, men and women smoking their cigarettes in silence . . . Just as memorable to me, perhaps, was to learn how long clover flowers could hold their color in the dusk," he concludes, in a nod to Whitman's homage to Lincoln, "When Lilacs Last in the Dooryard Bloom'd."[13]

The New Deal era opened up the possibility of cross-racial alliances and literary influences. Bellow was a Trotskyist while Wright supported Stalin, but if we shift focus to the FWP, we can perceive an unexplored connection. The competitive Bellow surely noticed that in 1938, Wright won the prestigious *Story* magazine's contest for the best piece of creative writing by an FWP employee, which enabled the publication of his story collection *Uncle Tom's Children* (1938). When the prizewinning "Fire and Cloud" appeared in the magazine, *Story* announced, "It is a tribute to the entire Federal Writers' Project that its assistance . . . should have enabled a talent such as Wright's to emerge."[14] In the summer of 1940, when *Native Son* was making Wright a national celebrity, Bellow came into money from an insurance policy and made a trip to Mexico with Goshkin. Passing through the Deep South on a Greyhound bus, Bellow became acquainted with Wright Country, as it were. He was "stunned when [his] bus was held up briefly by a chain gang doing road repairs," and also visited his uncle in Georgia, who sold secondhand clothes to Black sharecroppers. Bellow's interest in the topic of racial discrimination generated his earliest surviving manuscript, "Acatla" (ca. 1940), an unfinished

novel about an interracial American couple who have confrontations with big-
oted American tourists while traveling through Mexico.[15]

Bellow's experience with Jim Crow stimulated his first novel, "The Very
Dark Trees." In Atlas's account, the novel "concerned an English professor
named Jim, 'an enlightened Southerner' who, on his way home from teaching
at a midwestern university, is struck as if by a bolt of lightning and finds himself turned black. When he gets home, his wife doesn't recognize him at first,
then locks him in the basement so he won't alarm the neighbors."[16] Bellow's
friends found the satire of the liberal Southerner very funny, referring to the
manuscript as "White No More," perhaps alluding to George Schuyler's *Black
No More* (1931), which describes the opposite dynamic (a physician turns his
Black patrons white). "The Very Dark Trees" also sounds similar to Kafka's
Metamorphosis, and as Atlas observes, the professor's situation could be read
as a parable for an immigrant's transformation from Russian Jewish to American. It is telling that the Southern professor crosses over to the wrong side of
the color line shortly after he teaches in the Midwest, since Bellow's undergraduate institutions, Chicago and Northwestern, had established a tradition
of research into Black-white relations.

"The Very Dark Trees" was accepted by the Colt Press in 1942, and had it
seen print, our assessment of Bellow's racial politics might be different. But
to explain the circumstances of the manuscript's disappearance is also to narrate a shift in America's national identity. William Roth, the director of the
Colt Press, was drafted and suspended the press's operations. Bellow, deeming
the manuscript "an overambitious piece of youthful writing," threw it into
an incinerator chute.[17] His first published novel, *Dangling Man*, replaces the
social spirit of the 1930s with the cloistered feeling of *The Trial* (1925) and
Dostoevsky's *Notes from Underground* (1864). At the time, Bellow was hardly
enthused about the war effort; his antihero Joseph ends the novel by volun-
teering to fight while declaring sarcastically:

> Hurray for regular hours!
> And for the supervision of the spirit!
> Long live regimentation![18]

For Bellow, the state is no longer a progressive force.

It is telling that in *Dangling Man*, Joseph quits his job at a travel bureau. It
would be after World War II, when the travel industry was opening the world
to everyday Americans, that Bellow experienced a liberation of his creative

powers. Many critics have observed that *The Adventures of Augie March* rejects the collectivist outlook of an earlier literary generation, but it is important to stress the role that travel plays in Bellow's overwriting of his 1930s political commitments. The most striking example of flight occurs when he briefly becomes a union organizer. Augie abruptly takes up his lover's offer to travel to Mexico, where they will tame a wild eagle and sell the resulting photos and stories to a major magazine. "No, I just didn't have the calling to be a union man or in politics, or any notion of my particle of will coming before the ranks of a mass that was about to march forward from misery."[19] During this trip, a political struggle that was perhaps even more definitive for Mexico than the US, the Spanish Civil War, is kept outside the narrative frame altogether. At the novel's end, Augie is running business deals while based in "pert, pretty Paris," with its "maypole obelisk, . . . all-colors ice-cream, the gaudy package of the world."[20] Indeed, Bellow conceived the novel while he was on a Guggenheim fellowship in Paris. As Christopher Hitchens observes, "Bellow . . . boast[ed] that not one word of Augie March was written in Chicago; he took himself off to Positano, Rome, Paris, and London. There is nothing provincial about his Americanism."[21] The insight potentially opens up a discussion about *Augie March*'s relationship to the terrain of Saunders's *The Cultural Cold War*, but instead I would like to focus on *Henderson the Rain King*. This latter novel overwrites Bellow's Depression-era politics while reengaging with his racial concerns of the time.

Cultural Evolution, Cultural Relativism, and the American Frontier

In his 1994 op-ed "Papuans and Zulus," Bellow responded to the controversy generated by his now-infamous remark: "I was speaking of the distinction between literate and preliterate societies. For I was once an anthropology student, you see. Long ago I had been a pupil of the famous Africanist M. J. Herskovits, who had also devoted many decades to the study of the American Negro."[22] It is fair to say that Bellow did not mollify his critics, and multicultural and postcolonial readings of *Henderson the Rain King* (1958) have argued that the work stereotypes and marginalizes an Africanist other.[23] Nevertheless, Bellow's remarks are worth serious consideration, since his relationship to Herskovits has not been fully explored.[24]

Critics of *Henderson the Rain King* have focused on Bellow's indebtedness to nineteenth-century British travel writing and anthropology, instead of contextualizing his work within a twentieth-century American paradigm. For example, Eusebio Rodrigues's article "Bellow's Africa" (1971), which inspired a generation of critics seeking to give postcolonial readings of *Henderson*, mainly discusses the influence of Sir Richard Burton.[25] Accordingly, there has been a tendency to read Bellow as reproducing nineteenth-century discourse about the supposed dark continent. In the model of cultural evolution espoused by Victorian anthropologists such as Edward B. Tylor, cultures developed in a series of stages that paralleled the individual human being's development from childhood to adulthood, with the civilizational apex located in Northern Europe. Said presumably has cultural evolution in mind when he claims that anthropology has traditionally emphasized "the importance of temporality" instead of "the acquisition, subordination, and settlement of space."[26] For Said, this amounts to anthropology's disavowal of its basis in imperialism. As Robert Young points out, in its own time Tylor's doctrine was liberal and antiracist in intent; however, cultural evolution often served as a discursive justification for European control, as it arguably does in *Heart of Darkness*.[27] To be sure, Conrad was a critic of the greed and cynicism of Belgian colonialism, and the climax of his novella indicates that King Leopold II's corruption extends to the River Thames in London. Nevertheless, as Chinua Achebe argues, Conrad's critique is based upon depicting Africa as a region of "triumphant bestiality."[28] Hence Conrad did not attack colonialism as a whole, but rather endorsed the British imperial mission as an alternative.[29]

In contrast, Bellow was influenced by Jewish American anthropologists who criticized European colonialism. Anticipating Said's critique, Boas and his protégé Herskovits saw nineteenth-century anthropological knowledge as a direct reflection of the spatial power relations inhering in colonialism.[30] Boas contested the idea of the "human story as a unilineal development to a single socio-cultural end," instead emphasizing "different ultimate and coexisting types of civilization," each with their own particular histories.[31] Herskovits studied under Boas at Columbia in the 1920s and helped to codify the doctrine of cultural pluralism, which he labeled cultural relativism. His major work before the US entered World War II, *The Myth of the Negro Past* (1941), emphasized that American Black people had not been severed from their African heritage, but rather retained what he called "cultural survivals," which made the US a rich mosaic instead of an Anglo-Protestant melting pot.[32]

During the Cold War, Herskovits was an outspoken critic of US foreign policy, assaulting paternalistic attitudes toward Africa and supporting popular leaders such as the Congo's Patrice Lumumba.[33]

At Northwestern University, Herskovits established the Anthropology Department in 1938 and America's first African studies program in 1948. He has been accused of co-opting African studies from his intellectual rival Du Bois, but it is only fair to note that his work has been fertile for Black intellectuals.[34] Henry Louis Gates Jr. relies heavily on the two-volume *Dahomey: An Ancient West African Kingdom* (1938) for his projected connection between the African trickster figure Esu-Elegbara and the African American Signifying Monkey.[35] When she worked as an editor at Random House, Morrison oversaw the publication of Frances Herskovits's collection of her late husband's essays, *Cultural Relativism* (1972); Morrison's novel *Song of Solomon* (1977) arguably meditates upon Herskovits's theory of African cultural survivals.[36]

In the late 1930s Herskovits taught Bellow, who studied at Northwestern while the professor was working on *The Myth of the Negro Past*. Bellow summarized his teacher's approach to Black American culture in a limerick:

> There was a guy named Melville J.
> Who does oodles of work every day
> To prove that Brer Rabbit
> And blues on the Sabbath
> Came from Old Dahomey.[37]

As Atlas remarks, while the limerick would be considered racist today, it might also be perceived as "good-natured satire" from a minority writer who was himself scorned by anti-Semitic modernists like Eliot, Fitzgerald, Hemingway, and Pound.[38] Bellow was an attentive and capable student, which was attested to by Herskovits's glowing reference letter that gained him admittance to the University of Wisconsin's doctoral program in anthropology. Bellow dropped out while writing his dissertation, but his later fiction continues to display the influence of Herskovits's work. The mores of the cow-worshipping Arnewi tribe in *Henderson* are taken directly from Herskovits's first major publication, "The Cattle Complex in East Africa" (1926), while the militaristic Wariri tribe is based in part upon material in *Dahomey*.

In addition to anthropological details, Bellow's novel draws on Herskovits for its satire of colonial attitudes. When he arrives in Africa, Henderson initially imagines himself as a courageous white explorer "entering the past—the real past, no history or junk like that. The prehuman past" (*H* 46). Henderson's first thought upon seeing the Arnewi village is that it "must be older than the city of Ur" (47). He is therefore nonplussed when he discovers that the Arnewi's king has been educated abroad and is fluent in English:

> The antiquity of the place had struck me so, I was sure I had got into someplace new ... but here was someone who obviously had been around, as he spoke English, and I had been boasting, "Show me your enemies and I'll kill them. Where is the man-eater, lead me to him." And setting bushes on fire, and performing the manual of arms, and making like a regular clown. I felt extremely ridiculous. (52–53)

Learning that the drinking water for the Arnewi's cattle has been infested by frogs, Henderson decides to help the tribe by blowing the frogs out of the water with a homemade bomb: "Naturally I know a little something about explosives.... I had bought the .375 especially for this trip to Africa after reading about it in *Life* or *Look*" (94). Henderson's effort fittingly ends in "disgrace and humiliation," with the too-powerful gunpowder blowing up not merely the frogs but the entire cistern (112). One can thus read the scene, as Sukhbir Singh does, as a satire of "Americans' overwhelming sense of sufficiency [and] complacency."[39]

However, like the contemporaneous *The Ugly American*, the novel does not merely plead for cultural understanding: Bellow never actually went to Africa until 1970, after all. Instead, *Henderson the Rain King* turns cultural relativism into an attack on social conformity. Herskovits famously claimed that "there is no way to play this game of making judgments across cultures except with loaded dice," which the novel rewrites as a concern for the individual: "God does not shoot dice with our souls," Henderson states (*H* 85).[40] Bellow begins his novel with a striking reversal of Conrad, locating the heart of darkness squarely in America. As Marlow relates of Kurtz in *Heart of Darkness*, "Oh yes, I heard him. 'My Intended, my ivory, my station, my river ... Everything belonged to him—but that was a trifle. The thing was to know what he belonged to, how many powers of darkness claimed him for their own."[41] Living in New York, the wealthy Henderson is an impoverished, consumerist Kurtz: "A disorderly rush begins—my parents, my wives, my girls, my children, my farm, my animals ... I have to cry, 'No, no, get back, curse you, leave me alone!'" (3). In Africa, Henderson continues to resist systems of repressive norms in his quest for self-expression. Ruth Miller points out that the Wariri's affectations can be likened to those of suburbia, and they also have a well-developed bureaucracy: when Henderson first arrives in their village he passes through the equivalent of customs, where he is subjected to a physical exam and "a series of curious questions, such as my age and general health and was I a married man and did I have children" (142).[42] These are loaded questions for Henderson, given his desire to resist becoming "a rude, impoverished, mass-produced figure brought into being by a civilization in need of a working force, a reservoir of personnel, a docile public that will accept suggestion and control"—a passage that evokes Foucault's *Discipline and Punish* (1973), but which is actually from a 1961 lecture given by Bellow on D. H. Lawrence.[43]

Although the novel criticizes colonial attitudes, the ultimate goal of *Henderson the Rain King* is not to valorize African cultures, but rather map cultural anthropology onto the myth of the American frontier: like Augie March and Huck Finn before him, Henderson wants to light out for the territory. Here the fictional protagonist shares the concerns of the author: despite the fantastic plot, *Henderson* is just as autobiographical as *Augie March*, since Bellow was undergoing a divorce from Anita Goshkin at the time. The hyperbolic association of his domestic discontent with *Heart of Darkness* is typical for the period, although it is worth noting that Goshkin continued her career in social work.[44] In 1955, Bellow went on a road trip across the country to Nevada, where he would live for six weeks so as to claim residency, then obtain a divorce (eventually he was visited by Arthur Miller, seeking the same goal so as to be able to wed Marilyn Monroe).

Bellow's writerly journey helps to explain the terrain and characters in *Henderson the Rain King*, which are primarily those of the Wild West. In the vicinity of Reno, Bellow stayed at the Pyramid Lake Guest House, then in a cabin overlooking Pyramid Lake. As Leader observes, the "strangeness of the landscape sparked Bellow's imagination" and helped to produce "a novel mostly set in Africa . . . with a desert landscape very like that of Pyramid Lake."[45] When Henderson travels through "a region like a floor surrounded by mountains . . . hot, clear, and arid," he might as well be walking through arid Nevada.[46] One sees the same Western personages when *Henderson* is read alongside the short story "Leaving the Yellow House" (1958), which Bellow also wrote while living in Pyramid Lake. "Leaving the Yellow House" is the story of Hattie Waggoner, who lives by herself in Nevada and has a series of drunken misadventures, but also a nobility as an independent woman: "[Hattie] saw herself as one of the pioneers. . . . [S]he had lived on the range like an old-timer."[47] Hattie was based upon a woman Bellow knew and admired in Pyramid Lake; Hattie's physical characteristics, such as a large girth, are also those of the Arnewi princess Mtalba in *Henderson*. Atlas claims that the novel's "African women are notable mainly for their big behinds," but in Bellow's merging of the Arnewi village with Nevada, the frontier allows women relatively more autonomy than conventional society.[48] As Henderson says of the Arnewi's queen, "she had risen above ordinary human limitations and did whatever she liked because of her proven superiority in all departments" (*H* 75). Henderson himself, meanwhile, has the aspect of a gunslinger entering a frontier town, albeit one comically undermined.

Following Bellow into the American West reveals his novel's underlying concern with Native Americans. Henderson tells us: "My ancestors stole land from the Indians. They got more from the government and cheated other settlers too, so I became heir to a great estate" (*H* 21). In fact, *Henderson the Rain King* was composed on an Indian reservation. As Leader points out, Bellow's cabin was on the edge of the Paiute Pyramid Lake Tribe Reservation, which was established in 1859 and centers on Pyramid Lake. The relationship to Native Americans is apparent in the novel's title: although various cultures around the world have rainmaking ceremonies, the practice is mostly associated with southwestern Native American tribes, although not the Paiutes themselves. While we have associated Henderson's initials with those of Ernest Hemingway and thus a book like *Green Hills of Africa* (1935), a story like "Indian Camp" (1924) might be just as appropriate a parallel, as well as a work like Twain's *Roughing It* (1872).

In this view, the concept of Henderson, the Rain King, is about as archetypally American as one can get, highlighting frontier mythology and national identity. It is no wonder that Herskovits himself disliked Bellow's novel, and one guesses that Boas (who researched the Kwakiutl in British Columbia) wouldn't have liked it very much either. As Bellow told the *Paris Review*, "[Herskovits] scolded me for writing a book like *Henderson*. He said the subject was too serious for such fooling. I felt that my fooling was fairly serious."[49] Though Bellow took liberties with cultural anthropology, he took his creative power as a professional writer very seriously indeed. *Henderson* is a book with a racial conscience, albeit a problematic one, as Bellow advanced what might be termed a Jewish American exceptionalism enabled by globalizing American institutions.

Huck and Jim as Cosmopolitan Hybrids

Toni Morrison's *Playing in the Dark* famously criticizes "the parasitical nature of white freedom," which "has no meaning . . . without the specter of enslavement."[50] After extended discussions of Poe and Twain, and remarks on Faulkner, Hemingway, and William Styron, Morrison briefly critiques *Henderson the Rain King*. By the novel's end, Henderson has been invigorated by the shaman-like King Dahfu, who tragically dies. During the plane flight homeward, Henderson befriends an "American-Persian child" with whom he dances over the ice when his plane stops for fuel in Newfoundland (*H* 337). For Morrison, *Henderson* becomes a textbook case of white freedom based upon Black othering:

> In *Henderson the Rain King* Saul Bellow ends the hero's journey to and from his fantastic Africa on the ice, the white frozen wastes. With an Africanist child in his arms, the soul of the Black King in his baggage, Henderson dances, he shouts, over the frozen whiteness, a new white man in a new found land: "leaping, pounding, and tingling over the pure white lining of the gray Arctic silence."[51]

I am in agreement with Morrison that the novel celebrates a "new found land" of freedom—the immigrant child is headed for the frontier where Bellow composed the novel, "bound for Nevada with nothing but a Persian vocabulary" (*H* 339). Yet Morrison's lineage of white writers raises a question: does Bellow fit seamlessly, or does his Jewish American identity make the relationship vexed? This vexed relationship becomes apparent in the problematic identification of the novel's orphan as Africanist. It seems reasonable to draw a connection from Dahfu to the child, yet the latter is described as "very white" (335). "Persian," too, sounds rather indeterminate—the stewardess's remark that "his parents were Americans" does not rule out Asian as a racial marker (335).

Or, perhaps, could one call the child Jewish? This possibility raises the issue of Henderson's own race and ethnicity. As Stephen Gould Axelrod notes, despite Bellow's providing Henderson with a rarefied Anglo-Saxon pedigree, "throughout the novel, Henderson functions as both WASP and Jewish hero; an Ishmael out of both *Moby Dick* and the Torah."[52] Henderson's continual references to the Old Testament put his suicidalism and depression in Jewish terms; as Daniel Fuchs has shown, early drafts of the novel even had him exclaiming "oyoyoy!" during tense moments.[53] Henderson also has Jewish physical traits such as "hair like Persian lambs' fur," which makes for a direct connection to the Persian child in the plane (4). In short, *Henderson* raises the same issue that "Looking for Mr. Green" did—there seems to be a core of Jewishness inside a diverse array of white, Black, and implicitly red characters—except it is a globalized context instead of the 1930s New Deal context.

Bellow's novel is too self-reflexive for a white/Black binary, since Bellow was himself a careful reader of Poe, Twain, and Hemingway, and dealing with a fair amount of specifically Jewish American guilt as he wrote the novel. On his way to Nevada, Bellow drove through Illinois, so as to write an article for *Holiday* magazine called "Illinois Journey." In so doing, he returned to his Illinois Writers' Project days, and the racial concerns that animated his 1930s work. Bellow's essay was initially rejected by *Holiday* for being too grim: "They wanted me to cheer things up a little, like a true native son," Bellow complained in a letter to a friend.[54] Bellow's perhaps unconscious reference to *Native Son* is appropriate, since the essay's mood owes more to Wright than to the contemporaneous *On the Road*. While driving through southern Illinois, Bellow comes across an unlikely tourist attraction—"a roadside marker that read Old Slave House."[55] He follows the arrow to a Gothic mansion where a slaverunner named John Crenshaw did business:

> Because you know it is a slave house it looks evil, dangerous. . . . The evil is remote because slavery is dead. A sort of safe thrill passes through the liberal heart. But then, the evil is not altogether remote, because nothing has been done to make the house historic. . . . Its present owners live in the old mansion, and it is both domicile and museum.[56]

Bellow's thematic point is clear: instead of being a mere historical curiosity, Crenshaw's house is where the American people still live. Bellow thus highlights what MacCannell leaves out of *The Tourist* concerning history and racial politics. His tour through the house owes a great deal to Poe and the Gothic, and anticipates the points that Morrison would make over three decades later:

Slaves were imprisoned at the top of the house, in narrow cells no larger than closets. . . . Crenshaw tortured his captives on crude devices made of heavy beams. . . . His abuses of the black people were so horrible he was attacked by one of his own slaves and wounded in the thigh. The slave was cast alive into a furnace. . . . "Now, here," said my guide, "is Crenshaw's daughter. She was waited on hand and foot, and never even had to brush her own hair until after the Civil War was over." I must say that she sounded a little envious. Was she not the present lady of the house?[57]

A more visceral model of white freedom based on Black unfreedom could hardly be imagined; and, as per Morrison, white freedom only seems to have meaning when it is opposed to slavery. Yet as a Jewish American traveler, Bellow has a differential relationship to Crenshaw's white supremacy. On one hand, he is mobile, tooling through Illinois in an automobile at roughly the same time that the Montgomery Bus Boycott contested racial discrimination in public transportation. Yet Bellow is careful to note that Crenshaw's house is located in Egypt, Illinois, setting up a clear parallel between African Americans' enslavement by white people, and the Jews' entrapment by Pharaoh in the Book of Exodus. Bellow's essay ends by noting that there are white residents of Illinois, "the feuding blood still running strong in them," who demonize Lincoln.[58]

The novel that Bellow began shortly after, *Henderson the Rain King*, is precisely about whether a postwar Jewish American writer can pursue frontier freedoms without losing his social conscience. I believe that Leslie Fiedler's famous essay for the *Partisan Review*, "Come Back to the Raft Ag'in, Huck Honey!" (1948), can illuminate Bellow's approach to race. Fiedler argues for the centrality of a specifically American archetype in the fiction of writers like Twain and James Fenimore Cooper, that of "the mutual love of *a white man and a colored*."[59] In Fiedler's account of this mythic pattern, two central taboos for the white middle class, "overt homosexuality" and "love of the black," are fused into "the boy's homoerotic crush."[60] Although Fiedler stresses that the open water of rivers and oceans is the setting for this mutual love, one can also call the archetypal pattern a fantasy of the American frontier, insofar as the archetype postulates a space beyond conventional society where history and politics can be left behind: "Our dark-skinned beloved will take us, we assure ourselves, when we have been cut off, or have cut ourselves off from all others

... he will fold us in his arms saying 'Honey' or 'Aikane!', he will comfort us, as if our offense against him were long ago remitted, were never truly *real*."[61] Precisely because the fantasy is "sentimental . . . outrageous . . . [and] desperate," Fiedler argues that it is a dream of boyhood, not adulthood, and "too good to be true."[62] "Come Back to the Raft" suggests that for middle-class Jews as for white people during the Cold War, a political alliance with Black people amounted to little more than nostalgia for the dreams of boyhood. In particular, Fiedler's focus on homoeroticism anticipates the way many midcentury Jewish intellectuals replaced a stress on Black people's political agency with an admiration for their ostensible vitality and physical expressiveness, Norman Mailer's essay "The White Negro" (1957) being the classic literary instance of such fetishism.

Fiedler's essay can help us to understand the significance of Dahfu, who is often overlooked in criticism of Bellow's novel. In their readings of the therapy sessions in the cave underneath the Wariri palace, critics have traced Bellow's debts to the famous theorist of sexual liberation Wilhelm Reich, and the transgressive Freudian Paul Schilder.[63] Yet I think these theorists may have served as models of self-expression instead of libido per se. One might assume that Dahfu's royal harem would be the ideal setting for Reichian "cathartic total orgasm," yet Dahfu seems remarkably uninterested in his bevy of naked wives.[64] Meanwhile, when Henderson is poised to assume the kingship, he describes the position as if he were a put-upon husband. "No, I'd break my heart here trying to fill [Dahfu's] position . . . anyway, I am no stud. No use kidding, I am fifty-six, or going on it" (315).

Henderson's reference to his breaking heart is not mere hyperbole: as in Fiedler's account of the American archetype, the book's central love story entails an escape from heterosexual domesticity. During a royal ceremony, Henderson notes that Dahfu "was virile to a degree that made all worry superfluous . . . he ran and jumped like a lion, full of power, and he looked magnificent" (175). While this fetishization of Black physical prowess is fairly standard for the period, Dahfu for his part openly admires Henderson. "I will not conceal you are a specimen of development I cannot claim ever to have seen" (162). Despite his advanced age and his sagging gut, Henderson is a six-foot-four Army veteran who still "present[s] an appearance of utmost and solid physical organization" (163), drawing compliments from Dahfu that function as obvious double entendres: "I think you are like a monument. Believe me, I have never seen a person of your particular endowment" (155). Indeed, *Henderson the Rain King*'s continual references to the protagonists' mutual attraction functions as a running joke.[65] As Henderson emphasizes during the rainmaking ceremony, "I was [Dahfu's] friend then. In fact, at this moment, I loved the guy" (193). He repeats this declaration throughout the novel, most tellingly when he forgets to tell his wife that he loves her in a long letter—"By God! I goofed again" (289)—while stressing "I love Dahfu" (283).

Bellow professionalizes Fiedler's archetype, turning the forbidden interracial love into a highly intellectualized bond between Black mentor and white mentee. Here there is a real-life parallel, since Bellow specifically related "Come Back to the Raft Ag'in, Huck Honey!" to his friendship with Ralph Ellison. When Ellison roomed with Bellow in upstate New York in 1959, Bellow joked to a friend, "Don't tell Leslie."[66] Greif has speculated that Dahfu was modeled on Ellison, which would be anachronistic in terms of the houseshare, since *Henderson* had seen publication by this time. However, Bellow was indeed in correspondence with Ellison while in Nevada—in 1956, he wrote: "You wouldn't have known me, Ralph, with my casting outfit and a new reel pulling in rainbow trout. Sitting a horse, too [sic]."[67] The letter recreates Fiedler's model with Huck and Jim as literary professionals, and Ellison/Jim, still enjoying the wave of success from *Invisible Man* (1952), is even more successful and honored than Bellow/Huck.

This interracial relationship of creative writers parallels Dahfu and Henderson's relationship in Bellow's imaginary frontier. *Henderson the Rain King* develops an idiosyncratic right-center cosmopolitanism by merging cultural anthropology with Fiedler's account of the homoerotic frontier myth. The novel takes some trouble to overwrite Conrad and other European authors' colonial narratives, to defy expectations and make the native more well-read than the white American. In so doing, Bellow anticipates the postmodern turn in cultural anthropology, in which the native turns out to be just as cosmopolitan as the Western observer. As James Clifford notes, "[I]n the dominant discourses of travel, a non-white person cannot figure as a heroic explorer, aesthetic interpreter, or scientific authority."[68] Yet Dahfu figures as all of these things. As he explains to Henderson, "All preceding kings for several generations . . . have had to be acquainted with the world and have been sent at that time of life to school" (*H* 208). Traveling at will around the Middle East and South Asia, Dahfu begins professional training:

"Why, King Dahfu, Prince Itelo [of the previous tribe, the Arnewi] said you were interested in science."

"Did he tell you," said the guy with evident pleasure, "did he say that I was in attendance at medical school?"

"No!"

"A true fact. I did two years of the course." (178)

Dahfu reveals that he "was going for an M.D. degree, and would have done it except for the death of [his] father," which finally compelled his return to the Wariri (208). He therefore becomes a hybrid figure, with Henderson continually "try[ing] to picture him as a medical student in white coat and white shoes instead of the velvet hat adorned with human teeth and the satin slippers" (275). After several weeks with Dahfu, Henderson finds that his African adventure is turning into the equivalent of a cram session for an examination: "It was just my luck to think I had found the conditions of life simplified so I could deal with them—finally!—and then to end up in a ramshackle palace reading these advanced medical publications" (246). Although Dahfu is now confined within the remoteness of his village, he maintains his intellectual independence. As Henderson thinks admiringly, "What a person to meet at this distance from home. Yes, travel is advisable. And believe me, the world is a mind. Travel is mental travel" (167).

This mental travel involves a prototypical model of cultural hybridity, one that specifically emphasizes the autonomy of a creative professional. It is not difficult to see Bellow's doctors as figures for the literary artist. As Fuchs notes, Dahfu preaches "a textbook Romantic vitalism as the way back to health."[69] Dahfu encourages Henderson to be more creative, exulting, "Imagination, imagination, imagination! It converts to actual. It sustains, it alters, it redeems!" (271). In 1959, Bellow puzzled people by publishing "Deep Readers of the World, Beware!" in the *New York Times Book Review*, making fun of readers and critics who find symbols and hidden meanings everywhere in fiction. "We must leave it to inspiration to redeem the concrete and the particular and to recover the value of flesh and bone," he states, transferring power to the artist and away from the scholarly and critical establishment.[70] As Miller notes, Bellow was resistant to systems, to any establishment that would place limits on his own inspiration: he wanted "to turn his back on all respectable literature, and the scholars and critics who believed in its sanctity, and write a novel that defied every tenet or principle or category or system of analysis."[71] *Henderson the Rain King* models what might still be termed a nascent subfield, a kind of Lacanian non-anthropology that emphasizes how "the structure—the symbolic order—is never complete. There is always something left over; an excess or something that exceeds the symbolic."[72] This excess turns out to be Henderson's primary motive for travel, which redeems him from being an impoverished, consumerist version of Kurtz:

> I could just hear people back home saying, as at a party for instance, *"That big Henderson finally got his. What, didn't you hear? He went to Africa and disappeared in the interior. He probably bullied some natives and they stabbed him. . . . He was full of excess." "Listen, you guys, my great excess was I wanted to live. . . ."* (196)

It would be problematic to directly relate *Henderson* to Bhabha's later discussion of the postcolonial subject's "agonizing performance of self-images," since Bellow's genial comedy often verges on sheer silliness; moreover, King Dahfu does not share Bhabha's attempt to "represent a certain defeat, or even an impossibility, of the 'West.'"[73] Nevertheless, I would insist that much cultural theory at the turn of the millennium should be understood as part of a larger literary history of globalization. *Henderson the Rain King* does not display the anxiety over cultural and racial boundaries that scholars such as Kaplan see as constituting American middle-class identity. Instead, the novel precisely follows Kaplan's directive to "transform the traditional notion of the frontier from the primitive margins of civilization to a decentered cosmopolitanism."[74]

The novel's decentered cosmopolitanism is specifically that of a Jewish American intellectual, who will redeem the frontier for globalizing America, turning the violence of settler colonialism into the sacredness of healing. Axelrod notes that "[l]ike many another Jewish hero, Henderson learns to care less for himself and more for others."[75] It seems important to Bellow that one of these "others" serves as Henderson's spiritual and professional mentor. Henderson's first wife laughs at his ambition to go to medical school in his mid-fifties, which apparently helps speed their divorce. By contrast, Dahfu is receptive to the idea: "At first [Dahfu] exhibited a degree of reserve. But after I convinced him of my sincerity he really appeared to see a future for me . . . although I might be doing my internship when other men were retiring from active life" (239). Henderson's final address to his African guide, Romilayu, indicates that he will pursue Dahfu's profession:

> Romilayu, you and I will get together again one day. The world is not so loose any more. You can locate a man, provided he stays alive. You have my address. Write to me. Don't take it so hard. Next time we meet I may be wearing a white coat. You'll be proud of me. I'll treat you for nothing. (330)

Pointing to the book's frequent use of specialized medical terms, Eberhard Alsen notes that the book as a whole is written from the perspective of someone who has trained as a doctor.[76] Henderson expresses a particular admiration for Sir Wilfred Grenfell, which reinforces the book's connection to Native Americans as well as Black people, since Grenfell did medical missionary work among Inuit tribes in Newfoundland (where Henderson's plane stops for fuel). Yet Henderson's professional style is less like European paternalism and more akin to Kennedy's freewheeling Peace Corps of the following decade.

Bellow's Jewish American exceptionalist vision is certainly grandiose, since Henderson takes on the burden of America's sins against Black people and Native Americans by healing Asian people. "Naturally China is out, now. They might catch us and brain-wash us. Ha, ha! But we might try India. I do want to get my hands on the sick. I want to cure them. Healers are sacred" (*H* 285). Following Morrison, I would criticize this as an escapist fantasy, but on different terms. Instead of modeling a transhistorical white/Black binary, I would focus more specifically on the rearticulation of Bellow's role as a professional writer from the 1930s to the 1950s. As we have seen, the New Deal era and the FWP stimulated Bellow to criticize racism and social inequality. For all his declarations of autonomy during the early Cold War, Bellow was very much enabled by universities and financial grants—the Guggenheim awards that allowed him to write *Augie March* in Paris and *Henderson* in Nevada—and took part in foreign policy initiatives like a State Department-sponsored tour of Europe, during which he accompanied the Cultural Cold War stalwart Mary McCarthy. As with his friend Ellison, the price of this ticket was not merely anticommunism but a disavowal of progressive affiliations. Barbara Foley has devoted a book to the shift in Ellison's politics over a fifteen-year period, arguing in *Wrestling with the Left* (2010) that *Invisible Man* overwrites

Ellison's thirties leftism, especially in the way it demonizes the Communist Party as the exploitative Brotherhood.[77] At the time of *Invisible Man*'s publication, even Bellow found the criticism of the Brotherhood overdone, yet he shared in Ellison's antileftist turn.

In my view, the most effective critique of *Henderson the Rain King* proceeds not by arguing that it instantiates a rigid colonial self/other distinction, but rather that its Jewish American frontier elides collective movements for social change. As Brennan notes, the problem with the argument for hybrid cosmopolitanism "is not what the argument does so much as what it finds unnecessary or unappealing to do: hold out a sophisticated theoretical space for a defensive nationalism that relies, inevitably, on a grounded sense of sociocultural belonging to a polity."[78] It would be a stretch to argue that Bellow writes against African nationalism, since his novel only has a tangential relationship to the continent. Yet it is worth noting that the Wariri and their de facto leader, the Bunam, are akin to the Third World totalitarianisms that we saw in Burroughs's Mayan Empire and will see again in Bishop's Brazil and Wright's Gold Coast. "This is brain-washing," Henderson comments when he is quarantined by the Wariri after an extensive investigation into his documents and personal history (*H* 145). As Frank McConnell points out, the novel's climax, in which Dahfu is killed by the Bunam's subterfuge, is "a palace conspiracy no less complicated or sinister than those which have beset Versailles or St. Petersburg."[79] Despite the interracial friendship and cultural syncretism, Henderson and Dahfu are heroic individualists, unconnected to resistant nationalisms or, for that matter, the Civil Rights Movement.

While the concluding narrative of the "American-Persian child" may resist a model of racial binaries, it also suggests the novel's vexed relationship to Western Asian politics (337). In the 1930s the Reza Shah Pahlavi requested that foreign governments refer to Persia as "Iran," a diplomatic move that accompanied his modernization program. Since then, the term "Iran" has referred to a nation that, for better or for worse, has tried to follow an independent course in the era of globalization. This effort was famously stymied in 1953 by the Central Intelligence Agency, which arranged the overthrow of Mohammed Mossadegh, Iran's democratically elected, reformist leader, when he attempted to nationalize the country's oil industry. Melani McAlister points to the political and economic underside of Bellow's vision of transnational freedom when she mentions that the CIA thereby "secured the northern border of the new 'American frontier.'" In short, the novel's valorization of the airplane as a mobile container of cultural intermixture overlooks the political conflict taking place on the ground. At the time Henderson's plane flies over the area, Iran is being ruled by the US-supported dictator who replaced Mossadegh, a hard social reality that the book elides through its valorization of a benign, globalized medical professionalism.

Jonathan Freedman has argued that American Jews should be released from being Matthew Arnold–derived "symbol[s] of Culture or Anarchy," and while Bellow might seem to extend the line of culture through such self-appointed guardians as Allan Bloom, he anticipated Freedman's observation that "Jews are walking hybrids."[80] Although it has an affinity with *Partisan Review*–style cosmopolitanism, Bellow's selfhood is more capacious, anticipating the globalized models of later decades. *Henderson the Rain King*'s model of cosmopolitanism flummoxed the New York Intellectuals, who idealized a sophisticated domestic culture that would allow writers to be "simultaneously American and international," which served as a "positive source of attraction working in harness with the negative binding force of anti-Stalinism."[81] The generally nonplussed critical response supports McConnell's claim that Bellow "had to wait for the absurdist explosion of sixties fiction for his novels to be put in a true perspective."[82] If we take the title of *Henderson the Rain King* to allude to the rain ceremonies of the Southwest, the novel anticipates the counterculture's valorization of Native America. But Bellovian hybridity comes with no political guarantees, since he set himself resolutely against the counterculture, and I would like to end by looking at how his later work articulated a specifically Jewish American transnationalism.

Jewish and Black Atlantics

Carol Smith argues that Bellow constructs a "Jewish Atlantic" that sets Jewish Americans' elective migration to the US as the norm, erasing the traumatic history of the Middle Passage and slavery. Whereas Paul Gilroy's *The Black Atlantic* (1993) celebrates a Black counterculture of modernity and cosmopolitan hybridity, in novels like *Henderson the Rain King*, "signs of hybridity signal death."[83] In Smith's account, Bellow strategically deploys Blackness to underwrite Jewish inclusion within white America: "from the American shore, the Jewish Atlantic disappears through assimilation, the Atlantic and America whitens," guaranteeing Bellow his canonical status in American literature.[84] To an extent, Smith's argument is the opposite of mine: focusing on the American frontier, I have argued that *Henderson the Rain King* adumbrates a model of cosmopolitan hybridity, stimulated by a specifically Jewish American conscience regarding the violence of settler colonialism.

However, if one narrows the historical focus—from Smith's broad critique of modern "European liberal humanism" to the postwar privileges of the American Century—I agree that there is a basic continuity in Bellow's published oeuvre, instead of a "transition from the Young Saul to the Old Saul."[85] In the latter model, derived from his son Greg Bellow, the rebels of Bellow's early fiction were replaced by Old Testament patriarchs, as Augie March morphed into Artur Sammler. In my view, instead of rupturing, Bellow's idiosyncratic cosmopolitanism tacked rightward. Although his engagement with neoconservatism is beyond the scope of this chapter, I want to highlight the significance of travel for his cultural politics by giving a more substance to Smith's notion of a "Jewish Atlantic," which was not mere assimilation and disappearance.

Bellow's later years were marked by a deepening concern with the Holocaust as the defining event of the twentieth century, which also accompanied an interest in Israel as a space of refuge and empowerment. His coverage of the 1967 Arab-Israeli Six-Day War as a correspondent for *Newsday* made him sympathize with Israel as a beleaguered nation. I think it is fair to relate Bellow's affinity for Israel to the privilege of travel, which involved a rearticulation of what I have called his Jewish American exceptionalism. *Mr. Sammler's Planet* (1969) might seem to depart from Bellow's visions of mobility and freedom in the early Cold War, since it satirizes the hubris of travel to the moon and the counterculture's effort at self-reinvention, and apparently endorses an acceptance of groundedness and finitude. However, the novel valorizes the air travel of Sammler's nephew, the doctor Elya Gruner, between the US and Israel:

> "Uncle [Sammler], try some of these fruit jellies. The lime and orange are the best. From Beersheba."
> "Aren't you watching your weight, Elya?"
> "No, I'm not. They're making terrific stuff in Israel these days." The doctor had been buying Israel bonds and real estate. In Westchester, he served Israeli wine and brandy. He gave away heavily embossed silver ball-point pens, made in Israel. You could sign checks with them. For ordinary purposes they were not useful. And on two occasions Dr. Gruner, as he was picking up his fedora, had said, "I believe I'll go to Jerusalem for a while."

"When are you leaving?"

"Now."

"Right away?" ...

"Just as I am. I can buy my toothbrush and razor when I land. I love it there."

[Elya] had his chauffeur drive him to Kennedy Airport.[86]

Elya foregoes ostentatious trappings of wealth such as "Broadway musicals" and "private jet[s]," but he does have "one glamorous eccentricity," which "was to fly to Israel on short notice and stroll into the King David Hotel without baggage, his hands in his pockets. This struck him as a sporting thing to do" (283). Given the respect Sammler has for Elya, it is appropriate that he perceives the outbreak of the Six-Day War as a uniquely important world event. Although Sammler is "no Zionist," he "had suddenly become excited. He could not sit still" (142). For most of the novel Sammler is a physically feeble, crotchety character, but his advent on the battlefield invigorates him (and makes him a lot more like the novel's author). "It was curious, that. At the age of seventy-two on battlegrounds, wearing these shoes and a seersucker jacket and soiled white cap from Kresge's." This free space of adventure and entrepreneurialism between America and Israel is the one social formation that resists the larger cynicism of *Mr. Sammler's Planet*. In this view, Bellow was every bit as boundary-pushing as his countercultural antagonists.

I suggest that for Bellow, the appeal of a strident anti-Soviet foreign policy was the way such a policy would buttress the Jewish Atlantic, an ethnically specific model of autonomy through travel that amounts to a post-Six-Day War reformulation of the global frontier. This perspective can help to explain his major travel book, *To Jerusalem and Back* (1976). Although Bellow has a lack of sympathy for Palestinian nationalism, Emily Miller Budick has taken him to task for endorsing "a larger American tradition of thinking about Israel which resists the idea of Israel as a material place."[87] Bellow endorses Israel's material geography in various passages, but for him, the country's major appeal was not the preservation of an integral Jewish culture and this culture's relationship to scripture and tradition, but rather the way it enables an empowered, transnational Jewish middle-classness:

It seems to me often that life in this tiny country is a powerful stimulant but that only the devout are satisfied with what they can obtain within Israel's borders. The Israelis are great travelers. They need the world. . . . From the eighteenth century, European Jews, when revolution began to release them from their ghettos, hastened to enter modern society; they adored and hungered for it—its cities, its political life, its culture, its great men, its personal opportunities. Even the Holocaust did not destroy this attraction. And now, carrying Israeli passports, Germans or Poles no longer, they are nearly as eager and starry-eyed about the great world as their ancestors.[88]

As Budick suggests, we might read Bellow's Israel specifically as a Jewish American traveler's construction. Bellow points out that Israel is unique among nations in having to defend its right to exist, and points to a double standard: "Where Israel is concerned, the world swells with moral consciousness. . . . What Switzerland is to winter holidays and the Dalmatian coast to summer tourists, Israel and the Palestinians are to the West's need for justice—a sort of moral resort area."[89] It is only fair to observe that Bellow himself turned to Israel as a place for supercharged experience, full of meaningful landmarks and passionate conversations about politics and culture, which contrasts with Chicago's "bungalow belt" of "plainness, regularity, family attachments, dollar worries, fear of crime, acceptance of routine."[90]

I think this travel dynamic complicates our accounts of Bellow's turn toward neoconservatism: instead of disavowing the ideals of his youth, he seems to have relocated them to a foreign country. In effect, the Israelis are hardworking immigrants to the Middle East, paralleling his own immigrant generation to Chicago: "no people has to work so hard on so many levels as this one. In less than thirty years the Israelis have produced a modern country—doorknobs and hinges, plumbing fixtures, electrical supplies, chamber music, airplanes, teacups."[91] When Bellow describes the politically conscious Israelis of the 1970s, who are "actively, individually involved in universal history"—they "cannot afford to overlook the latest changes in the strategy of the French Communist Party nor the crises in Portugal and Angola . . . I don't see how they can bear it"—he might as well be narrating the Depression-era University of Chicago campus that he inhabited with Isaac Rosenfeld, passionately debating the day's issues.[92]

The problem here is that, as a traveler of the Jewish Atlantic, Bellow has attenuated his social imagination regarding the United States. He was not an ideologue regarding Middle Eastern politics: *To Jerusalem and Back* irritated Israel's hardliners, and in 1978, Bellow signed the "Letter of 37" in support of the Israeli Peace Now movement, which advocated a two-state solution to the

Israeli-Palestinian problem.[93] Yet it might be fair to observe that Israel will be more socially just, and a two-state solution more plausible, when the United States itself is more democratic, socially equal, and antiracist. Instead, Bellow's travel to Israel seems to have reinforced his racial model of undeserving welfare recipients. In his coverage of the Six-Day War, he argued that the Palestinians squander the largesse they receive from an overindulgent United Nations: "Now the number of refugees has increased enormously, and if the old system is followed, the UN will be supporting more dozens of rotting slums in which demoralized, idle young men can concentrate on 'politics.'"[94] For Bellow, a pathological culture fosters this unwillingness to work: "Arab music . . . induces torpor with its endless sweetish winding and its absurd insinuations and seductions. One not only hears it but feels it distressingly in the bowels, like a drug."[95] If we read Bellow transnationally, his attitude toward Palestinians and his attitude toward African Americans are of a piece: both groups inhabit bleak urban landscapes, parasitically relying on welfare regimes.

As we have seen, Bellow's "In the Days of Mr. Roosevelt" lionized the great reformer, and he often acknowledged his own productive relationship to the welfare state. Going through yet another divorce in the early 1970s, he joked: "If this keeps up, I'm going to have to go back to where I started—on the WPA."[96] Yet Bellow's blind spots regarding progressive government have been shared by various Americans over the past decades, when transnational forms of affiliation have become more exciting than solidarity with racial and class others within the US. I am not sure that Jewish and Black Atlantics, read over hundreds of years of history, could ever be reconciled. But we might try to rediscover Bellow's early commitment to a liberal, progressive nationalism, which is not only important for American literature but also for Bellow's own diminished reputation. "For after all . . . he *could* be found!" Grebe declares at the end of "Looking for Mr. Green," the Kafkaesque mood of the story suggesting that in the context of the bureaucratic and conformist 1950s, there is no difference between success and failure (109). In the 2020s, when the story's New Deal subtext has renewed fascination, it is worth renewing the search.

Chapter Four

....

The Imperial Eyes of the Outsider

Elizabeth Bishop, American Globalization, and the Cold War in Brazil

Always highly respected and honored, Elizabeth Bishop has undergone a posthumous sea change in her reputation: displacing Robert Lowell as America's representative midcentury poet, she has become one of the most revered writers of the modern era. This has involved a reevaluation of her social consciousness, stimulated by Adrienne Rich's "The Eye of the Outsider" (1983), which argued that "the essential outsiderhood of a lesbian identity . . . enable[d] Bishop to perceive other kinds of outsiders and to identify, or try to identify, with them."[1] Instead of seeing her as reticent or apolitical, critics now emphasize Bishop's differential gender and sexual identity, which made her not only sympathetic to lower classes and racial others but also a radical social critic. This political approach has been stimulated by the advent of the "New Elizabeth Bishop," which began with the publication of *One Art: Letters* (1994) and gained critical mass with *Edgar Allan Poe & the Juke-Box* (2006) and the volumes of prose, poems, and letters that have followed.[2] Scholars now draw on a hugely expanded oeuvre to argue that Bishop was a critic of midcentury American consumerism whose thought anticipates the Marxist theory of Fredric Jameson's *Postmodernism* (1991); that her letters from Brazil constitute an "epistolary citizenship" that "refuses . . . hegemonic discourse" by "contrasting the inaccuracies of newspaper reportage with the truth of personal witness"; and that the original draft of her book *Brazil* reveals that her "imperial social critique" was "too harsh" for *Life* World Library's editors, who "co-opted [her] into an American ethnocentric project full of mid-century sales pitches."[3] Even Bethany Hicok's richly detailed *Elizabeth Bishop's Brazil* (2016), which grants that Bishop could be racist in her representation of people of color, argues that she strenuously critiqued "authoritarian political systems" in Brazil while also making an "anti-imperialist critique of corporate America."[4]

This chapter argues that critics have overlooked the way Bishop participated in American globalization precisely as a lesbian writer.[5] We tend to persist in reading her as a poet of personal trauma—at most, complicit in structures of oppression, but not enabled by them. However, if Bishop's famous villanelle "One Art" can be read not just as her elegy for a lost lover, but, as Brett Millier suggests, "Bishop's elegy for her whole life," the poem reveals the mobility and socioeconomic privilege that informed her life and work[6]:

> . . . And look! my last, or
> next-to-last, of three loved houses went.
> The art of losing isn't hard to master.
>
> I lost two cities, lovely ones. And, vaster,
> some realms I owned, two rivers, a continent.
> I miss them, but it wasn't a disaster.[7]

In relation to the majority of Brazilians of the time, the lines highlight exceptional privileges, ones that go well beyond Bishop's relationship with the aristocrat Lota de Macedo Soares: the ownership of a colonial-era home in Ouro Preto; travel by car, boat, and airplane; and perhaps most of all, the capacity to represent the country to the US, as she did in poems, letters, a major article for the *New York Times Magazine*, and *Brazil*. "One Art" thus raises the question of whether Bishop's figurative ownership of "realms" and "a continent" can be criticized in the same terms as male travelers' representations— arguably a source of anxiety in Pratt's seminal *Imperial Eyes* (1992), which covers a very broad swath of travel writing and has trouble maintaining a distinction between the sovereign male traveler and the prerogatives of female travelers, especially where postwar American narratives are concerned.

In Jeffrey Gray's view, "that America's chief poet of travel is a woman refutes the received wisdom that travel is a male prerogative. . . . This is not to say, however, that Bishop's poetry calls on us to reconceive woman (or traveling woman) as empowered. Bishop herself did not feel empowered in or by travel."[8] To be sure, Bishop's family history was uniquely traumatic: her father died when she was eight months old, and the shock eventually confined her mother within a mental institution. As Helen Vendler puts it, "Bishop's mother, confined for life in a hospital for the insane . . . remained the

inaccessible blank at the center of all Bishop's travel. . . . Whatever knowledge
Bishop owned, it was the knowledge of the homeless and migrant."[9] At the
same time, Bishop did enjoy, if briefly, a happy childhood with her maternal
grandparents in Nova Scotia, Canada, and the lack of parental control led to
a strong sense of independence.[10] Joined to a modest yet extremely useful trust
fund and a first-class education that included a Vassar degree, Bishop's travel
enabled her to explore alternative sexual and gender roles.

I do not think that Bishop critics are wrong to argue that her feeling of
outsiderness in America—variously articulated as feminism, lesbianism,
and disability (asthma and alcoholism)—led to a heightened empathy with
marginalized people. But we might ask ourselves whether those feelings were
most productively articulated in a national context, as opposed to an international one. Axelrod asserts: "Bishop's queer politics consistently informed
and distinguished her social writing. It was the most radical side of her public
awareness."[11] In my view, an extended analysis of Bishop's relationship to the
New Deal is a major lacuna in the field.[12] The New Deal was hard to avoid in
Key West, since federal intervention saved it from certain financial ruin and
reinvigorated it as a tourist destination. Some of Bishop's most famous and
successful poems, like "Florida" and "The Fish," were stimulated by government policies. Key West enabled Bishop to make alliances across class and
color lines that are largely absent from her earlier and later work.

After World War II, Bishop bravely resisted Cold War norms and constructed her own transnational feminist literary network, yet this project was
enabled by American globalization. The next sections of the chapter attempt
to offer a more fine-grained analysis of Bishop's relationship to Brazilian politics and American influence. It is important not to uncritically accept Bishop's
terminology, and note, for example, that she frequently called democratically
elected presidents "dictator[s]" because she opposed their labor-friendly agen-
das.[13] In my view, Bishop critics mistake antistatist critiques for progressive
ones; in fact, Bishop's economic outlook can be exactly described as neoliberal
insofar as she favored US investment, the control of inflation at the expense of
populist initiatives, and America-friendly politicians such as her close friend
Carlos Lacerda. When Kennedy became president in 1961, Bishop committed
herself enthusiastically to the Alliance for Progress, which many Brazilians
came to view as a neocolonial project, especially when the US supported the
increasingly repressive military dictatorship that came to power in 1964.

Betsy Erkkila famously argues that Bishop's poems "take as their subjects

class consciousness, race and gender struggle, the culture of the commodity
and the machine, the relations of capital, property, and homelessness, and
the conflict between the dominant narratives of the West and the 'others'—
women, lesbians, blacks, Cubans, Indians, the lower classes, the body, nature—that those narratives subjugate and colonize."[14] Ironically, Bishop's contribution to the *Life* World Library series, *Brazil*, inscribes this list of others
within a US-centered modernization narrative based upon capital and property. Moreover, her poems, prose, and letters erase the political agency of reformist and radical Brazilians and people of color; the president of Brazil, Chinese communists, and farmers like Manuelzinho from the eponymous poem
are portrayed as corrupt, fearsome, or just contemptible. Although life as an
expatriate offered Bishop a great deal of freedom in terms of gender roles and
sexual expression, there is no guarantee that her politics will be emancipatory;
in fact, the public stances that she took were in keeping with her prerogatives
as a member of a global professional-managerial class. As I shall explain below,
although I will emphasize Bishop's globalized class privilege, this privilege is
difficult to separate from same-sex desires and practices. At the beginning of
the landmark essay collection *Fear of a Queer Planet* (1993), Michael Warner
states: "What do queers want? This volume takes for granted that the answer
is not just sex. Sexual desires themselves can imply other wants, ideals, and
conditions."[15] Bishop's expatriation, like that of Burroughs, suggests that the
things we have to fear on a Queer Planet are the same things we have to fear
on a Straight Planet: hyperindividualism, social inequality, and the oppression
of the Global South by the Global North.

Queer Poetics and the Welfare State in Key West

Many critics see Bishop turning southward to liberate herself from New England social mores and find broader self-expression as a woman and lesbian.
As Barbara Page puts it, "at the geographical periphery of the country, Bishop
found a place corresponding to her own disposition for the margins ... Bishop
needed a Key West of her own—in dreams and in the geographical peripheries
of real places—in which she might unravel the order that excluded her and
her kind."[16] However, there is a national amnesia where Florida is concerned,
as Steven Noll observes: although "conventional wisdom holds that modern
Florida began with World War II" and its "boom created by war-related industries ... modern Florida actually began in the 1930s with the government

programs of the New Deal."[17] In a 1935 article for *Harper's* magazine, Elmer Davis described Key West as a haven for writers and intellectuals, where "a group of men and women who had intended to make the rounds of the night clubs would stay at home instead, sitting up till two A.M. discussing problems of administrative technic, and having as good a time as they would have had at the night clubs."[18] In contrast to the money-oriented, hedonistic Paris of the Lost Generation, 1930s Key West functioned as a combination of bohemia and New Deal brain trust.

Did Bishop's bohemian lifestyle have a public valence? Commenting on the title poem of the collection *Edgar Allan Poe & the Juke-Box* (2006), Angus Cleghorn claims that Bishop's Key West poems extol an "erotic-tropical electric fulfillment" that, however counterintuitive given her shy persona, was entirely in keeping with her lifestyle at the time: "Who would have thought Elizabeth Bishop a 'honky-tonk woman'?"[19] Although this personal liberation was important in itself, it was also connected to the public world of the New Deal, which was still prominent in Key West several years after Davis's article, as a Bishop letter from March 1940 attests:

> *Partisan Review* has asked me to write them a "Florida Letter." . . . They are printing "The Fish" this month, I think . . . Mr. [Alfred H.] Barr [Jr., of the Museum of Modern Art] and his wife are in Key West and have been here. . . . The two boys who run the poetry magazine called *Furioso*— have you seen it? I just saw the first number with Wallace Stevens, E. E. Cummings, etc. in it—are here now and are "coming to call." . . . Wallace Stevens was here too at the "fancy" hotel, and Robert Frost . . . but the only person I saw of any importance was John L. Lewis chewing a cigar.[20]

As these letters and others indicate, Bishop was not isolated but networked, engaged in a national culture of arts and letters. In fact, it was New Deal government policies that initially brought Bishop to Key West. In 1934, the Federal Emergency Relief Administrator (FERA) for Florida, Julius F. Stone Jr. had faced three major options for Depression-stricken Key West: direct emergency relief; evacuation of the island; or the stimulation of the economy to make Key West self-supporting. He chose the last option, rehabilitating Key West through a work relief program that would convert the city into a popular tourist spot, which would attract private capital.[21] Stone's strategy was amazingly successful: while Key West might not have entered her consciousness beforehand, Bishop and her partner, the wealthy heiress and art patron Louise

Crane, were exactly the well-heeled travelers whom Stone wanted to lure to the island. "Louise enjoys fishing more than anything in the world," Bishop told a friend in January 1937, and Crane's eventual role as homeowner and patron functioned as significant economic relief (*OA* 53). "New Deal Awakens Key West, America's Tropical 'Problem City,'" a *New York Times* headline announced on May 2, 1937; Bishop settled there in January 1938.[22] It is no exaggeration to say that the most personal details of Bishop's Key West life were the effects of government policy. For example, local relief administrators helped property owners to repair and renovate houses for tourists, while enabling low rental rates.[23] This was most likely the situation of Mrs. Pindar, who was Bishop's landlady during her first extended stay in Key West (*OA* 67). Even Bishop's attire and mode of transportation was a realization of Stone's vision for the transformed island; Stone not only used federal funds to refurbish nightclubs so as to appeal to tourists, but also encouraged bicycle riding and the wearing of shorts, which scandalized the modest locals.

Bishop's working-class aunt and uncle Maud and George Shepherdson also relocated themselves to Key West. Bishop regularly ate dinner with them, and given the federal government's important role in Key West, it is likely that they were supported by the WPA. "Everybody lived on the W.P.A. I seemed to have a taste for impoverished places in those days," Bishop said later.[24] This helps to explain Bishop's excitement in a 1939 letter to her mentor, the poet Marianne Moore: "Yesterday we had the great thrill of seeing our PRESIDENT [Franklin Roosevelt]. All Key West stood on the curb all dressed up, holding little flags and clapping respectfully. He is much better-looking than I had thought" (*OA* 80).

Bishop Studies, and literary studies in general, tends to valorize an anti-governmental version of cultural activism, but a state-centered politics might be "much better-looking than [we] had thought," informing poems that seem to focus on private epiphanies. Commenting on the poem "Florida," Eleanor Cook says that "the coastline . . . is seen as if by a walker, not a sailor," and features "detailed description of a natural scene, realistically, with suggestive patterning on closer inspection."[25] Yet Bishop made no attempt to hide the genesis of this poem in touristic experience. One could draw a parallel with the later "2,000 Illustrations and a Complete Concordance" and argue that if an illustrated family Bible frames the episodes of the latter poem, some of the exotic scenes of "Florida" are generated by brochures, in particular the Key West Administration's 1935 pamphlet that sought to lure tourists to the island.

The lines "The alligator, who has five distinct calls / friendliness, love, mating, war, and a warning" (*PPL* 25), were inspired by a visit Bishop made to the famous naturalist Ray Allen, who wrestled alligators and imitated their calls in shows for tourists, and whose advertising brochure Bishop sent to Moore.[26] Despite the claim that in the moonlight, "the careless, corrupt state is . . . the poorest / post-card of itself," Bishop's "state with the prettiest name" is arguably a series of touristic images—"Here are my best snapshots, so far, of Key West," Bishop enthused to Moore in January 1938 (*OA* 67).

Bishop's "Florida" can be read alongside the American Guide Series, since Moore was one of the originators of the idea for these travel guides. Having traveled through Europe before World War I, Moore "knew the value of a guidebook," and urged the Civil Works Administration (a precursor of the WPA) to hire unemployed writers to prepare guidebooks and state histories.[27] The congruence of the FWP writers' and Bishop's work is precise enough to suggest that she intended her work to sync with the publication of the guides. Bishop published "Florida" in the *Partisan Review* in January 1939, which was followed by several Key West-themed poems in various magazines; meanwhile, *Florida: A Guide to the Southernmost State* came out in 1939, followed two years later by the *Guide to Key West*. Having famously broken with the Communist Party, Philip Rahv, the editor of the *Partisan Review*, worked for the FWP and contributed to its guide to New York City.

Bishop thus entered a national conversation regarding the guidebooks. "Florida" might be said to have a self-reflexive, performative quality, insofar as Bishop's mapping of Florida accompanied a New Deal-funded mapping of American states. As Millier observes, "In a characteristic manipulation of scale and perspective, the poem looks both close up and from the air at Florida, as we shift from seeing single animals, flowers, and swamps to viewing 'a state full'—the entire coastline in one sweep. Bishop appreciated the cartographic richness of the state of Florida" (*M* 115). This is not to simply conclude that "Florida" encouraged more tourists to visit the state, although it may well have. The larger point is that what Susannah Hollister has called Bishop's "geographic feeling," which involves "turning away from the social in order to pursue it," here becomes aligned with government-sponsored reform efforts.[28] Far from retreating to a geographical periphery, Bishop was part of a collective effort to bring an economically distressed region to public attention.

Although "The Fish" has been shorn of its social context, reprinted in anthologies as a stand-alone effort, it is important to see that the poem recounts

an aesthetic and moral experience produced, in part, by "putting the government into the tourist business."[29] The "little rented boat" indicates that the
poem's speaker is a tourist with money to spend, as opposed to a fisherperson
whose economic survival is involved (*PPL* 34). Millier remarks that the poem's "accumulation of detail forces its conclusion" when the speaker lets the
fish go (154), but one could also argue that some sort of epiphany of "rainbow, rainbow, rainbow!" was desired before the poetic speaker ever boarded
the boat (*PPL* 34). Since the speaker's fishing is done for pleasure instead of
production, "The Fish" is oriented toward experience *in itself,* toward the desire for self-knowledge and broadening of personal horizons. The transaction
underlying "The Fish"—of a tourist paying, not for a physical object, but for
experience, in the context of a New Deal effort to stimulate just such touristic experience—arguably involves a certain attitude toward economic policy.
In this reading of the poem, the fish himself might be seen as an exemplar
of classical liberalism—an aquatic individualist persevering in the midst of
Depression-era hardship. Yet while the fish is given his due as a hardy survivor,
he is also decentered and unmanned by the speaker's decision to toss him back
into the water, insofar as the poem valorizes play instead of work—leisure
and a certain excess of technology and experience. "The Fish" thus announces
a transition to a different economic regime, one that we might identify as
Keynesian in its concern with consumerism and the stimulation of demand.[30]

If Bishop can be aligned with modern liberalism and opposed to *laissez-
faire*, she can also be opposed to the classical individualist Ernest Hemingway, and given Hemingway's legendary status in Key West, a brief comparison might be helpful. Hemingway had watched in consternation as his once
placid getaway turned into a vacation hotspot. He was famously hostile to
the New Deal, condemning it as "[s]ome sort of Y.M.C.A. show. Starry eyed
bastards spending money that somebody will have to pay."[31] In contrast, he
claimed "the sanctity of his individualism" by identifying himself "squarely
as a *producer* of goods as opposed to a worker whose services, like those of
the WPA writers Stone imported to Key West, are contracted to benefit a
larger collective."[32] Hemingway was thus horrified when he himself became
a Key West tourist attraction, number 18 on the list of attractions in a WPA
pamphlet.[33] Bishop herself later remembered "her stay in Hemingway's house,
where I had to chase tourists out of the front yard all the time" (*OA* 290). To
be sure, there is a rich irony in Hemingway's anti-New Deal rhetoric, insofar
as he arguably functioned as a New Deal unto himself for Key Westers who

desperately needed the aid. According to a historian of Key West, Maureen Ogle: "By early 1933, as the nation slipped closer to outright despair and bank runs became a daily event, about the only things keeping Key West afloat were the Hemingways' remodeling jobs, Ernest's bar tabs and fishing jaunts, and the yacht-setters who showed up hunting for fish or a piece of the growing Hemingway legend. . . . [H]e made sure they paid their bills and treated townspeople fairly."[34] But this economic stimulus, as important as it was, was inadequate; the government had to step in and do what Hemingway's private initiative couldn't, and I argue that Bishop was broadly supportive of this government effort.

Here I would like to emphasize the activities of Bishop's partner Crane, who was not merely a wealthy socialite. Crane's mother, Louise Boardman Crane, was associated with John Dewey's progressive museum movement, and she and her daughter were friends with Holger Cahill, the director of the WPA's Art Program. This provides context for Bishop's essay "Gregorio Valdes, 1879–1939." Ogle notes that while "Bishop regarded Valdes as her own personal discovery . . . in truth, he had already developed a small reputation as a primitive painter."[35] Bishop's particular contribution was to enable a Cuban American artistic circuit from South to North even as she herself went from North to South. According to Bishop's essay, she saw a painting by Valdes in a nondescript barbershop, and finally bought it for three dollars, then commissioned him to paint a painting of her White Street house (*PPL* 326–27). Valdes had worked for the WPA, and his painting of a house in which Bishop wrote various same-sex love poems serves to locate the house within a network of New Deal connections. As Bishop writes in a letter that indicates how socially expansive her life in Key West was: "we were so proud when Mr. Cahill, who is the head of the W.P.A. Art Project, was here and saw it [Valdes's painting]. He said it was very good and wanted the local W.P.A. Art Project to give a *Valdes Show*" (*OA* 79). Bishop's article on Valdes, which appeared in the *Partisan Review*, is for its own part reminiscent of cultural accounts in the WPA guidebooks, functioning as a historical sketch of the Cuban American community in Key West (which is where Valdes was born).

This dynamic brings up a criticism leveled at New Deal cultural programs: was Valdes merely an ethnographic object—a bit of local color for metropolitan readers? Bishop's account of Valdes's earlier work in cigar factories seems to bypass a history of labor-management strife, and her assessment of Valdes's work is marked by condescension: "although he certainly belongs to the class

of painters we call 'primitive,' sometimes he was not even a good 'primitive'"
(*PPL* 331–32). Nevertheless, it is only fair to note that Bishop saw the worth
of Valdes's paintings when not everyone did, enabling a career that took on a
life of its own. Valdes had several paintings displayed at prestigious galleries
in New York, including MoMA. Although Valdes tragically died soon after
the exhibitions of his work, his paintings continued to circulate; as Bishop
noted in 1944, "the best one of all was owned by Orson Welles" (*OA* 121).
This might not be the radical/contrarian figure that Bishop Studies desires,
but a New Deal-oriented Bishop perhaps reveals something more valuable for
progressive alliances: that, as David Kurnick puts it, "there's something queer
about the welfare state."[36]

Bishop thus gives us a model of the interwar poet-critic who is generally
enabled by, and sympathetic to, government policies.[37] In this light, her classic
poem "Roosters" does not criticize the intrusion of the military into an impoverished, yet culturally appealing idyll, but rather the transition from New
Deal reform to security-state apparatus. As Bishop lamented in a 1942 letter,
"They [the US Navy] are just tearing down all the good work the government
has been doing here in the last ten years, and when the war is finally over,
Key West will be more ruined than ever" (*OA* 106). Although "Roosters" is
a prescient criticism of what later became known as the military-industrial
complex, I want to argue that Bishop herself took part in America's general
rightward shift after World War II. As an expatriate, she criticized Brazilian
analogues of Roosevelt, and while travel enabled a greater autonomy than she
would have found in the US at the time, we need to seriously consider whether
her personal freedom ran counter to the interests of the majority of Brazilians.

Gender Trouble on the Brazilian Frontier

Many critics have noted that Bishop reevaluated her childhood and became
empowered to write about it in Brazil, but this writing also involved a resistance to America's Cold War containment culture. The first short story
Bishop completed and published, "Gwendolyn," functions as an allegory for
her resistance to what Betty Friedan famously called a "comfortable concen-
tration camp" for middle-class white women.[38] Gwendolyn "stood for everything that the slightly repellent but fascinating words 'little girl' should mean
… blond, and pink and white … [and] 'delicate,' which, in spite of [my] bron-
chitis, I was not."[39] "She had diabetes," the narrator adds, and, coddled by her
indulgent parents, Gwendolyn dies of this disease. Shortly after Gwendolyn's

funeral, the narrator plays in her large yard with her cousin Billy, fighting "for the possession of insects in matchboxes," and has the inspiration of retrieving a doll from her aunt's bedroom: "we played vaguely at 'operating' on [the doll's] stomach . . . Then we had the idea of adorning her with flowers. . . . The game was more exciting than 'operation.' I don't know which one of us said it first, but one of us did, with wild joy—that it was Gwendolyn's funeral, and that the doll's real name, all this time, was Gwendolyn" (*Pr* 60–61). Both girls suffer from sickness, but the narrator has a rugged health and capacity for the "wild joy" of survival. For Bishop, to write and publish this story was to become the adult version of the rustic heroine who functions as counterpoint to medicalized, embalmed Gwendolyn, and thus one of the independent career women whom Friedan celebrated. In an April 1953 letter, Bishop disparaged the story but emphasized the *New Yorker*'s generous payment, which she elsewhere called a "huge sum" (*OA* 267): "The first story they took, before Christmas, I am not proud of—and it is very short—and with one thing and another I've already been paid about $1,200 for it. It's quite crazy" (*OA* 259). It is this empowerment, I think, that gives Bishop the quality of being tangential to second-wave feminism (she refused to appear in women-only anthologies) and anticipatory of third-wave feminism, in particular the concept of the performativity of gender advanced in queer theory.

The paradox here is that while Bishop resisted "naturalized and reified notions of gender that support masculine hegemony and heterosexist power," she was enabled by the global expansion of American power and technology.[40] As she wrote in a 1953 letter, "[W]here I am living and what I am doing seem to suit me perfectly for the first time in ages—and surely at this stage of history and airplanes and the wireless we don't have to brood too much about expatriation" (*OA* 282). Gillian White argues that Bishop felt "intense queasiness over U.S. culture at midcentury," which included "the excesses and reach of high capitalism" and an "automobile-driven economy."[41] But it's not clear how Bishop's disparaging remarks about mass culture are any different than those of New York Intellectuals of the time.[42] Moreover, if we turn our critical lens southward, we can see that despite her relocation to Samambaia (Soares's estate, two hours from Rio), Bishop continued to participate enthusiastically in American consumer culture. A striking detail about the publication of "In the Village" is that it enabled the purchase of a sportscar, stimulated by "an ad for an MG for sale in the Sunday paper. . . . Finally in my excitement Lota and I rushed to Rio and I *bought* one" (*OA* 273). In another letter Bishop likens herself to a character in a film, "an awful picture with Ginger Rogers and

Cary Grant taking some kind of youth-elixir—and the first thing Cary G
did after taking it was to rush out and buy a car exactly like mine to symbol-
ize adolescence" (*WIA* 147). In filmic terms, one might say that the clanging
blacksmith's hammer that famously concludes "In the Village" dissolves into
the MG, "zoom[ing] up the mountains—rather slowly, to tell the truth—with
the cut-out open. It is fun driving; I'd never driven before. I am going abroad
in February—mostly Italy" (*OA* 284). Bishop's adoption of the persona of a
male film star has an element of parody, but it also represents economic success
that enables further global mobility.

    Instead of seeing Bishop as retreating to a rural aerie in Samambaia, we
should see her famous cliffside writing studio as highly networked, which
enabled a feminism that articulated itself transnationally and was largely individualistic in orientation. It is in this light that I would like to read the
introduction to her translation of *The Diary of "Helena Morley"*—Bishop's
1957 translation of Alice Dayrell Caldeira Brant's *Minha Vida de Menina*
(1942)—"a consuming labor of love" that lasted five years (*M* 257). Millier
says that "she [Morley] is not at all an Elizabeth figure; sturdy and outgoing,
unscholarly and vain, she is rather a type Elizabeth admired" (257). However,
there is a self-reflexive quality to the introduction insofar as Bishop rewrites
the young frontier heroine as a globalized writer-professional, ultimately prov-
ing to be more "sturdy and outgoing" than the book's author, Brant, ever was.
When Bishop said later in life that she had always had strong feminist princi-
ples, she had good reason to make this claim, since her 1957 translation was an
attempt to recuperate the silenced voices of literary Brazilian women. As she
writes in her draft for *Brazil*, "For three hundred years [women] were rarely
taught to read or write. . . . Some of the talent wasted can be guessed at. *The
Diary of 'Helena Morley'* (Alice Brant) is an authentic diary kept in Diaman-
tina in the '80s by a young girl, certainly a novelist *manquée*" (*Pr* 235). Bishop
then adds, "Women are now prominent in Brazilian letters," going on to name
among others Clarice Lispector, whose work she also translated. Bishop thus
anticipates second-wave feminism's recovery of woman-authored texts, although, instead of constructing an alternative canon, she works to broaden
and integrate the existing one. Although Alice Brant herself may be unscholarly, Bishop gives the diary a literary pedigree: "Certain pages reminded me
of more famous and 'literary' ones: . . . Wordsworth's poetical children and
country people, or Dorothy Wordsworth's wandering beggars" (*Pr* 273–74).
Dissolving distinctions between genders, Bishop provides the canon with a

gender-troubling lineage in which Dorothy Wordsworth stands right alongside her more famous brother, and in contemporary terms, resists Lowell's
condescending remark that her own poetry was merely "the best written by a
woman in the twentieth century."[43]

Bishop's validation of literary Brazilian women also involved the manipulation of newfound professional opportunities. Ironically, Hicok's recent
book on Bishop and Brazil overlooks the way in which Bishop's midcentury
life represents a globalization of the female community of "queer birds" that
Hicok eloquently depicted in her important 1999 article about Bishop's Vassar
College writings. "[The student journal] *Con Spirito* allowed Bishop to 'come
out' as both a writer and, perhaps much more provisionally, a lesbian. Moreover, the *Con Spirito* writers seemed to share a fantasy of a productive female
community. . . . Bishop built this fragile network at Vassar and maintained it
in suggestive ways in the poetry and prose she published throughout her life."[44]
When she took Soares on a seven-month tour in the US to meet editors and
tour literary New York, Bishop incorporated both Soares and Brant in her own
transnational literary network. During this same time period, Bishop was shop-
ping "The Shampoo" to various magazines; as Millier notes, it "is clearly a love
poem between women" (248), although in a letter Bishop jokingly called it
"the little poem Mrs. White [Katharine White, her editor at the *New Yorker*]
couldn't understand" (*OA* 241). Bishop's laughing subversion of Cold War
norms makes one wonder if we should continue to describe her as in any way
shy or closeted. I would suggest that if Brazil allowed Bishop to reimagine her
childhood, it also enabled her to recuperate visions of gender variability and
sexual freedom expressed in her earliest published work. Many critics have
noted that stories like "A Flight of Fancy" and "Then Came the Poor" are quite
open regarding same-sex desire. Indeed her late-1920s poem "I introduce Penelope Gwin" reads like a proleptical resistance of 1950s containment culture:

> I introduce Penelope Gwin,
> A friend of mine through thick and thin,
> Who's traveled much in foreign parts
> Pursuing culture and the arts.
> "And also," says Penelope
> "This family life is not for me.
> I find it leads to deep depression
> And *I* was born for self expression." (*PPL* 203)

When one understands that "bird" was "a code word for lesbians in the 1930s," the poem becomes a straightforward tale of pursuing sexual adventures abroad ("She fed grilled almonds to the birds, / And spoke to them with honeyed words" [204]), while staying one step ahead of a chaperone-like aunt.[45] Bishop's early Brazilian years allowed her to recover the spirit of Penelope Gwin, a kind of flaneur/flapper who is enabled by the expansion of American economic influence in Europe during the Roaring Twenties, although to be sure "The Shampoo" is a more mature account of same-sex love.

Turning a quotation from a later Bishop letter into a chapter title, Millier calls Bishop's mid-1950s years in Brazil "A Deluxe Nova Scotia" (252). One might also call this time period a Deluxe Vassar College or even Deluxe Walnut Hill boarding school, because of the way in which Bishop reevaluated her youth, achieving financial success in the process. Yet one would probably not call Brazil a Deluxe Key West, despite the country's racial and cultural diversity. In New Deal-era Florida, governmental programs and a sense of national alliance had enabled an earlier Bishop to cross racial and class lines. In the postwar global economy, her sense of professional opportunity, adventure and travel put her at odds with the more workaday lives of Brazilians associated with Samambaia, as she noted herself: "You should see our 'yard' now—three English cars, all the finest, sitting in it, and why the workmen on the house don't murder us all as dirty capitalists I don't know" (OA 273). Here I am in agreement with Fiona Green's analysis of Bishop's relationship to the New Yorker, which highlights Bishop's orientation toward the marketplace and the way in which the strength of the US dollar enabled her travel. In effect reading Bishop's poetry through Immanuel Wallerstein, Green models an economic world system of poetry production, arguing that peripheral Brazil provided poetic raw materials for the literary core of Manhattan: "It was in part the income from poetry published in the New Yorker that provided the dollars that kept her comparatively rich in inflation-bound Brazil, and the relative poverty of her adopted country that gave her some of the raw materials for that verse, its authenticity adding to its value."[46] I would add that Bishop's economic relationship to the literary metropole entailed specific political positions.

This is an aspect of The Diary of "Helena Morley," which contains diary entries written from 1893 to 1895, shortly after slavery was abolished in Brazil. Hicok notes that the book is "packed with references to freed slaves who continue working as servants. . . . These passages would have been a minefield for an American translator in the racially charged context of the United States in the 1950s."⁴⁷ Yet Hicok's judgment about the "minefield" of translation strikes me as anachronistic. A key passage in Bishop's introduction names another famous account of the aftermath of slavery, and explains why she was so confident the work would be "a real blockbuster" in 1950s America (which, as Maria Machado points out, was a major reason for her undertaking the translation)⁴⁸: "Occasionally entries referring to slavery seemed like notes for an unwritten, Brazilian, feminine version of Tom Sawyer [sic] and Nigger Jim" (*Pr* 274). The reference to "Nigger Jim" is stark indeed, and indicates the kind of literary-political discourse that the Morley translation entered. As Jonathan Arac reminds us, "It was only after the Second World War that *Huckleberry Finn* achieved massive canonicity in the schools, as the great spiritual representative of the America that had become the dominant power in the world, and that aimed to embrace alien peoples with the loving innocence that Huck offered Jim; yet these same years were the time [of] the assertion of African American civil rights . . . the importance of this cultural work overrode the offense the book generated among many of its newly authorized, but also newly obligated, African American readers."⁴⁹ The "unwritten, Brazilian, feminine version" of this Twain novel was arguably one that Bishop produced herself in the act of translation. To be sure, Morley does not light out for the territory with a dark other, since her story is more familial and town-centered. Nevertheless, insofar as Bishop insists in the introduction that it "could have happened in any small provincial town . . . at almost any period of history" (*Pr* 272), and that Morley herself "has many friends, old and young, black and white" (286), the book in Bishop's view takes on a "national and global political function as an icon of integration."⁵⁰

In other words, Bishop's translation project does not merely reproduce pre-existing racial prejudices, but bears a specific relationship toward social change in the 1950s. To return to Fiedler's famous analysis, the American veneration of *Huckleberry Finn* entails an escape from politics and even from adulthood altogether, toward a fantasy of juvenile interracial camaraderie, "the boy's homoerotic crush."⁵¹ Bishop's putting *Morley* in the lineage of Twain suggests that Fiedler's critique might be relevant across gender positions: whatever good feelings she had toward racial others, she had trouble conceiving of their autonomous political agency. This was certainly the case in Brazil, where Bishop tended to blame the poor for their problems, suggesting in various poems and letters that children were the victims not of social or racial inequality but rather of bad parenting, as for example in "Mother's voice, ugly as sin," in "Squatter's Children" (*PPL* 76; see also *M*, 272–73). As Hicok observes, "'Helena Morley' herself loved 'little black babies,' but that love tended to wear off when they grew up," which parallels Fiedler's observation of "the white boy and the black we can discover wrestling affectionately on any American street, along which they will walk in adulthood, eyes averted from each other, unwilling to touch."[52] Generally speaking, *Helena Morley* seems an attempt to reconcile Black and white people "through juvenile classics . . . on the shelves of the Children's Library."[53]

To judge from Bishop's letters, the original Brazilian text of *Minha Vida de Menina* (1942) roughly paralleled *Huckleberry Finn*'s role in Cold War America; simply referring to the book as a Brazilian classic overlooks its relationship to turbulent political energies. As Bishop says of the book's author, "She wrote really beautifully; the characters, the Negro servants, the old grandmother, etc., are really well presented, and it is funny. (I have seen a dignified lawyer here laughing his head off, reading it.) . . . [I]t gives a beautiful little picture of a way of life that has vanished" (*OA* 269). The reference to the "dignified lawyer" highlights Bishop's social milieu, which included Soares's traditional landed elite and a growing class of urban professionals, many of whom were perhaps nostalgic for a time of supposed social harmony. As the historian Thomas Skidmore relates of the late 1950s, "Taken together, the signs of awakening mass politics in the urban and rural sectors were bound to frighten those groups which had most to lose if the power equilibrium should be disturbed by the populist politicians: the rural landowners, never before threatened . . . the urban middle class, still linked by many personal ties to the rural landowners . . . and the military officer class."[54] Not merely a cultural intermediary but an active agent of American globalization, Bishop had strong views about populist politicians, which we should consider if we want to claim her as "a revolutionary lesbian poet."[55]

Bishop's Critique of Brazilian Big Government

While Bishop may not have published explicitly political writing in the 1950s, she was eager to take the position of the insider who knew the truth behind US newspaper headlines. For example, following the election of the left-liberal president Juscelino Kubitschek de Oliveira, Bishop wrote to Lowell in November 1955, "The old dictator gang is back in again. (If you happen to read of it in the papers don't believe what they say. The *NY Times* had it completely the wrong way around,—another step for 'democracy,' etc." (*WIA* 172). In effect, "The old dictator gang" is Bishop's term for Brazil's political regime from 1930 to 1964. In 1930, a defeated presidential candidate, Getúlio Vargas, took the office through armed insurrection; he abolished elections in 1937, engineering a state-driven modernization project that paralleled European efforts. Vargas stood aside for democratic elections in 1945, retook power as president by a landslide vote in 1950, and committed suicide in 1954 in a dramatic episode that I shall discuss below. His protégés were Kubitschek (president from 1955 to 1960) and João Goulart (president from 1963 to 1964).

Bishop did not simply reproduce Soares's aristocratic views; rather, she had her own set of political interests in Brazil. As she wrote in an August 1953 letter: "it is very strange to me to live in a country where the ruling class and the intellectual class are so very small. . . . It's certainly bad for the 'arts' too. . . . Well, it's all because of NO MIDDLE CLASS" (*OA* 271). On this point, it is extremely important to analyze Carlos Lacerda, Brazil's "first great leader of the middle class," a political gadfly who aspired to the presidency and helped to depose Vargas and Goulart.[56] Originally a member of the Communist Party, Lacerda joined the União Democrática Nacional (UDN) in the 1930s, a party that "espous[ed] classically liberal democracy, individualism, and free markets" and disdained "the blue-collar rabble perceived to be overly privileged by the patron state."[57] As the historian Bryan McCann relates, "[Lacerda] favored international investment and disparaged state control."[58] It is not an anachronism to call Lacerda a "neo-liberal" politician, since this term is used by Skidmore in 1967 in his classic account of midcentury Brazilian politics.[59]

Lacerda was also arguably a certain kind of feminist; according to McCann, "the greatest innovation of [his] middle-class populism" was "its appeal to women."[60] In Bishop's letters and in various accounts of her life in Brazil, Lacerda is a frequent visitor to Soares's household, a genial next-door neighbor. But this was also a part of his recruitment strategy, which "brought politics into the well-ordered, middle-class Brazilian home": "Lacerda was the first major politician to summon housewives into the political fray. He organized *comícios em casa* (rallies at home) to reach out to these women. These were gatherings of approximately fifty to a hundred supporters in private middle-class residences. . . . Lacerda then built on the rallies by appointing women to key positions."[61] Soares herself was an aristocratic landowner and hence a more independent version of the women to whom Lacerda addressed himself, but she shared in the trend toward female autonomy and middle-class consumption. When Lacerda was elected governor of the newly formed Guanabara district (the Rio area) in 1960, Soares was rewarded with a job designing a new park. Bishop herself considered Lacerda to be a feminist, writing to Lowell in March 1961: "it is about time [Soares's] poor country made some use of her brains, and it shows how superior Carlos is that he insisted on her accepting. (He also goes to my darling female doctor in N.Y., and took some more Brazilian men to her, too, which is probably a huge step forward for the cause of feminine equality in Brazil!" (*WIA* 352–53).

Bishop here conflates the growth of a Brazilian middle class with her own globalized American status, since it is hard to see why Lacerda seeing a German American female doctor in New York (Anny Baumann) necessarily advances feminine equality in Brazil. It is important to stress that Bishop found Lacerda appealing precisely because he was pro-American in his ideology; as she wrote to the *New Yorker* in 1953: "He is one of the anti-Vargas editors, and one of the few who has dared to be sensibly and courageously pro-American in his policies all along. He may even get to be the president-after-next if he isn't shot first (he's always being shot at, called a 'Yankee lover,' etc.)."[62] Where neoliberalism is concerned, Lacerda's opposition to restrictions on foreign investment suited Bishop's own transnational strategies. "You can live like a princess [in Italy] on your trust fund," Lowell wrote to Bishop in 1952 (*WIA* 132), but she had far more ambitious plans, telling him in December 1957: "Our [her and Soares's] financier friend, Oscar, is here. . . . We sat up till two like a group of wicked old capitalists, conniving. At one point I mentioned you, and immediately Oscar was off again, scribbling away and figuring the fantastic interest on $30,000 in 2 1/2 years. I went to bed seeing us all millionaires" (*OA* 347). I do not think it would be accurate to see Bishop merely performing a voice for Lowell here; in fact, managing her money in a developing country seems to have led Bishop to develop an economic perspective that was more sophisticated than Lowell's was, although it is important to emphasize that this perspective can be classified as neoliberal. As Skidmore describes the Brazilian situation: "The neo-liberal formula was based on the assumption that the price mechanism should be respected as the principal determinant in the economy. . . . Government budgets should be balanced. . . . Foreign capital should be welcomed and encouraged as an indispensable help to a capital-poor country. . . . The leading spokesman for this formula was the well-known economist Eugenio Gudin."[63] Bishop closes her original draft of *Brazil* with a lengthy quotation from "Eugenio Gudin, Brazil's most highly respected economist," and herself goes on to emphasize the control of inflation, the evil of "wild government waste," and the necessity for "educated nuclei" who will help "industrial and material progress . . . [to] take place at a tremendous rate" (*Pr* 249–50). Bishop's endorsement of Lacerda and Gudin is entirely in keeping with her globalized autonomy as an American expatriate, which includes her proto-third-wave feminism.

The relationship between Bishop and Lacerda is every bit as interesting as that between Bishop and Soares, and involves political intrigue at the highest level of Brazilian government. In August 1954, an associate of Vargas tried to assassinate Lacerda, who had been a blistering critic of the Vargas government, wounding Lacerda and killing his bodyguard. The ensuing controversy led to the military calling upon Vargas to resign; instead, he wrote a famous suicide note, and shot himself. Bishop's poetic response to this event, "Suicide of a Moderate Dictator," can be said to discredit Vargas, whom it associates with misinformation and bureaucratic red tape, and extol a social stability associated with the poem's dedicatee, Lacerda: "This is a day that's beautiful as well, / and warm and clear. . . . / At eight two little boys were flying kites" (*PPL* 236). It is important not to lionize Vargas or see him as a victim of imperialism (as one might see his contemporary in Central America, Jacobo Arbenz of Guatemala); ultimately Vargas's goal was more to control workers and the poor than to emancipate them. Nevertheless, Bishop's poem goes against popular feeling regarding these sensational events, which created "a state of shock unparalleled in [Brazil's] history": as Robert M. Levine puts it, although "the elite had abandoned him . . . [Vargas] remained the hero of the people."[64] Far from the calm represented in "Dictator," when Vargas was killed Brazil went into tumult; initially the recipient of sympathy due to the botched assassination attempt, Lacerda found himself go from hero to goat when Vargas committed suicide, and was forced to go into hiding.

Bishop's involvement in this political turmoil complicates the assertion that her "queer politics . . . [was] the one area in which she moved far beyond her era's liberal consensus."[65] Attacking Vargas and jockeying for his own presidential bid, Lacerda resorted to nativist, anti-Semitic, and finally homophobic invective; although Bishop objected to comparing him to Joseph McCarthy, Lacerda seems to have exploited similar fears.[66] He spurred a government investigation into *Última Hora*, a Vargas-friendly newspaper owned by a Jewish publisher, Samuel Wainer, and while Vargas's circle was indeed tainted by corruption, "Lacerda's rise to political stardom depended in no small measure on painting Wainer as a malignant, foreign, communist Jew."[67] After the attempt on Lacerda's life, Lacerda discredited Vargas by accusing the president of having a homosexual affair with his bodyguard, Gregorio Fortunato, railing on his radio broadcast: "Fortunato enjoyed an intimacy of the bedroom, of the bed, with Getúlio Vargas. . . . Gregorio Fortunato is the bedmate of Getúlio Vargas!"[68] As McCann notes, "Fortunato's appearance—tall, muscular, and Afro-Brazilian—undoubtedly lent this sensationalist allegation an extra frisson. . . . Lacerda used it as a final justification for Vargas's removal from office by any means necessary."[69] We are thus left with the irony that someone who was a potential target of the Lavender Scare in Washington, DC (while she was Consultant in Poetry at the Library of Congress) celebrated a politician who engineered a Lavender Scare in Rio. One might of course argue that Bishop was unlikely to have been parsing Portuguese-language radio broadcasts, yet Lacerda's charismatic persona spread far and wide in this time period, and he was after all her next-door neighbor. Bishop was eager to promote him to US audiences in 1955, writing various friends as well as the *New Yorker*, precisely because he was directly responsible for Vargas's death: to Lowell, she wrote, "A friend and neighbor of mine, Carlos Lacerda . . . [was] the young man who was really responsible for the fall and suicide of president Vargas"; to Marianne Moore, "[Lacerda] knows who you are and would very much like to meet you. . . . He's a newspaper editor, a Representative, a very brilliant young man and certainly the most interesting Brazilian I've met" (*OA* 311; a significant statement, if we include Soares in the category of Brazilians). These letters are not a criticism of liberal consensus but rather bear a direct relationship to American globalization, emphasizing individual autonomy coupled with a belief that their author has a special role to play in guiding the world. If we insist that Bishop's social writing in Brazil was radical in its public awareness, then we seem to be articulating queer politics in a straightforwardly American exceptionalist idiom.

Here I would like to stress the appeal that Lacerda's maverick style held for Bishop's own expatriate persona. She feared violence due to her association with him, though there is more than a touch of pride in an August 1954 letter:

> Carlos Lacerda, of whom you have probably read now, just happens to be one of my best friends and a neighbor here. The friend I am staying with is also involved politically, so there has been little time to think of 'work,'

as I'm sure you can imagine. I am in my studio in the country now, and incredible as it seems to me, with a .22 at my side. (*OA* 299)

It is surely no accident that Bishop composed her poem about crossdressing and gender stereotypes, "Exchanging Hats," in this time period, nor that, over the past three decades, we have come to see her as a more transgressive poet than contemporaries such as Lowell: associating herself with violent regime change in a developing country, openly engaging in a lesbian love affair with a Brazilian aristocrat, wearing men's clothing and driving about the countryside in a luxury sportscar, and working independently in her rustic studio with a shotgun ready at hand, Bishop was as gender troublesome as it was possible to be. And yet her politics were significantly to the right of a mainstream liberal publication like the *New York Times*.

Is it possible to be a right-wing queer? This designation for Bishop does not discredit the sophisticated critiques that she makes of government policies, as for example in her major political work of the late 1950s, "A New Capital, Aldous Huxley, and Some Indians." Although Bishop is commonly read alongside Claude Levi-Strauss (whose *Tristes Tropiques* she was reading at the time), her essay seems prescient in anticipating postmodern anthropological criticism, in particular James C. Scott's landmark work *Seeing Like a State* (1998).[70] Scott notes that the combination of utopian aspirations for a "totally transformed future" (95), and a population labeled as "technically backward, unschooled, [and] subsistence-oriented" (96), often leads to alienating urban spaces and, at worst, outright tyranny. In particular, Scott criticizes a technocratic "authoritarian high modernism" that he ascribes to the architect Le Corbusier, whose protégés designed Brasília, "about the closest thing we have to a high modernist city," the new capital that replaced Rio de Janeiro in 1960 (118). Forty years earlier, Bishop made a similar critique, highlighting the desire to transcend the actually existing Brazil by starting anew: "The site of Brasília is an empty, barren, slightly rolling plateau. . . . I was not prepared for quite such dreariness and desolation" (*Pr* 295). The difficulty of orienting oneself in Brasília becomes a running joke—"the driver got lost and we ended up back at the Palace of the Dawn again" (319)—a point made in the essay's form, which traverses various interiors and landmarks in a disorienting manner. Most importantly, Bishop observes that despite the architect Oscar Niemeyer's communist convictions, Brasília will exacerbate social inequality instead of solve it. For example, she chastises him for putting servants in a "sunken wing" of the president's residence, noting that "In the old days, slaves were often kept in the dank basements of Rio houses." In Bishop's view, Niemeyer's response to potential social problems has been to "put them underneath, or underground, like a lazy housewife shoving household gear out of sight underneath a deceptively well-made bed" (304).

As the comparison of Niemeyer to a "lazy housewife" indicates, the essay criticizes conventional gender and sexual identities as they relate to race and nation. There is an overlap of the essay "A New Capital" with Bishop's earlier poem of Washington, DC, "View of the Capitol from the Library of Congress," which, as Axelrod argues, functions as "queer political assertion."[71] As in the poem, "A New Capital" deflates "masculinist official discourse" and its figures[72]: "As we left, a group of small soldiers, members of the Brasília Guarda Especial, marched solemnly past changing guard, pounding with their heavy boots; in their unstarched green uniforms, they always look like wilted string beans" (Pr 305). Meanwhile, Huxley himself is equated with the high modernist project, since the future author of the utopic Island (1962) takes on a propagandistic role for the government's ideal city. Huxley's role is undermined when the party visits the indigenous people, where he comes across as very straight, very white, and a figure of fun: "[Huxley] is a very handsome, aristocratic-looking man, but the Indian's final opinion, given in a tactfully lowered voice, was, 'Homely . . . homely . . .'" And under the circumstances Huxley did appear, not homely, but exceedingly long, white, refined, and misplaced" (Pr 315). For her part, Bishop lacks a modernist preoccupation with supposedly vanishing tribal cultures, since her Indians are camera-ready and culturally resilient: "these Indians knew all about cameras and were happy to pose, in rows" (Pr 314) Bishop remarks, as conventional Indianness becomes something to be performed: "when asked to pose for a photograph he politely removed his clothes" (Pr 315). Bishop comes off as postmodern insofar as she demotically aligns herself with the Indians and self-reflexively foregrounds her physical presence as narrator, as in the following exchange: "The man who so admired my earrings . . . pointed to his chest and said he was a widower, then talked away in Nu-aruak to the brighter friend, who started to laugh. He had asked if I would stay behind and be his wife. This produced a great deal of tribal merriment" (318). This cultural syncretism and potential racial miscegenation is in keeping with the sexual desire that Bishop has already expressed: "Their rounded behinds and childishly smooth legs, in both sexes, are remarkably pretty," she remarks (317), anticipating her later description of Friday in "Crusoe in England" as "Pretty to watch; he had a pretty body" (*PPL* 155). The Indians' village thus arguably becomes what Axelrod, drawing on Foucault, calls a "heterotopic site," open to "sexual license, gender confusion, [and] racial multiplicity."[73]

However, we should not assume that a critique of government in an American context will necessarily have the same ideological valence in the context of a developing country. One reason that Axelrod's reading of "View of the Capitol" is so convincing is that in McCarthy-era Washington, DC, Bishop's gender was marginalized and her sexuality was criminalized. Enabled by the privileges of American globalization, Bishop's sexual identity disengages from the progressive causes that we might want to link to it. It is only fair to note that Kubitschek's project united Brazilians from various ends of the political spectrum, and that he celebrated the "anonymous titan, who is the *candango* [manual laborer], the obscure and formidable hero of the construction of Brasília" (qtd. in Scott, 129); Kubitschek ended up honoring the workers' demands for their own land and access to urban services. Meanwhile, where Bishop's affinity for the Indians is concerned, the title "A New Capital, Aldous Huxley, and Some Indians" does not give them much political agency. Her paean to Portuguese colonialism is straightforwardly paternalistic, or (with Soares's landownership in mind) maternalistic: "The Indians seem to inspire a deep affection in almost anyone who has to work with them . . . it may be partly due to the childlike charm of the Indians themselves and partly almost to the old Portuguese colonizing gift; they were (and are) almost completely without racial or color prejudices and treated whatever strange races they ran across with the same amused, affectionate familiarity that they had for each other" (*Pr* 319–20). Brazil declared its independence from Portugal in 1822, and we might ask what Bishop's contemporary social alternative to Brasília was. Her desired model is a developmentalist one based upon the example of the frontier in the United States: "The founding of small towns and villages in the interior, and help with their industries and agriculture—especially by means of railroads . . . [this] is what would really open up the interior, and not a new capital" (293–94).

With Green's critique in mind, Bishop's essay ultimately orients itself not toward the causes of the labor that built Brasília, or the rights of natives encroached upon by such modernization projects, but toward the lucrative North American literary market. In keeping with the argument that Bishop rewrote Morley's frontier figure as a globalized professional writer, we should note that the Indian's "tactfully lowered" comment about Huxley, which Bishop is privileged to hear, will then be relayed to the *New Yorker's* national audience. Axelrod argues that in her poem "View of the Capitol," Bishop identifies the Library of Congress "as a home territory of intellectual and artistic freedom . . . a renegade cultural site more likely to be associated with nonconformist than with nationalist, capitalist, and heteronormative values."[74] In effect, the essay "A New Capital" ends with a figure emerging from the library—Anthony Trollope, whose negative comments about Washington, DC, are quoted by Bishop so as to apply to Brasília: "For myself, I do not believe in cities made after this fashion. Commerce, I think, must elect the site of all large congregations of mankind. In some mysterious way she ascertains what she wants, and having acquired that, draws men in thousands around her properties" (qtd., *Pr* 321). Although Bishop grants that Washington, DC, ultimately worked out and that Brasília may succeed also, the quotation from Trollope gets to the core of her critique of Brasília, which she emphasizes in her draft for *Brazil*: it is an ostensibly "sensational and never-to-be-forgotten public work" that will only create "economic crisis" and a "spiral of inflation" (*Pr* 200–201). There is truth to this accusation, but it is important to note with whom Bishop's sympathy ultimately lies: the "national disgrace" of inflation, she emphasizes in her 1965 *New York Times Magazine* article, "produces an atmosphere unlike any other. . . . It is the very small middle class that feels the pinch the most" (*Pr* 350).

This orientation toward middle-class empowerment gives Bishop unlikely ideological bedfellows, since her critique is in line with the contemporaneous bestseller *The Ugly American*. As we saw in the first chapter, the novel criticizes ethnocentric foreign-service bureaucrats who advocate large-scale public works projects such as dams, and valorizes instead egalitarian middle-class travelers who learn foreign languages and develop small businesses that will fight communism at the grass-roots level. Although the novel is a libertarian frontier fantasy, Bishop is exactly the kind of traveler Lederer and Burdick wanted her to be: an intense student of Portuguese and appreciator of Brazilian music and food, a critic of big-government boondoggles, and stridently pro-capitalist and virulently anticommunist. To be sure, "A New Capital" went unpublished after the *New Yorker* rejected it, while John F. Kennedy distributed copies of *The Ugly American* in the US Senate in an effort to raise awareness of the global communist threat. Nevertheless, Bishop herself was galvanized by Kennedy's election as US president in 1960. This led to her publication of explicitly political writing and a direct engagement with Kennedy's "Janus-faced policy for the Western Hemisphere," as John DeWitt terms it: "A grandiose plan to promote economic development and democracy was announced with great enthusiasm. Hidden from public view was the counterinsurgency program designed to prevent at all costs the expansion of communist influence in Latin America."[75]

The Alliance for Progress, the Reforms of João Goulart, and Bishop's *Brazil*

Saunders has meticulously analyzed the CIA's funding of American intellectuals in *The Cultural Cold War*. Yet while Lowell's brief trip to Latin America—during which he extolled Hitler in a speech in Buenos Aires and "stripped naked and mounted an equestrian statue in one of the city's main squares" before being subdued with a straitjacket and Thorazine—comes in for a great deal of criticism, Bishop escapes such scrutiny, despite her being in Brazil for fifteen years.[76] I suggest that Bishop didn't publish more overtly political material because her political outlook didn't suit the temper of the times; she even claimed that her jaded "From Trollope's Journal," which can be read as a criticism of the staid Eisenhower establishment, was held for publication until after the 1960 elections (*M*, 313–14). At this point Bishop sought out the White House and various well-connected literary figures, instead of the other way round.

In the 1950s, Bishop's attitude toward Brazil had paralleled that of Washington, DC's leaders. According to Millier, Brazilian culture attracted Bishop "not for its political progressiveness, but for its population of relatively primitive, uneducated people . . . she was convinced that the Brazilian lower classes were uneducable" (242, 272). As Michael Latham relates, Washington strategists "looked on the peoples of the region as emotional, irrational, and unworthy of serious U.S. consideration"; George F. Kennan, a major architect of Cold War policy, thought "Latin Americans [were] . . . beyond redemption."[77] All of this changed when Fidel Castro took power in Cuba, which made Latin America "a major arena of ideological struggle in the Cold War," stimulating Kennedy to announce the Alliance for Progress, which enlisted economic aid in the struggle against Communism. In the summer of 1961, *Life* magazine gave extended coverage to Kennedy's initiative, arguing that the Alliance represented "a depth of mutual commitment between Latin America and the

United States that even Che Guevara, Cuba's romantic revolutionary hero, could not unsettle. . . . Irrational Communists had little chance of standing in the way of U.S. achievements."[78]

Bishop's June 15, 1961, letter to Lowell functions as a kind of policy document for her new role as a public poet; as she remarks, "I told Lota I wanted to be a 'poet engagée' and she said I wanted to be engagée to Kennedy's insolent chariot" (*WIA* 362). Although this is a humorous exchange with her partner Soares, Bishop is quite serious about putting her knowledge of Brazil directly in the service of Kennedy's new Embassy personnel. "I've been thinking I'd like to do something for our new regime here, something like give advice! I realize I have picked up a vast amount of information in almost ten years here. . . . I had this idea before but I have been sternly ignored by the Embassy here and the 'cultural attaches' have been so low-class there didn't seem to be much use in trying." In the same letter to Lowell, she gives an account of a dinner party that is worth quoting at length for its combination of anticommunism and Yellow Peril rhetoric:

> Unfortunately someone had had the idea of bringing along a Chinese Trade Commission that had just arrived from a stay in Cuba—8 or 10 small-sized, slovenly-looking, youthful, long-haired Chinese who wouldn't touch alcohol and pinned people down, in French or bad English. (Mao-Mao—pronounced like Mow—means "bad-bad" in Portuguese and is a common expression. After they all refused Scotch and wine, again, looking grimmer & grimmer, Roberto [Marx, the famous architect] said "Mao-Mao-Tse-Tung.") I tried talking to one whose English was very limited and when he told me "Castro-strong-strong" shaking his fist, and "Batista bad-bad" (as if I wouldn't have heard of him, probably) for the first time, I think, a really cold shudder of fear and horror of Communism went down my spine. They were dreary, ignorant-looking little men, their eyes burning with righteous passion—and there we were all being very gay, admiring plants and Roberto's collection of Brazilian antiques, etc., and stuffing ourselves—and about to reap what we sowed. (*WIA* 362)

Bishop then goes on to speculate how she might ally herself with New Frontiersmen such as Kennedy's new Ambassador to Brazil, Lincoln Gordon: "I don't know about the new Ambassador here, Gordon, an economist from Harvard. I could call on him, but it would all be much easier if I had some kind of recommendation from Washington—if I could get it. I'll write [Archibald] MacLeish, anyway" (*WIA* 362–63).

Bishop's plan is not insincere. As I emphasized at the beginning of this chapter, she had previously shown a public-spiritedness in her support of various New Deal initiatives. One of the advantages of moving from a paradigm of Bishop-as-reticent to Bishop-as-empowered is to be able to see that her role of "poet engagée" was in keeping with a longstanding commitment to public service, one that in some ways paralleled MacLeish's.[79] Nevertheless, Bishop's concept of public service took a decidedly rightward turn in this era, which might make us qualify the political claims we make for her correspondence. Recently Siobhan Phillips has argued that Bishop's letters from Brazil constitute an "epistolary citizenship" that "contrast[s] the inaccuracies of newspaper reportage with the truth of personal witness," which "contains a progressive potential even if her reaction to specific policies did not."[80] However, in terms of both specific policies and "hegemonic discourse," Bishop's epistolary citizenship supports US-friendly politicians and Cold War initiatives.[81] Although Hicok claims that Bishop objected to Lacerda's "cynical and murderous tactics" when he was governor of Guanabara (Rio), Bishop went back to supporting him during the upheavals of the mid-1960s[82]: "Riots in the Senate about Carlos. . . . Goulart would do almost anything to get rid of him, but at the same time doesn't want to make a martyr of him, of course, because then he'd be apt to get elected President. That clipping you sent from the N.Y. *Times* was so wrong. How can they get things so wrong, I wonder. I'd like to know what Gordon really thinks. I'd like to call up Kennedy!" (*WIA* 507). Indeed, in Bishop's account, Kennedy displaces Goulart as a political leader and, in a sense, a father figure for the Brazilian people. I find the following passage from a letter striking, insofar as it endorses the idea of assassinating the president of a developing country[83]: "President Kennedy's death really overwhelmed Brazil. It was very moving. . . . Even now the taxi drivers, storekeepers, etc., when they spot my American accent, make me little speeches—and always conclude with 'If only it had been *our* John instead of yours.' (Joao Goulart, the President.)" (*OA* 423). It is important to emphasize that the statements in Bishop's letters portended actual violence. Skidmore notes that after the military deposed Goulart, "Rio had two centers of torture," one associated with "anticommunist Governor Carlos Lacerda's state government, [which] had been primed to go after the left. Lacerda's police were delighted to round up union, church, and student organizers."[84] Meanwhile, Goulart may have been assassinated in 1976 as part of the CIA-backed Operation Condor, a coordinated program of South American governments to eliminate leftists and dissidents.[85]

This is not to make Goulart a savior figure; Bishop seems correct that some of his actions were opportunistic, and there is evidence that he imagined taking dictatorial power in a coup from above modeled on Vargas's 1937 maneuver.[86] Nevertheless, many people who wanted to change Brazil's status quo supported Goulart—including, in effect, characters from Bishop's own poetry. On August 26, 1963, Bishop writes that

> Friday night was the fatal anniversary of Vargas's suicide. President Goulart staged a monster mass meeting.... However, it was a great flop, to the relief of most people. Goulart is a coward and Brazilians do have a small sense of 'fair play' and a big sense of the ridiculous.... We watched intermittently on TV because rumors of revolution were rife, of course. The best moment was when a farmer handed the President up a monster *mandioca* root—about 25 lbs., a huge phallic symbol. This was so Brazilian—giant vegetables are revered. I have a 'pumpkin big as the baby,' you may remember, in a poem. Just another proof of primitivism. (*OA* 417)

Bishop refers to "Manuelzinho," in which the "world's worst gardener since Cain" brings the landowner-speaker "a mystic three-legged carrot, / or a pumpkin 'bigger than the baby'" (*PPL* 77). Here we can turn to Rich's reading of this poem, which observes that Manuelzinho—"exasperating, picturesque"— has "qualities traditionally attributed to the colonized" by the "liberal landowner."[87] Not only is it questionable whether "Manuelzinho" opens up a critique of the landowner's perspective, but one could turn Rich's own perspective on Bishop inside-out. Her argument for the "the essential outsiderhood of a lesbian identity" and "other kinds of outsiders" has helped to foster what we might call Bishop's academic hypercanonization.[88] Yet the new editions of Bishop's work not only reveal that her globalized American feminism ran counter to leftist Brazilian politicians and the initiatives of workers and peasants, but also reveal fissures within potential queer alliances.

On this point, Caetano Veloso's autobiography is perhaps more valuable for providing a Brazilian perspective on Bishop than Carmen Oliveira's *Rare and Commonplace Flowers* (1995), which focuses on the bureaucratic infighting related to Soares's construction of Rio's Flamengo Park. There is a certain

overlap between Veloso and Bishop: Veloso was an artist (a musician who participated in the countercultural *Tropicália* movement), an admirer and friend
of Clarice Lispector, and a sexually transgressive figure who claims he would
"make a great queer" because "those suggestions of androgyny, polymorphism,
and indeterminacy that colored the . . . pop music scene still threaten the
conventions that underlie many acts of oppression."[89] Most importantly, he
was a participant in the cultural and political events that Bishop narrated,
insisting that in the early 1960s, "the Left consisted of every Brazilian who
deserved to be one, and all human beings worthy of the name" (6): "with the
students behind President João Goulart . . . we were moved to write political
plays and songs. The country seemed to be on the verge of implementing reforms that would transform its profoundly unjust face and allow Brazil to rise
above American imperialism" (37). According to Veloso, the military coup was
"planned by Lacerda" (197), who "had become a relentless opponent of nationalism and 'pro-labor' policies. . . he was the Left's number one enemy" (196).
The irony here is that the social forces that supported Goulart were once the
social forces with which Bishop had made a provisional alliance in Key West.
In Brazil, Bishop saw this reformist, anti-imperialist drive as a kind of political adolescence that the US had already passed through; as she remarked of a
student whom she and Soares mentored: "He brings me all the student magazines—from the *other* university—the communist one—ghastly dead stuff
about Sacco & Vanzetti, Esso-congresso—etc.—etc. They seem to be trying to
go through the early thirties all over again" (*WIA* 462). It is thus understandable that Veloso, a student himself in the early 1960s, would emphatically deny
that an American expatriate would have the right to speak for the country,
noting his amazement that "someone—a woman poet at that!—might thus
sum up the military coup that sent to jail some of my finest schoolmates and
professors: 'A few brave generals and the governors of three important states
got together and, after a difficult forty-eight hours, it was all over. The (favorable) reactions have been really popular, thank God.' Apparently there was
such a thing as right-wing good intentions" (6). While the rightward shift
of Bishop's good intentions might have been partially due to the long-term
influence of her partner's views, I have argued that a desire for autonomy and
control, economic self-interest, and a kind of frontier individualism were also
major factors, which comes across in the overlap of her thought with American modernization theory.

In terms of sales, the *Brazil* edition of the *Life* World Library series put Bishop more in league with James A. Michener than with Robert Lowell, since the book reached millions of households across the USA. *Brazil* has been a thorn in the side of Bishop critics, who emphasize that her artistic vision was corrupted and even, in the case of Angus Cleghorn, that her political critique was erased: "It is clear that the American Life editors found Miss Bishop to be too blunt and bitter in her social diagnoses. Is she too harsh in her imperial social critique?"[90] But is Bishop criticizing American imperialism, or making an American imperialist critique of Brazil? Cleghorn's defense of Bishop is based on a tourist/traveler opposition, which emphasizes the cultured good taste of the traveler: while *Life*'s "tourist initiative presents Brazil as a golden country with an exotic past and a prosperous modern future," Bishop's "geo-poetics of mapmaking . . . stresses long, slow, deep time occurring through historical events."[91] Following Edward Said, many scholars who relate travel writing to imperialism have questioned this tourist/traveler opposition. It is striking that Cleghorn objects to the following excision (all of the following quotations are from Bishop's original draft):

> Both the U.S. and Brazil remained rather cautiously imitative for two hundred years or more, and both have suffered from (let us face it) inferiority-feelings at different periods in our histories. But we laugh at the same jokes, enjoy the same movies, and have almost the same legends of the "frontier," Indian chiefs, gold-rushes, pioneers, hunters, and savage beasts. Americans and Brazilians are equally quick to sympathy, on the side of the under-dog, hospitable, and kind; both have a sense of national destiny, of great things ahead, and the word "democracy" can still move us deeply. (*Pr* 247)

The passage puts Bishop squarely in line with the American Exceptionalism underlying the Alliance for Progress's reworking of the theme of Manifest Destiny. As William Appleman Williams and later critics such as Latham note, postwar modernization theorists took the American frontier as a universal model of development, thereby disregarding class conflict and racial exploitation: "Like the older ideologies of imperialism and Manifest Destiny, modernization on the 'New Frontier' defined the virtue of a benevolent United States in terms of its ability to assist peoples trapped in lower positions on a hierarchical, cultural, and developmental scale."[92] In Bishop's *Brazil* as in Rostow's contemporaneous *The Stages of Economic Growth*, peoples can be arranged quite precisely along a continuum of developmental stages, from "20th-century men with 20th-century problems" to "the really timeless, prehistoric world of the Indians" (*Pr* 168). Like Rostow, Bishop wants Brazil to advance toward capitalist modernity ("transport is one of the basic problems which Brazil must solve before it can begin real exploitation of its truly magnificent resources" [209]) and contain subversive influences ("the northeast ... is indeed a highly explosive area, ripe for Communist infiltration" [207]).

I do not share the view that modernization narratives are necessarily bad things, but Bishop, in other contexts exhilarated by "a constant sense of readjustment" (*PPL* 8), does not seem ready to look at development from alternate points of view. To be sure, she briefly dwells on the perils of modernity in a passage that can be likened to various 1950s critiques: "human-man, poor as he may be, is still more important than producing-man or consuming-man or political-man" (*Pr* 250). Nevertheless, "Brazil is going to push and be pushed into industrialization" (250), and Bishop is concerned to discredit any critics of American influence: "The anti-American nationalist is almost always one of two types.... His business has been granted privileges and strong government protection. Naturally he is afraid of foreign competition, particularly American large-scale competition and particularly if his own product is inferior or producing unfairly big profits. The other type of anti-American nationalist is, as is usual everywhere, the man who feels he must blame all his troubles on others: Jews, Negroes, or another nation. In political office such men can stir up anti-American feeling among the poor and ignorant" (248–49). Bishop's draft is prescient in forecasting the military coup, since she notes that army officers are "afraid of Goulart's leftist politics" and that Goulart is "suspected by the military heads of being red" (246).

Bishop's endorsement of the dictatorship (which began in 1964, took a more repressive turn in 1968, and finally ended in 1985) is not an aberration, nor does it reflect naivete; rather, it is perfectly in keeping with views she had expressed for over a decade. Her letters were emphatic: "the military in Brazil have never in all its history tried to seize power *or keep it*—and Castelo Branco was reluctant to be President.... The suspension of rights, dismissing lots of Congress, etc.—had to be done, sinister as it may sound. Otherwise it would have been just a 'deposition' and not a 'revolution'—and many of Goulart's men would still be there in Congress" (*WIA* 530). Bishop also endorsed the dictatorship, and portrayed Branco as a kind of modern-day Cincinnatus, in "On the Railroad Named Delight," which appeared in the *New York Times Magazine* in May 1965. Narratives of Bishop's life in Brazil are painful to read at this point; the illiterate Manuelzinho could not read or respond to Bishop's representations of Brazil, but urban, literate Brazilians could. Although Oliveira's book is a problematic mixture of fiction and nonfiction, it does make it clear that Bishop's critics objected not only to the cultural and racial attitudes expressed in "Delight," but also to her endorsement of US influence: "Pieces like this only served to strengthen the conviction in the average U.S. reader that outside of his own country there flourished an immense desert of underdevelopment, waiting for the paternalistic assistance of the United States government. . . . Bishop didn't need to amplify the misinformation of her countrymen, who ignored the fact that the Alliance for Progress wasn't a philanthropic expedition but a financial investment."[93]

Bishop's letters and essays, the original draft of *Brazil*, and various poems in *Questions of Travel* (1965) form a straightforwardly reactionary take on Brazilian politics in the 1960s. This certainly does not mean that we should demonize her, but in my view, an attempt to recuperate an overlooked radical Bishop would also be a misguided effort. Instead, perhaps we should rearticulate literature's relationship to the nation-state. Must our treasured poets be radical? As I have argued, Bishop critics often mistake antigovernmental positions for leftist ones.[94] In so doing, they overlook an earlier time in which Bishop had a generally positive relationship to state-centered politics. This may reflect a broader problem with the transnational turn in literature and American Studies (which is probably giving way to a new era, albeit one still dimly glimpsed, as of this writing): while it has encouraged us to study an engagement with Brazil that we might not have otherwise, it has caused us to overlook the good things that a national government can do.

Are we ever liberated from making judgments about human nature? And why does it matter so much what we look like, or who we sleep with? As it stands, Bishop's marginal identity does not liberate her from criticisms that we might make of other travelers—gay as well as straight, female as well as male, queer as well as normal. Bishop's "Arrival at Santos," a Brazilian port, involved the fantasy of "a different world," where one "somehow never thought of there *being* a flag," and where a figure of state authority—a "six-feet-tall" police lieutenant, Miss Breen—can morph into a figure of transgressive sexual desire (*PPL* 71). But one can't get away from nation-states, and Bishop's

1950s and '60s writings were a response, at once anxious, assertive, and very American, to turbulent Brazilian political energies. Inescapably, her various travels and relocations—national in Key West, international in Brazil—raise the issue of what role poets and professionals can play toward government and social reform. In my view, this is the most profound question that Bishop asked regarding travel.

Chapter Five

·······································

A Native Son on the Global Frontier

Richard Wright's Antiracist
Modernization Theory

"As a major novelist, a famous expatriate writer, and the author of three travel books, Richard Wright stands as the single most important African American literary traveler," John Gruesser remarks.[1] At first it might seem unlikely to relate Wright's travel writing to the postwar discourse of the frontier. In his classic work of Black nationalist literary criticism, *Long Black Song* (1972), Houston A. Baker Jr. argues that Black American identity is constituted by its exclusion from the Turnerian paradigm:

> When the black American reads Frederick Jackson Turner's *The Frontier in American History*, he feels no regret over the end of the Western frontier. To black America, frontier is an alien word; for, in essence, all frontiers established by the white psyche have been closed to the black man.... When the American grab bag was opening—when new territories were being annexed and handed out to humble homesteaders—the black American was toiling from day clean to first dark ... [and] sold or bartered back and forth as chattel.... The black American's perspective on history, his patterns of social organization, his life style as a whole, are significantly different from those of white America.... The differences stem largely from the fact that the black man was denied his part in the frontier and his share of the nation's wealth.[2]

Various studies have complicated this model of total exclusion, making a case for Black pioneers who fought racism.[3] However, my focus is on middle-class professionalism, which is suggested by Baker's phrase "When the black American reads Frederick Jackson Turner's *The Frontier*." The tremendous success of *Native Son* and *Black Boy* empowered Wright to explore the privileges of postwar American travel, which involved a blurring of Black and white identities. Shortly after entering the "Spanish frontier" in *Pagan Spain* (1957), Wright claims: "I have no race except that which is forced upon me. I have no country except that to which I'm obliged to belong. I have no traditions. I'm free. I have only the future."[4] Although he claims that he "ha[s] no country," Wright might as well be cutting-and-pasting from Turner, who valorizes "a gate of escape from the bondage of the past . . . freshness, and confidence, and scorn of older society, impatience of its restraints and its ideas, and indifference to its lessons, have accompanied the frontier" (*FJT* 59). Even as he highlights the racism that Turner disavowed, Wright embodies the prerogatives of the American Century, demanding that we distinguish between criticizing racism while extolling Black American culture, and actually believing in the existence of races.

The first half of the chapter argues that Wright was largely a creation of the FWP, and as such, is our preeminent thinker of the artist's relationship to progressive government. Deemphasizing Wright's relationship to the Communist Party (CP), I focus on a more important element in his writing, an investment in upward mobility and socially responsible professionalism. Here I return to McGurl's observation that the FWP "established the legitimacy of [the government's] own form of institutional support for artistic production."[5] This was, in fact, the major institutional alternative to the MFA program, and Wright's ideological manifesto, "Blueprint for Negro Writing" (1937), extols a professional autonomy that was enabled by his status as an FWP director. In particular, Wright creatively reworked the American Guide Series of travel books into poems as well as stories that criticized racial inequality. Wright first became an American celebrity through attacks made upon him in congressional hearings, during which white supremacist politicians demonized federal arts programs and the New Deal as a whole. *Native Son* responds to these attacks by defending the institution that enabled its writing: in a convergence of author and protagonist, Bigger Thomas functions as a militant FWP tour guide for Chicago's Black Belt. Drawing on recent scholarship that reveals how the Solid South used government programs to maintain and further white privilege, I argue that *Native Son* envisions an antiracist New Deal, an aspect of the novel that was clarified by Arnold Rampersad's 1991 restoration of the original text.

The next section of the chapter follows *Native Son* to Argentina, where a New Deal-era document, centered on racial and class conflict, morphed into a form of American exceptionalism. Although the film is usually dismissed as a failure, it has power when reread as a criticism of the racial inequality of the GI Bill (the same program that empowered Sal Paradise in *On the Road*). The film draws attention to the government's creation of unprecedented affluence for America's white middle class while the Black middle class was comparatively underserved. Yet *Native Son* nevertheless presents the problem of the yawning gap in age between the ostensibly twenty-five-year-old Bigger and the forty-one-year-old Wright, who played his own famous character and whose stardom was the film's main selling point. Wright's unlikely embodiment as Bigger highlights the author's privilege as a relatively wealthy traveler. He developed an antagonistic relationship with the leftist presidency of Juan Perón, which reveals that what Paul Gilroy called the Black Atlantic can become enmeshed with imperial structures. The film of *Native Son* signals a transition in Wright's politics, from leftism to what we might call the Black Vital Center.

The chapter then follows Wright and *Native Son* to the decolonizing Gold Coast (now Ghana). Criticized by African intellectuals, Wright's travel book *Black Power* (1954) was also defended by the Pan-Africanists Dorothy and George Padmore, while recent scholars, inspired by Gilroy, have read it in terms of an empowering Black cosmopolitanism. Instead of a new departure in Wright's oeuvre, *Black Power* can be read as an extension of his earlier role as a writer of travel guides for the federal government. Wright struggles to balance his 1930s social concerns with the freedom of the postwar frontier, as he draws on his own work for a model of African decolonization. In effect, he tries to export a Black New Deal to Africa, and *Native Son*, serving as an ideological template for *Black Power*, itself becomes an African American exceptionalist text. This explains what is both compelling and troubling about Wright's rhetoric, as he develops an antiracist modernization theory that contests neocolonialism while accepting modernization theory's premises. While it would be too strong to call Wright a Black Ugly American, his final betrayal of the Pan-Africanist leader Kwame Nkrumah to the State Department indicates that his project is enabled by global American power.

The chapter concludes with *Pagan Spain,* which has not drawn much attention from Black Studies or postcolonial criticism. Wright's final travel book can be likened to treatises discussed in earlier chapters such as *The Lonely Crowd*, since he speculates about how the individualism celebrated by the Frontier Thesis might be modified for the postwar era. Especially relevant is the work of Walter Prescott Webb, who framed the American frontier in global terms: "always, for some three centuries, to the west of the settlements there stretched an empty country inviting entrance, luring the venturesome toward the sunset. . . . [But] the American process was but an example . . . of a parallel but more complex development that was going on wherever European people were appropriating land in the New Worlds."[6] Following Turner's emphasis on the closing of the frontier, Webb argues that the world's empty lands are now fully peopled, and the era of individualism has passed. *Pagan Spain*, too, identifies the American frontier as part of a larger global development, albeit one that involves racial terror and exploitation, since Wright was well aware that neither the Old West nor the "New Worlds" had been empty countries. Instead of rejecting the Frontier Thesis, Wright reinvigorates it precisely as a Black American intellectual, one who is more creative and autonomous than any white traveler. Yet even as *Pagan Spain* celebrates Wright's unfettered autonomy, the book also indicates the suppression of progressive social alternatives abroad as well as the legacy of the New Deal at home.

Wright as Upwardly Mobile Professional

The decisive factor in Richard Wright's early career was an upbringing in a family that valued education and achievement, and the way this ethic meshed with government support of the arts. Highlighting his undeniably brave resistance of Jim Crow segregation and his impressive autodidacticism, we risk endorsing a myth of total individual autonomy. In the second volume of his autobiography, *American Hunger*, Wright argues that the Communist Party betrayed America's core ideals: "The spirit of the Protestant ethic which one suckled, figuratively, with one's mother's milk, that self-generating energy that made a man feel, whether he realized it or not, that he had to work and redeem himself through his own acts, all this was forbidden, taboo. And yet this was the essence of that cultural heritage which the Communist party had sworn to carry forward."[7] The admixture of a model of total dependence ("mother's milk") with one of total independence ("self-generating energy") is striking. As Wright's major biographer and archivist, Michel Fabre, remarks, "All through his life Wright remained an American (brought up in spite of himself on Horatio Alger and the Bible)."[8] While Wright objected to Alger's emphasis on economic success, he did endorse a model of rationalist Protestant individualism, a middle-class ethos imbibed in childhood.

Wright's frequent allusions to Max Weber's *The Protestant Ethic and the Spirit of Capitalism* (1904) are not accidental. He spent much of his childhood with his maternal grandmother, a strict Seventh-Day Adventist, and in an early draft of *Black Boy*, he boasted that he had taken his religion "neat."[9] As Fabre stresses, Wright was enabled by a Black puritanism that emphasized achievement and discipline. "If Richard did not become the delinquent that poverty and racial discrimination could easily have made of him, it was largely due to the influence of his maternal grandmother, although he did not fail to revolt against her in due course. He also learned from his mother, uncles and aunts to value learning."[10] In the recently published essay about Margaret Wilson, "Memories of My Grandmother" (ca. 1941–42), Wright acknowledges that "my grandmother would pray that I acquire knowledge to get on in the world ... and she took great pride in all good reports she heard of my progress in school."[11] At this time Wright lived among cultivated middle-class Black families. In a minor but telling detail in his essay "The World and the Jug," Ralph Ellison notes that "the boys who helped Wright leave Jackson [Mississippi] were the sons of a Negro college president."[12]

To be sure, Wright's youth was scarred by periods of poverty, including a growth-stunting diet that initially prevented his employment in the post office when he moved to Chicago in 1931. Yet his stellar performance on the written exam testifies to an investment in meritocratic upward mobility. Instead of insisting on Wright's proletarian identity, we might question the raced nature of terms such as "white collar." Despite Wright's claim in *Black Boy* that he "had no hope whatever of being a professional man," his manifesto "Blueprint for Negro Writing" (1937) represents his role as a writer in terms of socially responsible professionalism.[13] "Negro writers should seek through the medium of their craft to play as meaningful a role in the affairs of men as do other professionals," he states. "But if their writing is demanded to perform the social office of other professions, then the autonomy of craft is lost and writing detrimentally fused with other interests."[14] According to Wright, the writer's "subject matter," the Black social world, has become "far more meaningful and complex" than the world dealt with by "the so-called Harlem school of expression," which means that "the Negro writer ... requires a greater discipline and consciousness" than ever before (47). Hence, "[w]riting has its professional autonomy" (48).

In keeping with Wright's focus on professional autonomy, I would like to read "Blueprint" as a self-reflexive meditation on the writer's institutional status. As Evan Kindley points out in *Poet-Critics and the Administration of Culture* (2017), the masterpieces of interwar poetry are unimaginable without their "manifestos, personal statements, ... and justifications."[15] In this perspective, *The New Negro* (1925), the master document of the Harlem Renaissance, might be read as making a case for largesse from patrons insofar as it showcases an array of young Black poets, accompanied by Alain Locke's framing essay "Negro Youth Speaks." When the patronage system collapsed along with the rest of the economy in 1929, "poet-critics" used their expertise to make a case for funding and employment in an era of bureaucratic institutions. Although the university eventually became the institutional home of poet-critics, this was only one of several possible outcomes.

Before he was known as a novelist, Wright was a promising young poet, and in the mid-1930s he explored alternatives that went outside the modernists' foundations and universities. His early poetry was inspired by the Communist Party-sponsored John Reed Clubs, and has an appropriately militant tone for someone who worked relief jobs as a ditch digger, street sweeper, and hospital orderly. As he writes in "Child of the Dead and Forgotten Gods," which was published in the proletarian journal *The Anvil* in 1934:

> O you innocent liberal!
> O you naïve darling! . . .
> Do tell us of the enchanted oil you would spread upon the
>   bitter and irreconcilable waters of the class struggle![16]

But there is an irony in Wright's revolutionary rhetoric, since these militant poems functioned as a portfolio testifying to his professional expertise. The moment the Illinois-based office of the FWP was formed, Wright approached his relief caseworker, Mary Wirth, with his dossier of poems. As biographer Hazel Rowley relates, "Mrs. Wirth immediately signed him on as a supervisor. . . . In terms of integrated work, he had probably scored the most prestigious job for a black man in the whole of Chicago."[17] Skilled writers earned $93.50 per month; the supervisor position paid $125 and enabled Wright to move his family to a roomier apartment at 3743 Indiana Avenue (close to Bigger Thomas's address at 3721 Indiana Avenue, a parallel that I shall explore below).

Wright's position as FWP supervisor is fundamental for the tone of self-confidence in "Blueprint for Negro Writing." "Blueprint" is famous for castigating the Harlem Renaissance, "that foul soil which was the result of a liaison between inferiority-complexed Negro 'geniuses' and burnt-out white Bohemians with money" (37). Yet Wright's essay appeared in *New Challenge*, a little magazine financed by a Black bohemian with money, Dorothy West, who precisely sought to continue the Renaissance. West pulled the plug after one issue, but this was hardly devastating for Wright, since the John Reed Clubs, as well as the magazine he edited, *Left Front*, had been canceled in 1935; more-over, membership in the Communist Party had never paid the bills in the first place. In the late 1930s, West herself began working for the FWP. To quote from Langston Hughes's classic account of the Harlem Renaissance in *The Big Sea* (1940), the 1929 crash eventually sent West as well as Wright "rolling down the hill toward the Works Progress Administration."[18]

A number of scholars have commented on Wright's FWP background, and his writings for the Illinois project have been published in their entirety.[19] Yet we have not fully related his employment by the state to his creative writ-ing. If government policies helped to inspire Bishop's poems "Florida" and "The Fish," the influence on Wright was still greater, since he was an FWP employee for over three solid years. Wright's essays for the Illinois Writer's Project covered a plethora of topics, from Black nightlife to agriculture, and he engaged in similar activities after transferring to the New York office. Fus-sell opposes the Baedekers to today's consumerist fare, but if we shift focus to classic American travel guides, Wright's essay for *New York Panorama* (1938), "Portrait of Harlem," provides a richly detailed account of Black history and society in New York. Wright also shows that the federal government invigo-rated Harlem just as it had Bishop's Key West, fostering artistic culture and not mere survival:

> The FERA, [and] its successors . . . brought a new lease on life to Har-lem's underprivileged. WPA's monthly checks constitute a considerable part of the community life-blood. . . . The Federal Art Project in New York has discovered an immense amount of latent artistic talent among the Negro children of Harlem. . . . Harlem's boast that it is an area where new dance steps are created is indisputable. . . . [They] can be seen in Harlem's dance halls, at house parties, on beaches, and in the streets in summer to the tune of WPA Music Project bands.[20]

Wright also brings a creative self-reflexivity to what was supposedly a rote ex-ercise. As Fabre observes, Wright probably has himself in mind when "Portrait of Harlem" discusses the recent literary renaissance[21]: "For a few years Negro writers created more than they ever have before or since that period. Joyce's *Ulysses* influenced some of them; and even the gospel of Gertrude Stein claimed a number of Negro adherents."[22] Wright has subtly transformed himself from a tour guide into a local landmark, since his Joyce- and Stein-influenced *Uncle Tom's Children* appeared in the same year.

To draw on Paul Gilroy's deeply influential *The Black Atlantic* (1993), we might call the 1930s Wright hybrid and cosmopolitan, except his political ideals were centered on American locales and institutions. As discussed in the introduction, his poem "Transcontinental" was inspired not only by Louis Aragon's "The Red Front" (more specifically, E. E. Cummings's translation of this French-language poem), but also by the American Guide Series. In Gilroy's terms, the FWP enabled the exploration of routes as well as roots, and quite literally, since Wright's transition from Chicago to New York was made in the expectation of transferring to the FWP's New York office. His position as editor for the CP's *Daily Worker* was a six-month stopgap, and the recent publication of *Byline Richard Wright* (2015) reveals that his journalism was embedded within a constellation of causes, many of them involving federal initiatives.[23] The key issue is whether we see the nation-state as merely a repressive container of violence and domination, or whether Wright's transnational outlook can be reconciled with nation-based progressivism.

This issue can be clarified by analyzing Wright's early masterpiece "The Ethics of Living Jim Crow." "Ethics" eventually developed into Wright's autobiography *Black Boy*, in which the same anecdotes are used, and like *Black Boy*, "Ethics" can be read as a criticism of fascism, whose genesis Wright locates in the American South.[24] But the contexts for the works are different. *Black Boy* and the midcentury autobiography of which it is a part, *American Hunger* (fully published in 1977), are written in the emergent "discourse of the crisis of man," which defends human nature against the dehumanizing force of totalitarianism.[25] In contrast, "Ethics" first appeared in the FWP anthology *American Stuff* (1937), a collection of stories, poetry, and folklore. In this ecumenical collection, "Ethics" was publicly recognized as "easily the most powerful piece of writing."[26] Not only Wright's breakout effort, it was also his most successful performance to date in a professional exam or competition. Lawrence P. Jackson notes that "the anthology was one of the earliest examples of a modern, impartial selection process in the history of American letters."[27] It is thus appropriate that "Ethics" was the lead piece for the 1940 reissue of *Uncle Tom's Children*, which, until the publication of *Native Son*, was the FWP's most successful creative literary project. Wright was later to locate human liberation in the decolonizing Third World, but it is important to see that in the late 1930s, his hopes were centered on solidarity in America, and articulated through the institutions of an activist state.

These national institutions had powerful enemies, notably the Dies Committee, which is mentioned only in passing in Wright scholarship but is fundamental for the composition of *Native Son.* The year 1938 marked the advent of the House Committee to Investigate Un-American Activities, headed by Martin Dies Jr., often identified as a precursor to Joseph McCarthy. Dies had been a longstanding enemy of Black political agency; during his campaign in 1930, he criticized the first Black congressperson since Reconstruction, Oscar De Priest of Chicago's South Side: "Had I been a member of congress when Oscar De Priest made a speech assailing the southern white man, I would have taken a swing at that nigger's jaw."[28] Dies was relentless in his attacks on the FWP, calling *American Stuff* communist propaganda and specifically targeting "The Ethics of Living Jim Crow" in a congressional hearing. As FWP editor Jerre Mangione emphasized in his memoir, Dies's accusations, which put his committee "on the front page of every American newspaper," were "a means of trying to discredit the entire New Deal."[29]

In effect, Wright himself had become a symbol of the New Deal. According to Susan DeMasi, HUAC claimed that "[he] was an 'alien,' not born in the United States ... in a racist harbinger of the 'birther' movement that plagued President Barack Obama."[30] During the time that he was identified as alien and other, Wright wrote and revised *Native Son,* having been approved by Alsberg to write his own fiction full-time. Perhaps because we continue to see Wright as mainly a naturalist writer, we have located *Native Son's* extraliterary inspiration in the contemporaneous Robert Nixon murder trial in Chicago, overlooking the way *Native Son* defends and, in a sense, embodies the institution that enabled its writing.

Native Son in Chicago: Wright's African American Guide

[Bigger] put on the gloves and took up the pencil in a trembling hand and held it poised over the paper.... *Don't go to the police if you want your daughter back safe.* ... His scalp tingled with excitement; it seemed that he could feel each strand of hair upon his head. He read the line over and crossed out "safe" and wrote "alive." ... There was in his stomach a slow, cold, vast rising movement, as though he held within the embrace of his bowels the swing of planets through space. He was giddy.—Wright, *Native Son*

> In an effort to capture some phase of Bigger's life that would not come to me
> readily, I'd jot down as much of it as I could. Then I'd read it over and over,
> adding each time a word, a phrase, a sentence...a new and thrilling relationship
> would spring up under the drive of emotion, coalescing and telescoping alien
> facts into a known and felt truth.... It had a buoying and tonic impact upon
> me;...my temperature would rise as I worked. That is writing as I feel it, a kind
> of significant living.—Wright, "How Bigger Was Born"

"Who doesn't love creativity?" McGurl asks. "The fervor of our lip service to
creativity is matched only by the enthusiasm of our paeans to personal experience."[31] McGurl claims that our biographical readings of fiction are more
savvy than naïve, insofar as such readings highlight "a mediated experience
of expressive selfhood."[32] For the FWP-based Wright as for the writers of the
later Program Era, an institution enabled the storytelling, which to an extent
merges Wright's experience with Bigger's.[33]

Ellison famously remarked that "Wright could imagine Bigger, but Bigger could not possibly imagine Richard Wright."[34] This is a Cold War-era reassessment of *Native Son*, since in 1940 Ellison had celebrated the character:
"Would that *all* Negroes were psychologically as free as Bigger and as capable
of positive action!"[35] However, Ellison's reevaluation has lasted, whether one
lauds or criticizes the novel. Rampersad states that Bigger has "no pretense
to a sophisticated education, to anything more than rudimentary reading...
intellectually he is a creature of the movie house, where he is an easy prey to
fantasies constructed by Hollywood."[36] In *Native Son* criticism, the most-used
adjective for Bigger is probably "illiterate."

Yet this emphasis on brutishness and illiteracy is puzzling, since to start
with, Bigger is a speed reader. Following the progress of his own crime in
newspapers, he "scan[s] the print quickly...looking for some clue that would
tell him something of his fate," duplicating the work of Wright as well as his
FWP colleague Margaret Walker, who sent Wright clippings of a murder trial
in Chicago throughout his writing of *Native Son*.[37] Bigger also thinks criti-
cally about the mass media and its relationship to economic power. In the late
1930s, the 20-year-old Bigger would not have been old enough to vote in a presidential election, but he engages in a very politically aware form of signifyin(g)
when he "play[s] 'white'" with his friend Gus:

> "Hello," Bigger said. "Who's this?"
> "This is Mr. J. P. Morgan speaking," Gus said.

"Yessuh, Mr. Morgan," Bigger said, his eyes filled with mock adulation and respect.

"I want you to sell twenty thousand shares of U.S. Steel in the market this morning," Gus said.

"At what price, suh?" Bigger asked.

"Aw, just dump 'em at any price," Gus said with casual irritation. "We're holding too much." . . . [T]hey bent double, laughing. (*NS* 18–19)

Bigger and Gus are creatures of the movie house like any American youths, but Gus's laughing "I bet that's *just* the way they talk" indicates that they have invented the dialogue themselves (19). Indeed Bigger has a close interest in local politics that is probably unusual for any youth in the country, Black or white, as revealed when he sees "a huge colored poster [on] a signboard":

"That's Buckley!" He spoke softly to himself. "He's running for State's Attorney again. . . . I bet that sonofabitch rakes off a million bucks in graft a year. Boy, if I was in his shoes for just one day I'd *never* have to worry again." (13)

Pace Ellison, throughout the novel Bigger imagines himself as Richard Wright, especially insofar as he functions as a kind of renegade FWP employee. Here *Native Son* repeats the dynamic of the poem discussed in my introduction, "Transcontinental," turning travel guides into a stimulating narrative that highlights racial inequality. Initially Bigger is a disempowered tour guide, enduring a humiliating visit to the South Side with Jan and Mary, the white leftist sightseers who insist on bypassing tourist attractions and seeing how the locals really live: "We want one of those places where colored people eat, not one of those show places" (*NS* 69). As a criminal storyteller, Bigger uses the travel guides' maps and attractions to his own advantage, displaying an expert knowledge of the area that parallels Wright's itineraries as a Chicago-based FWP writer.

Valerie Smith remarks of Bigger's developing autonomy, "it is as if Bigger takes the pen from Wright and rewrites his story into the tale he wants it to be."[38] When his girlfriend Bessie claims that he has trapped himself with his ransom scheme, Bigger responds confidently, "I know the South Side from A to Z. We could even hide out in one of those old buildings . . . Nobody ever looks into 'em" (*NS* 149). Smith observes that Bigger's story has elements of true crime, but I would emphasize that Bigger's tale is pedagogical and not merely sensational, since he foregrounds racial strife that was left out of the

Illinois travel guide. In his major essay for the Illinois Writers' Project, "Ethnographical Aspects of Chicago's Black Belt" (1935), Wright recorded white people's violent response to the Great Migration: "A form of organized resistance to the moving of Negroes into new neighborhoods was the bombing of their homes and the homes of real estate men, white and Negro, who were known or supposed to have sold, leased, or rented local property to them. From July 1, 1917 to March 1, 1921 the Negro housing problem was marked by no less than 58 bombings. Arson, stoning, and many armed clashes added to the gravity of the situation."[39] For Wright's fictional protagonist, knowing the South Side from A to Z includes knowing the history of these housing struggles: "[Bigger] saw dusty walls, walls almost like those of the Dalton home. . . . Some rich folks lived here once, he thought. . . . He remembered that bombs had been thrown by whites into houses like these when Negroes had first moved into the South Side" (*NS* 182). Bigger's remembrance is not strictly realistic in terms of character (he would have been a very young child in Mississippi at the time), but it is true in the sense of what we might call an urban "racial wisdom" operating in tandem with government-sponsored research projects.[40]

In this view, *Native Son* does not merely attest to the value of the institution that made its writing possible, but to the broader possibilities of the New Deal itself. I think we overlook this dynamic because we continue to read the text through the prism of Cold War liberalism, which cast suspicion upon an activist state. In Baldwin's critique, Bigger recalls "the auction-block and all that the auction-block implies" in terms of slavery's legacy of self-hatred.[41] However, while we have criticized Baldwin's reliance upon a redemptive New Critical language of "complexity . . . ambiguity, [and] paradox" and his dismissal of Marxism, we might also reconsider his portrait of the late 1930s (13). "[*Native Son*] was published . . . very few years after the dissolution of the WPA and the end of the New Deal and at a time when bread lines and soup kitchens and bloody industrial battles were bright in everyone's memory" (25). New Deal programs and their offshoots, especially the GI Bill, were structuring Black/white relations at the very time Baldwin wrote, in a way that rivaled slavery for fostering present-day racial inequality.

The political scientist Ira Katznelson's work has changed the way we think about the New Deal and race. In his magisterial *Fear Itself: The New Deal and the Origins of Our Time* (2013), Katznelson reveals that Southern congressional Democrats initially led the movement to create a modern welfare state. However, the Southern power structure enabled progressive legislation on condition that Black labor was kept rigorously excluded. In the later 1930s, the New Deal assumed a more racially confrontational stance, as the South "observed growing black aspirations and outmigration, demands for better education, the heightened activism of an assortment of liberals, union organizers, Communists, and socialists. . . . New Deal initiatives, ranging from agriculture to industry, threatened to destabilize Jim Crow."[42] Wright's nemesis, the Texas Democrat Martin Dies, illustrates this transition, since he had begun the 1930s as an enthusiastic supporter of Rooseveltian reforms. In 1937, Dies told the House: "There is a racial question here. . . . [Y]ou cannot prescribe the same wage for the black man as for the white man."[43] When Dies formed HUAC in 1938, Richard Wright embodied everything that he now hated about the New Deal.

Native Son is the paradigmatic novel of this second phase of the racial New Deal, envisioning the extension of its reforms across the color line, a road not taken in government's relationship to race. One of the few scholars to highlight Bigger's Southern upbringing, Virginia Whatley Smith, notes that "the reach of Southern whites interjects itself into Northern domains."[44] Southern newspapers make a running commentary on Bigger's case—"Down here in Dixie we keep Negroes firmly in their places" (*NS* 281)—and the Chicago district attorney Buckley becomes an agent of this repression through manipulating Bigger to confess:

> "That was not as hard as I thought it would be," Buckley said.
> "He came through like a clock," the other man said.
> Buckley looked down at Bigger and said, "Just a scared colored boy from Mississippi." (310)

While Buckley would be aware of the Great Migration, his targeting of Bigger specifically as a Mississippi native suggests a figure like Dies or Theodore Bilbo, the white supremacist Mississippi senator who defended lynching in a 1938 congressional debate. In Whatley Smith's Foucaultian reading, Buckley is a "human panopticon" who figures "the towering eye of the prison state" that incarcerates young Black males, reducing Bigger's humanity to a case study in deviance.[45] However, it is important to note that *Native Son* specifically identifies Buckley as part of a faction of reactionary white people who want to roll back the WPA, union activity, and progressive taxation (*NS* 386). As Bigger's lawyer Boris Max states, "All of the factors in the present hysteria existed before Bigger Thomas was ever heard of. Negroes, workers, and labor unions were hated as much yesterday as they are today" (385–86).

"Negroes, workers, and labor unions" suggests a broad alliance centered in "New Deal town," the sociologist Horace Cayton's term for Black Chicago in the late 1930s.[46] When he first met Wright, Cayton was doing research at the University of Chicago under the aegis of Louis Wirth, whose wife hired Wright for his FWP supervisor position. Stressing the importance of the Chicago school of sociology for Wright's work, we have overlooked this school's enabling connection with an activist state. Published after World War II, Cayton's classic co-authored study *Black Metropolis* (1945) had been a WPA project that employed over a hundred people during its research-gathering phase. In a 1941 essay, Cayton claimed: "[F]or every move that Bigger took, we have a map; for every personality type he encountered we have a life history. . . . We could also write a book about Chicago, but it won't sell three hundred thousand copies nor reach one per cent of that number of readers nor have the social impact of Wright's book."[47] For Cayton, *Native Son* was the fictional expression of his WPA-funded enterprise.

The concept of New Deal Town helps to illuminate Max, surely one of the most controversial characters in American literature. We have focused on the expurgation of references to interracial desire in the 1940 edition of *Native Son*, but just as importantly, Rampersad's restored edition reveals Wright's insistence on a Black/Jewish alliance: "And, because I, a Jew, dared defend this Negro boy, for days my mail has been flooded with threats against my life," Max declares (*NS* 385). Various critics have noted that Max is not identified as a communist, and importantly, his interview with Bigger emphasizes not class revolution but rather thwarted upward mobility (353–54).[48] Max might best be characterized as a socially responsible Jewish professional who recognizes the desire for achievement of youths like Bigger (who had earlier been intrigued by fascism). In keeping with Katznelson's argument that the New Deal engineered contemporary race relations, *Native Son* confronts the public welfare directly, even criticizing inequality in food safety, as well as in housing, education, and health care (344). One could argue that it was precisely a Black writer who had to identify the nascent American welfare state as such, not to discredit it but rather to demand an extension of its protections and privileges.

As Szalay observes, in part 3 of *Native Son* it is not only Bigger but the New Deal itself that is on trial, and this was quite literal in the case of the HUAC hearings.[49] Recent scholarship on the Program Era has shown that the novels of university-based creative writers contain figures for mentors like Iowa's Paul Engle and Stanford's Wallace Stegner.[50] In like fashion, *Native Son*'s Max performs the role for Bigger that Alsberg performed for Wright and the FWP. As DeMasi observes, before Alsberg became the FWP director, his major interest as a writer and activist was prison reform. Drawing on Gandhi as well as leftist currents of the time, Alsberg argued in essays like "Prisoners' Swaraj" (1930) that America's incarcerated should develop a nonviolent resistance movement: "The criminal . . . must develop an active conviction that poverty and lack of opportunity are his greatest crimes."[51] Alsberg's role as an anti-panoptic prison activist helps to explain why he chose Wright for his "secret creative writing unit," allowing Wright to work solely on his tale of racial crime and punishment for a year and a half.[52] During the HUAC hearings, Alsberg "t[ook] particular offense about the claim that Wright, born in Mississippi, was not a citizen, calling it 'the most fantastic of all charges.'"[53] This explains the reflexive quality in part III of *Native Son*, when the novel tells itself back to the reader in the courtroom scenes. The defense that Max makes of Bigger accords with the arguments that Alsberg made on behalf of the American Guides and the FWP: "In him . . . is what was in our forefathers when they first came to these strange shores hundreds of years ago" (*NS* 393). In effect, *Native Son* declares itself to be more American than Dies and his proto-Birther movement.

This is not to say that Alsberg was effective in his role as a public defender: fallible like Max, his FWP was gutted in 1940, and Alsberg himself was fired that August. Bigger thus declares his autonomy at the end of *Native Son*—"what I killed for, I *am*!" (429)—which is in keeping with his concern throughout the novel that the tale of criminality has been his own. "[Jan] didn't have a damn thing to do with it! I—I did it!" he imagines telling a policeman (245). These declarations can be read as what McGurl terms autopoetics, and Valerie Smith terms self-authorization. Insofar as Bigger is himself a storyteller, his self-authorization corresponds to Wright's ownership of *Native Son*. Wright's editor at Harper's, Edward Aswell, said it was "a fine thing that the Federal Government, through WPA, is making it possible for a man of Mr. Wright's caliber to continue his creative work," and even suggested giving the FWP credit on *Native Son*'s book jacket.[54] In my view, the latter idea seems paternalistic—one wouldn't give the GI Bill credit on the cover of Norman Mailer's *The Naked and the Dead* (1948), or suggest the Guggenheim Foundation was a co-writer of *The Adventures of Augie March*. Nevertheless, while *Native Son* was Wright's own intellectual property, the FWP did enable the storytelling project, which contradicts our image of the government as a blob-like enforcer of conformity and routine, or a mere provider of relief checks. *Native Son* might justifiably mock the South Side Boys' Club, where ineffectual philanthropists want Black youths to play ping-pong, but Wright was a steadfast supporter of the FWP, which he and Alsberg wanted to make a permanent institution. While Wright did not succeed in turning the FWP into a "People's Art Project," the effort highlights his commitment to progressive American government.[55]

Wright never wrote a eulogy for Joseph Stalin. In contrast, he was deeply traumatized by the death of "FDR, . . . who really gave me a chance to write books." While working at the Chicago FWP, he visited the New York office and sang jubilantly to his fellow employees:

> Roosevelt! You're my man!
> When the times come
> I ain't got a cent,
> You buy my groceries
> And pay my rent.
> Mr. Roosevelt, you're my man.[56]

But Wright was not merely on relief, an unfortunate phrase that is often used in connection to his FWP period. Funding *Native Son* was a major boon for the federal government, since the novel was a kind of literary Keynesian multiplier, not only generating health within the publishing industry but a big windfall in taxes from Wright himself. "One's mind reels when one tries to figure out what changes will be wrought by FDR's death," Wright wrote in an April 12 diary entry, and in a letter to Gertrude Stein he said, "The death of Roosevelt simply knocked all the optimism out of people."[57] As in Du Bois's *Worlds of Color*, the comments reveal a perhaps surprising emotional investment in a progressive presidency. Wright's post-*Native Son* career, which includes a significant body of travel writing, has little to do with communism but a great deal to do with the vicissitudes of liberalism, as America and its institutions globalized.

Native Son Goes to Argentina

In our analysis of Wright's life and work in the late 1940s and early 1950s, we have focused on his relationship to communism and existentialism. Wright denounced his nation's racial hypocrisy in his article "Not My People's War"

(1941), published in the CP-sponsored *New Masses*: "Who can deny that the Anglo-American hatred of Negroes is of the same breed of hate which the Nazis mete out to Jews in Germany?"[58] In 1942, Wright was commanded by the Party to back America's war effort and overlook segregation in the military. Wright quietly quit the Party before his public break two years later, when his jeremiad "I Tried to Be a Communist" was published in two installments in *The Atlantic Monthly* (later reprinted in the 1949 bestselling essay collection *The God That Failed*). Wright's search for meaning led to a rich engagement with French existentialism, culminating in his novel *The Outsider* (1953). Scholars have argued that, despite his anticommunism, Wright continued to use a Marx-influenced approach in anticolonial travel narratives like *Black Power* (1954), in which he transferred his hopes for humanity to the Third World.

Yet the Party and its strictures were less important for Wright's career than a broad transformation in American culture and transatlantic political relationships. After he quit the CP, his activities paralleled Roosevelt's transition from "Dr. New Deal" to "Dr. Win the War," which involved the elimination of Federal One accompanied by new opportunities for writers and intellectuals.[59] While Wright was hardly eager to serve in a segregated army, he was keen on a position in the psychological or propaganda services. To support his application for various war agencies, Wright wrote a lengthy article called "Mobilization of Negro Opinion." The title's affinity with "Blueprint for Negro Writing" suggests the value of Wright's professional expertise regarding Black American culture. In "Mobilization of Negro Opinion," Wright "outlined an extensive propaganda campaign (using specific facts conveyed by radio, the press, church, schools, posters, songs and black intellectuals and artists) aimed at convincing the black population that the Fascist regimes were fundamentally racist."[60] Wright also tried to get a position on the editorial board of *Yank, the Army Weekly*, and teamed with Paul Robeson to provide morale-boosting radio programs for the Office of War Information.[61] A new book jacket for *Black Boy* urged the reader to buy war bonds.

Wright thus joined the national fight against fascism, but this admirable effort also suggests a close relationship to the globalizing institutions of postwar America. William Maxwell's *F.B. Eyes* (2015), which discusses African American writers' fraught relationship to J. Edgar Hoover's regime, notes that FBI surveillance "returned with a vengeance . . . in the early 1940s" following an "anomalous break during the Great Depression."[62] His book takes its title from a poem that Wright wrote on a ship bound for Argentina, "The FB Eye

Blues" (1949), which complains, "every place I look, Lord / I find FB eyes / I'm getting sick and tired of gover'ment spies."[63] In Maxwell's account, the poem reveals "[Wright's] suspicion that the F.B. eye was just as able as he to board a master symbol of Black Atlantic mobility."[64] For Maxwell, contemporary models of mobility such as Gilroy's Black Atlantic entertain the fantasy that one can elide a state power that remains ever-present. However, despite the trouble that the FBI and CIA often caused for Wright, he was also enabled by American globalization, which makes for an overlap of his itinerary with Washington, DC's designs for the world.

This topic can be explored by deemphasizing a Paris-centered account of Wright's midcentury career and instead following his ship to Buenos Aires— something that literary critics have been reluctant to do, since it involved making the problematic film version of *Native Son*. Although Wright had earlier rejected offers to film *Native Son* (including a proposal that made Bigger Thomas a persecuted white immigrant), he cowrote a highly successful play. Working at the Federal Theatre Project in Chicago in 1936, Wright wanted to stage Paul Green's one-act drama about a Southern chain gang, *Hymn to the Rising Sun* (*BB* 347). In 1940, Wright and Green cowrote the script for *Native Son*, which was directed and produced by the wunderkind Orson Welles. Canada Lee, an actor/activist whom Michael Denning describes as a "classic Popular Front proletarian star," played Bigger to acclaim.[65] As Denning observes, Welles's innovative set design involved the audience as a participant, in the manner of contemporaneous plays like Clifford Odets's *Waiting for Lefty* (1935); the actor who played lawyer Max "stood at a railing on the apron and directly addressed the audience, as if they were the jury."[66] The play helped to form the public image of Wright as well as *Native Son*. "My own image of Richard was almost certainly based on Canada Lee's terrifying stage portrait of Bigger Thomas," Baldwin relates, adding that when he visited Wright for the first time in Brooklyn, "Richard was not like that at all" (*B* 253). Eventually the staging of *Native Son* took on a reflexive character: just as Max tried to save Bigger's life, a progressive coalition in New York defended the play from right-wing attacks.

In 1948, Wright received an offer to film *Native Son* from a French film producer, Pierre Chenal, who had been working in Argentina since the Nazi occupation. Wright bought the rights to *Native Son* from Green and Welles for $6,000 (roughly $65,000 in 2021 dollars). "It was a financial risk, but Wright anticipated large profits."[67] A movie based on a classic novel is often disavowed by the author, but in this case Wright was directly responsible for the 1951 film that he wrote, produced, and starred in. This latter role has been a source of outright embarrassment for many friends and critics. Walker remarks that "nothing short of inordinate conceit and ego could have made him willing to play the part of Bigger Thomas," while Baldwin recalls Wright's return to Paris "from wherever he had been to film *Native Son*. (In which, to our horror, later justified, he himself played Bigger Thomas.)"[68] Indeed, while Wright was a passionate filmgoer whose writing style was influenced by techniques such as expressive lighting and jump cuts, the idea of a novelist embodying his own most famous character just seems *wrong*—as it would be if George Orwell had starred as Winston Smith in a film version of *1984*, or J. D. Salinger had played Holden Caulfield in *The Catcher in the Rye*, or J. R. R. Tolkien had played Frodo in *The Lord of the Rings*. Wright was forty-one years old at the time, and while the film tries to finesse the situation by identifying Bigger as twenty-five, there nevertheless remains the incongruity of a middle-aged man playing a symbol of urban youth.

Reviewers were not kind to the film, which moreover had been heavily cut by New York state censors, creating a truncated version that was then sold to European chains. The film has not played much better in videocassette or DVD format. Ellen Scott notes that in addition to its choppy story and "forced and unconvincing performances," the film is "hard to watch," with "over-dark cinematography . . . literally frustrating our vision."[69] She makes a virtue of these negative elements by relating *Native Son* to film noir (a genre that Wright's naturalist fiction influenced), arguing that the film's exposé of racism was deliberately offputting, "a Black leftist anti-colonialist critique that was Blacker than noir."[70]

Due to the efforts of the Library of Congress, which preserved a negative of the uncut film, and the film scholar Fernando Martin Peña, who discovered a print of the Argentinean theatrical release, the original version of *Native Son* has been restored.[71] Meanwhile, the distribution company Kino Lorber has done Wright scholars a great service by making the film available through a Blu-ray disc as well as online venues such as Amazon.[72] Although I agree with Scott that one must read the film against the grain in order to redeem it, the restoration reveals that Wright's film was not meant to be discontinuous or too dark to watch. One is often impressed by the cinematography, and we can readily perceive that the film displays postwar affluence more than it does squalor, as well as a remarkable amount of skin. For example, although played by an amateur actor, Jan Erlone can be described as a tall Hollywood hunk, shirtless when the detective collars him in his apartment. Bessie has a much bigger role in the film, which transforms her from a domestic worker into a nightclub chanteuse who even has a brief moment of female bonding with Mary Dalton. For Wright's part, the cigarette-smoking Bigger is not merely a Humphrey Bogart–like noir character but also an action hero, ripping off his shirt during a gunfight with the police as well as in a dream sequence. Our readings of the restored film need to deal with this element of glamour, especially the visual representation of Bigger Thomas as a kind of sex symbol.

Is the film a dated look at Great Depression America, or a film actually set in the 1950s? The setting seems to be precisely 1950 and not the novel's late 1930s, which clarifies its political agenda and might alter our evaluation of Wright's performance. In an essay called "The Shame of Chicago" (1950), which was stimulated by his visit to film *Native Son*'s exterior city scenes, Wright claimed that the South Side's poverty and "ugliness" was the same as what he had experienced in the 1930s.[73] Yet as Fabre notes, the South Side *had* changed: Wright noted the new cars, stores and hotels, and his venue for "The Shame of Chicago," *Ebony*, was a glossy pictorial inspired by *Life* magazine. As with the unexpurgated version of Bishop's book on Brazil, scholars might want to rediscover a radical film repressed by New York's censors, but Wright himself made key changes. For example, the pamphlets that Jan gives to Bigger have similar titles to the ones in the novel—the novel's "Black and White Unite and Fight" and "Race Prejudice on Trial" (*NS* 98) become the film's "Labor Leads the Fight" and "Smash! Jim Crow!"[74] However, while the

FACING PAGE

Top: Bessie (Gloria Madison) serenades Bigger (Richard Wright), Mary (Jean Wallace), and Jan (Gene Michael) in the film adaptation of Richard Wright's *Native Son*, which turns the novel's Ernie's Kitchen Shack into a swanky nightclub. Whereas the novel had emphasized 1930s deprivation, the film has elements of postwar affluence, more in keeping with the milieu of *Ebony* than proletarian magazines.

Bottom: Bigger as action hero: the shootout with the police in the film adaptation of Richard Wright's *Native Son*. In the novel, Bigger is a youthful victim of racism and the Great Depression; in the film, he is more akin to a war veteran, with a personal style influenced by stars like Humphrey Bogart. In institutional terms, the nation-centered progressivism of the Federal Writers' Project has been replaced by a multinational film production centered in Buenos Aires, where this rooftop scene was filmed.

pamphlets in the novel were *"Issued by the Communist Party of the United States,"* the film's pamphlets are issued by "Social Science Publishers," which indicates the influence of Gunnar Myrdal more than Karl Marx.

Yet the tempering of progressive politics does not discredit the film, especially given that Wright was never a strict adherent of Marx. As Wright stressed in the conclusion of his photo essay *12 Million Black Voices* (1941): "The differences between black folk and white folk are not blood or color, and the ties that bind are deeper than those that separate us. . . . What do we black folk want? We want what others have, the right to share in the upward march of American life."[75] I suggest that whereas the novel criticized racial inequalities in the New Deal and sought to extend the power of an activist government, the film *Native Son* addresses the racial inequality of the GI Bill. According to Katznelson's *When Affirmative Action Was White* (2005), Jim Crow politicians were largely successful in making sure that white veterans were the main beneficiaries of state support for education, job training, and home loans, as "the Gordian knot binding race to class tightened" and America "missed [its] chance to fashion black mobility and create a robust African American middle class."[76] The film's Bigger might thus be understood not as an urban delinquent, but a returned war veteran. In the novel, Bigger wore his own clothes as the Daltons' chauffeur, but in the film, Bigger wears a military-style uniform and is even called "The General" at one point. Wright might not be believable as a young person, but as a mature veteran, his performance is quite decent.

In this reading of the film, Bigger reenters a postwar world in which white people benefit disproportionately from home loans, job training, and higher education. The story of *Native Son* continues to criticize inequality and racist stereotypes, including that of the Black male rapist. However, in the film, Bigger is not a symbol of dire poverty but rather challenges white peoples' domination of the spaces of postwar affluence, as when he takes Bessie to the fairground in the Daltons' car, then on a trip to the beach. While the novel looked to a broad transformation of America's race and class system, the film might be likened to *A Raisin in the Sun* (1959) by Lorraine Hansberry, another work that stressed the thwarted ambition of an upwardly mobile Black middle class. This approach to the film can make sense of the single biggest change from the novel, the character of Bessie. Whereas the novel downplayed Bessie's death and foregrounded Mary Dalton's, in the film it is the reverse: Bigger murders Bessie because he thinks she has told the police where they are

Bigger picks up Mary at her home in the film adaptation of Richard Wright's *Native Son*. This image might serve as a visual representation of Wright's own relationship to the so-called Third World masses, and his ideological transition from *Native Son* to later works like *Black Power* and *The Color Curtain*. Although sympathetic to decolonizing countries, he wanted them to avoid the temptation of communism in the passage to capitalist modernity.

hiding, but in the closing scene, Max reveals to Bigger that a local stool pigeon informed on him. "So she didn't snitch on me. She stuck to me. She was true!," Bigger exclaims, accepting the likely fate of a death sentence.[77] Instead of a weeping accomplice to Bigger, Bessie is an autonomous woman with dreams of success as well as the film's only truly noble character, with whom Black female viewers could potentially identify.

Nevertheless, to read the film in this way is admittedly to read it against the grain of its creators' intentions: Bigger *is* supposed to be twenty-five, after all. A different intervention would be to read the film as precisely about the contrast between Bigger's status as a young man, and the middle-aged, globally recognized writer playing him.[78] In other words, we could read the 1951 film of *Native Son* as an implicit travel narrative. Wright's unlikely embodiment as Bigger highlights his own globalized privilege as a relatively wealthy American, and thus a new way of inhabiting what Whatley Smith calls "the black body in motion."[79] If we shift focus from the national to the global level, the GI Bill takes on a different significance. A major element in Baldwin's critique of Wright was that the latter's 1930s-style politics were incongruous for a postwar context. He was skeptical about Wright's Franco-American Fellowship, which was intended to pressure overseas American businesses to adopt fair hiring practices, but which Baldwin called "this extraordinary organization": "most of the Negroes I knew had *not* come to Paris to look for work. They were writers or dancers or composers, they were on the G.I. Bill, or fellowships. . . . I had no reason to suppose that any of them even *wanted* to work for Americans" (*B* 262–63). Baldwin's list of occupations parallels Federal One, which has now been supplanted by alternative sources of funding, especially the GI Bill, which enabled creative agency for expatriate Black Americans.

In my view, Wright's political activism in France was important, but his socioeconomic situation had changed greatly from what it had been fifteen years before: he was not enabled by government programs but rather by his own bank account, ample from the proceeds of *Native Son* and *Black Boy*. Wright moved away from Chicago in 1937 and had not set foot in the city in eight years when he flew into O'Hare Airport in 1950, in a sense inhabiting the plane that Bigger views in an early scene in the novel (Bigger's dream is to be an aviator). Segregation was alive and well in postwar Chicago, but when Wright argued that nothing had changed since the 1930s in his *Ebony* article, he seems reluctant to register his own dollar-enabled global mobility, which turned Chicago itself into a tourist attraction. *Native Son* itself now enters the postmodern world of what thinkers as varied as Boorstin and Jean Baudrillard described as pseudo-reality or the simulacrum. The Depression-era Bigger was confined to his street corner, but Wright and Chenal's film crew bribed local white policemen to film the exteriors for *Native Son*'s depiction of Chicago, which indicates a new fluidity in race and class hierarchies.

Wright's excursion into film noir expressed what we would now call a midlife crisis. Fussell remarks in passing that whereas social scientists have made various attempts to define tourism, the tourist industry is familiar with a desire that is seldom openly revealed: "to realize dreams of erotic freedom."[80] This desire was as important for Wright in Buenos Aires as it was for Burroughs in Tangier, Bellow in Paris and Arizona, and Bishop in Rio de Janeiro. It might not be too cynical to view Wright as paying thousands of dollars for a packaged tour, one which facilitated a deeply meaningful activity (the making of a socially conscious film), yet also realized the worldwide daydream of being a movie star and sex symbol. If we take Wright as embodying his protagonist, Bigger was able to have an uninhibited affair with Mary Dalton: Wright romanced Jean Wallace, the actress who played Mary, as well as several other cast members. American readers were disoriented by the way Wright's public persona morphed from family man to international playboy and back again. In 1953, *Ebony* ran an article entitled "Black Boy" that illustrated Wright's Parisian life, which included a cook and maid, elegant family dinners, and strolls to bookstores and cafes. As Rowley remarks, "Not long before, *Ebony* readers had shaken their heads in wonderment at photographs of Wright the film star, surrounded by adoring young women in Argentina. This time, Wright had metamorphosed into a devoted family man, enjoying the bourgeois life on the Left Bank."[81] Meanwhile, Wright's wife Ellen had long talks with Simone de Beauvoir, telling her of Wright's infidelities, showing her promo stills of a half-naked Wright acting out *Native Son*'s dream sequence, and deciding she would respond by having her own affair. Despite her leftist background and partnership in an interracial couple, Ellen Wright's middle-class ennui is similar to that criticized by Catherine Jurca in her study *White Diaspora* (2001), and like her husband, Ellen Wright wanted to escape it (she succeeded in her own bid for autonomy, becoming an international literary agent).

The director of Sono Film, Attilio Mentasti, held the world premiere of *Native Son* aboard a Pan American "Strato-clipper," a huge Boeing-designed luxury airplane that featured sleeping berths and a cocktail lounge.[82] This might seem an incongruous venue for telling a story that inspired writers like Frantz Fanon, but in its transition from novel to film, *Native Son* takes on an imperial aspect. Anna Shechtman claims that "the shared quality of life in first- and third-world poverty lent the film an unplanned, and unspoken, internationalist politics."[83] But is it not just as likely that many Black and white Latin American filmgoers, while sympathizing with the film's critique of racism, also envied and admired Bigger and Bessie as they tool through downtown Chicago in a limousine? Studying *Native Son*'s production in a country that was less developed vis-à-vis the US, one finds racial indeterminacy instead of transnational antiracist alliances. As Rowley relates, "Chenal had not realized how difficult it would be to find black people for the South Side scenes. As opposed to other countries in Latin America, the population of Argentina was overwhelmingly European. Local blacks spoke Spanish. Chenal had to dub

Bigger and Mary cruise through downtown Chicago, in the film adaptation of Richard
Wright's *Native Son*, on a pleasure trip to the fair and then the beach (scenes that do not
appear in the novel). Here *Native Son* enters the world of what Daniel Boorstin would later
call the image and still later Fredric Jameson would call the postmodern. In a US context,
Wright was racialized as a Black person; globally, he was perceived as American—in the
historian David Potter's phrase, one of the people of plenty.

their voices with those of local white Americans, who did their best to imitate
black American ghetto speech."[84] Instead of taking on a professional role vis-
à-vis the Black working class in "Blueprint for Negro Writing" or "Mobilization of Negro Opinion," Wright was now helping to manage a transnational
enterprise that manufactured a "Black American" voice.

We indeed must put "race" in quotation marks here, as Henry Louis Gates
Jr. would want us to do, but in a way that undermines the concept of a racial
identity and the political affiliations that we would base on this identity.[85] The
question of political affiliations raises the issue of why Argentina would support the making of *Native Son* in the first place. The nation's once-healthy film
industry was in decline after World War II, partly because of their neutralist

stance during the war and increasing competition from the US. This strained relationship to the US meant that Argentina did not share France's fear that supporting a *Native Son* film might affect Marshall Plan aid. Instead, *Native Son* was made by Argentina's oldest and most respected film company, Sono Film, with the goal of bringing prestige to the industry. In Thy Phu's account, the film "can be seen to recast [the novel] *Native Son* as a story of nationalist struggle. . . . The nascent Argentine industry, which staked its ambitions to that of Wright and the story of Bigger Thomas . . . [found] in this unlikely antihero a seemingly apt figure heralding a new era of international acclaim."[86] Wright's novel synced with the leftist agenda of Juan Perón, who had been elected president in 1946, as well as his wife Eva Perón, a labor activist who was later the subject of the musical *Evita* (1976). "The socialist class analysis pivotal to *Native Son*, and made explicit in Max's courtroom speech, might have had resonances for the recent class struggles in Argentina in which Perón had mobilized labor unions and the working classes more broadly in his rise to power against the rightist dictatorships of the 1930s and early 1940s."[87] For Phu, these socialist sympathies made *Native Son* feel "'native' to Argentina," where the national film industry benefited from protectionist policies that ensured a domestic audience.[88]

Since she was not able to view the complete film, Phu is better at explaining why the Perón-guided film industry, inspired by the novel, approved the film's production. The restored version of the film is less progressive than Phu indicates, and there is also a tension in Wright's supposed ideological affinity with Perón. Wright begins *Pagan Spain* by stating: "God knows, totalitarian governments and ways of life were no mysteries to me. I had been born under an absolutistic racist regime in Mississippi; I had lived and worked for twelve years under the political dictatorship of the Communist party of the United States; and I had spent a year of my life under the police terror of Peron in Buenos Aires" (*PS* 3). Bishop did not have to endure Jim Crow, but in terms of Cold War politics, Wright's view of Perón is remarkably similar to her view of Vargas and Goulart. Like the Brazilian leaders, Perón was a populist who enjoyed the support of the working class and unions, and confronted opposition from the military; he defeated a coup attempt in *Native Son*'s year of release, won re-election in 1952, and was deposed and exiled by a military coup in 1955.

Wright did not try to undermine Perón in the way that Bishop celebrated Carlos Lacerda's campaigns against Brazilian presidents, but he shared her desire to escape paying taxes. Although Wright lived and worked in Argentina for a year, he never applied for a work permit, so as to stay off the government's books; when he received a large sum from Sono Film for the distribution rights, denominated in Argentine pesos, he transferred the money secretly to the US. As Fabre remarks, Wright's shenanigans with Chenal and Mentasti "resembled a spy story," and one gets the feeling that the making of *Native Son* was itself worthy of film treatment.[89] Yet I am not sure that Wright's avoidance of taxation was admirable, although Perón indeed persecuted his opponents and engaged in surveillance. One good outcome of Peronism was a social safety net that has persisted to this day, and when we use the discourse of corrupt state bureaucracies and dictatorships, we might be reproducing our own American prerogatives as well as an antistatist ideology. If Wright sympathized with the Argentinean working classes or racial minorities, he has left no record of it save a glancing allusion in *Black Power*, which emphasizes elites' resistance to modernization. Ellen Wright became especially distressed with her husband when she found out that he had bought a car for one of *Native Son*'s actresses, which might be likened to Bishop's acquiring a new MG. In short, there is a general overlap of globalized American privilege, instead of transnational progressive affiliations.

As the quotation from *Pagan Spain* indicates, it was during Wright's time in Argentina that he accepted the Cold War equation of leftist and rightist regimes. For Wright, both were "totalitarian," even as he remained critical of racism in the US. Modifying the title of Arthur Schlesinger Jr.'s 1949 book, we might call Wright the Black Vital Center, since he claimed to be more authentically free and quintessentially Western than his white American compatriots.[90] As he puts it in *White Man, Listen!* (1957): "My imagination is constantly leaping ahead and trying to reshape the world I see . . . toward a form in which all men could share my creative restlessness. . . . I regard my position as natural, as normal, though others, that is, Western whites, anchored in tradition and habit, would have to make a most strenuous effort of imagination to grasp it."[91] Wright's reshaped world parallels Turner's frontier, in which the pioneer, full of "restless energy, . . . had the creative vision of a new order of society. In imagination he pushed back the forest boundary to the confines of a mighty Commonwealth" (*FJT* 95). Wright's desire for a reshaped world drew him to the Gold Coast (now Ghana) in his travel book *Black Power*, which imagines a mighty Commonwealth through what I am calling antiracist modernization theory.

Black Power: A Black New Deal for Africa?

In 1958, Wright wrote to a friend: "Did you read *The Ugly American?* It is badly written but a true novel and it makes you wonder and wonder."[92] But the prescient Wright is not giving himself enough credit, since his travel book about the Gold Coast (now Ghana) anticipated Lederer and Burdick's defense of overseas Americans; in fact, to summarize *Black Power* is to provide the general narrative of *The Ugly American.* Like the diplomat Louis Sears in Haidho, the capital of Sarkhan, who maintains a manicured lawn that separates his Embassy from "the confusion and noise of the road" (*UA* 11), Wright is anxious about perceived noise and disorder during his bus ride to Accra:

> The kaleidoscope of sea, jungle, nudity, mud huts, and crowded market places induced in me a conflict deeper than I was aware of; a protest against what I saw seized me. As the bus rolled swiftly forward I waited irrationally for these fantastic scenes to fade; I had the foolish feeling that I had but to turn my head and I'd see the ordered, clothed streets of Paris.[93]

In Accra, Wright is placed in a "modernistic bungalow" with obsequious servants who ask "Massa want chop?" at mealtime, and stymied by a native leader who seems friendly but is disturbingly evasive (67, 68). When a newspaperman asks to reprint a speech that Wright has just given at an outdoor political rally, Kwame Nkrumah quietly censors the attempt, reading Wright's notes and then "push[ing] the notes into the top breast pocket of [Wright's] suit," a "meaningful gesture" that leaves Wright baffled (105). Meanwhile, Wright is suspicious of large-scale projects such as Nkrumah's plan to build a dam on the Volta River: "does not this Volta scheme sound as though the British were exchanging political for economic control?" (232).

Like *The Ugly American's* expatriate professionals, Wright recovers his autonomy through a frontier narrative. At first he conducts his "excursions into the 'bush'" by taxi (*BP* 251), then goes on an extended road trip with "Battling Kojo," an ex-boxer who drives Wright's rented car (252). Yet Wright is not going just to rough it—"I had no desire to wander at random in the jungle," he remarks (291). Instead, he advises impoverished Africans to use creativity and individual initiative, as when he advises a young man to invent a machine that will help produce a local food:

"How many times a day do they make this *fufu*?" I asked.

"In the middle of the day and night, sar."

"Now, look—you are an electrician. Why don't you invent a machine to pound that stuff?"

His mouth dropped open and he stared at me, then he tossed back his head and laughed.

"I'm serious," I said. (182)

Wright does not go into business with the electrician to make fufu-pounding machines, as he might in *The Ugly American*, but his activity anticipates that of Peace Corps volunteers, with whom Nkrumah would have an uneasy relationship in the following decade.[94]

In his preface, Wright says his book will "openly use, to a limited degree . . . Marxist instrumentalities of thought," but his statement that "the Communist instrumentality which I once held in my hands has built up a slave empire of 800,000,000 people" draws a line in the Cold War sand (12, 10). *Black Power* urges Africans to adopt capitalism, despite Wright's condemnation of the slavery that built cities like Liverpool (28). Like other Cold War thinkers, Wright is concerned that "the greatest incentive to the growth of Communism in Africa today would be the attempt on the part of the West to throttle the rise of African nations" (13). The problem is that "capitalism has to buck a strange set of conditions in the Gold Coast" (364). Wright is critical of "the system of native African communism," in which extended families and kin networks serve as a kind of welfare system (295–96). "Individual initiative is not very popular in Africa," Wright is told. "Why amass a lot of money? You'll have to give it away anyhow" (296). Hence, "African business firms are conspicuous by their shabby triviality," as Wright complains (329): "African capitalism is practically nonexistent; it seems that the African possesses little or no desire to launch ambitious financial schemes" (367–68). Demonstrating an inventive and egalitarian character instead of an ugly one, Wright embodies what modernizing Africans should aspire to be. "Self-reliance is the only sure way to freedom," he emphasizes (392). This experience on the African frontier enables Wright to end his book with an impassioned jeremiad, an open letter to Nkrumah that exhorts him to chart an independent course between Russian and Chinese communism on one side, and British neocolonialism on the other.

Wright's open letter has affinities with *The Ugly American*'s "Factual Epilogue," which urges complacent American readers to fight the global communist menace, yet it also recalls the lawyer Max's speech at the end of *Native Son*. More than any other writer in this book, Wright had been committed to the New Deal, and his postwar frontier individualism is correspondingly more vexed, as *Native Son* itself transforms into an imperial discourse in an African context. Drawing on the work of Wilson Jeremiah Moses, Gruesser puts *Black Power* in the lineage of "Ethiopianism," a Black American discourse that imagined for Africa a glorious past and even brighter future. The term derives from Psalm 68:31 in the Bible: "Princes shall come out of Egypt; Ethopia shall soon stretch out her hands unto God."[95] Ethiopianism was often a kind of missionary discourse that "assert[ed] that because of their experiences in the New World black Americans were the people most qualified to redeem Africa religiously and politically."[96] Gruesser argues that *Black Power* constitutes a final rejection of Ethiopianist discourse, since Wright "avoids exceptionalism, refusing to envision himself in a leadership role vis-a-via Africa and looking [instead] to the continent for guidance."[97] I share Gruesser's emphasis on Wright's residual Christianity, but someone who declares "Our people must be made to walk, forced draft, into the twentieth century!" seems to desire a leadership role (*BP* 413).

Although *Black Power* draws on Conrad's *Heart of Darkness* (1899) and Gide's *Travels in the Congo* (1927), its most important influence is Wright's own early work. Instead of seeing Wright's travel literature as a new departure in his oeuvre, we might view it as a return to the ethnography and research he did in the 1930s as a contributor to the FWP's guidebooks. However, in a Cold War context, his traveler's approach to Africa merged with the tenets of modernization theory. As several critics have pointed out, his paradigm especially resembles Daniel Lerner's *The Passing of Traditional Society* (1958).[98] Lerner began his career by getting an MA in English literature from New York University, publishing articles on Turgenev and Henry James. He worked for the Office of Strategic Services (the precursor of the CIA) during World War II, pursuing something akin to Wright's aborted OWI career. In the 1950s, Lerner became known as the founder of development communication theory, a form of modernization theory that postulated that people became modern and cosmopolitan by consuming media, which allowed them to imagine alternate selves and life in other places. According to Lerner's intellectual biographer, his perspective on modernization was based on his early literary scholarship on Henry James. In Lerner's view, "James consumed media (novels), liked what he read about Paris, imagined himself in those places, actually traveled to those places, and, once there, 'transcended national origins and developed a cosmopolitan outlook.'"[99]

If Lerner's modernization theory grew out of World War II, Wright's grew out of the New Deal, and both applied the research techniques and developmental paradigm to the Third World. While Lerner valorized Henry James, Wright takes himself as a model for the cosmopolitan modern self, as well as his semi-autobiographical character Bigger Thomas. For example, Wright finds Gold Coast newspapers wanting in relation to African American newspapers: "The Gold Coast press differs sharply from the press of the American Negro. If one ignored the names, one would never know that the press was giving news of black people. Words like discrimination, lynch, race, Jim Crow, white people, etc., are conspicuously absent" (*BP* 230). These are the topics that Wright covered in Illinois Writers' Project essays like "Ethnographical Aspects of Chicago's Black Belt," as well as in his many pieces for the *Daily Worker* newspaper. In Wright's case, reading and writing inspired him to join the Great Migration to Chicago and then later to move to Paris, not merely to escape a humdrum culture à la James but to experience life beyond America's color line. Yet Africans do not have this desire for mobility and self-reinvention: "The African newspaper, like the African himself, is a local thing. African ideas and culture do not fare well on alien soil, and the African has no hankering for foreign parts" (230).

In this view, Bigger Thomas, despite being oppressed by American racism, is an example of a media-consuming self—reading newspapers, watching films, and desiring a better life. Bigger is also politically astute, even providing a leftist political reading of Buckley's campaign poster. In Africa, Wright's fictional model of Black agency and potential upward mobility takes on an imperial aspect. Whatley Smith notes that Wright was familiar with only one African novel in English, Amos Tutuola's *The Palm-Wine Drinkard* (1952), and was disappointed by its lack of a strong protagonist: "A source of frustration for [Wright] is that the African hero is no Bigger Thomas self-empowered to move things on his own volition."[100] In the open letter to Nkrumah, Wright's description of the supposed African mentality—"[not] sharply defined; there is too much cloudiness in the African's mentality, a kind of sodden vagueness"

(*BP* 410)—is the way Bigger described his brother Buddy in *Native Son*: "Buddy was soft and vague . . . with no sharp or hard edges" (*NS* 108). In the Gold Coast, *Native Son*, and in particular its polemical Book Three, becomes *Black Power*'s modernization theory, which is antiracist in the sense of resisting colonialism but also stereotyping in relation to Africans.

Like white American modernization theorists, Wright stigmatized developing nations if they did not follow his model. Pratt's *Imperial Eyes* contrasts white male "monarch-of-all-I-survey" discourse with Wright's persona, providing the following quotation (which I have abbreviated slightly) from *Black Power*. In this section, Wright is traveling through the northwestern Gold Coast, formerly an independent empire, the Ashanti Kingdom:

> Night comes suddenly, like wet black velvet. The air, charged with too much oxygen, drugs the blood. The scream of some wild birds cuts through the dark and stops abruptly, leaving a suspenseful void. A foul smell rises from somewhere. . . . An inexplicable gust of wind flutters the window curtain . . . Fragments of African voices sound in the darkness and fade.[101]

Connecting Wright to the British writer Mary Kingsley, Pratt argues that "in the dark the cult of the seeing-man dissolves," replaced by "incomprehension [and] self-dissolution" that gives rise to "a serene receptivity and intense eroticism."[102] But students of Wright will recognize that the passage in *Black Power* is heavily indebted to Poe, in the vein of the Gothic that was a major element of his oeuvre. In his first published story, "Superstition" (1931), Wright similarly described his protagonist's visit to a place that "time had forgotten": "In the far distance [there was] the mournful whistle of a departing train, the faint and musical tinkle of a cowbell, a solitary dog bark, the monotonous beat of the rain. . . . The sizzling sound of green burning logs filled the room, giving off a queer, pungent odor" (*W* 218–19). In his writing on America, Wright used Poe to criticize the effects of racism, as he made clear in his essay "How Bigger Was Born": "we have in the oppression of the Negro a shadow athwart our national life dense and heavy enough to satisfy even the gloomy broodings of a Hawthorne. And if Poe were alive, he would not have to invent horror; horror would invent him."[103] Even in the supposedly free northern US, segregated housing condemns families to Gothic environments; as Fabre has shown, the tenements that Bigger and Bessie hide in, with their windows "like the eye-sockets of empty skulls," are described in ways that recall Poe (*W* 31). Again, this is a way in which Wright took the supposedly rote exercise of research for FWP travel guides and turned it into literary creativity and social critique in *Native Son*.

In contrast, in *Black Power*'s long final chapter, "The Brooding Ashanti," the Gothic becomes a way of stigmatizing a foreign culture and political system. Wright says that after Nkrumah's victory, the Ashanti "now had the modern, streamlined Convention People's Party against them *and* the armed might of the British," which set up the likelihood of a standoff between Nkrumah and the Ashanti chiefs (*BP* 331). For Wright, this "vaguely Oriental" stronghold of African "Divine Communism" is a totalitarian state: "It's here that even until today society is basically religious, military, and political—all one organic whole" (328). Like Burroughs's imaginary Guatemala in "The Mayan Caper," Wright's Ashanti is a forbidding place, as he might be said to invent the genre of the Cold War Gothic. "What was down those narrow paths leading into the jungle—paths so shaded and black and wild [?] . . . Africa was a dark place, not black but somber, not depressing but slightly haunting" (292–93). Several critics have noted Wright's indebtedness to *Totem and Taboo* (1913), but "The Brooding Ashanti," with its account of human sacrifices and vengeful spirits, might also be described as Freud read through Poe: "The tribal African thinks that when he confronts you dramatically with a detached human head, and you fall down in a faint, he has demonstrated some awful spiritual power" (370). "The Fall of the House of Usher" is especially relevant, since in Wright's view, Ashanti's material and moral decay is a retribution for the transnational slave trade that eventually produced Wright himself.[104] He emphasizes that the Ashanti were eager participants in the trade, and still maintain the practice of household slavery: "[People] were a kind of currency; one could pawn one's children, one's nieces or nephews. . . . When the West saw these pawns in the African households, they called them slaves and felt that these people would be fit to labor on the plantations in the New World" (316). Wright here identifies slavery as an indigenous Original Sin that gave rise to Gilroy's Black Atlantic. Wright, meanwhile, is the betrayed son who has made good, now returning from across the sea to view the impoverished condition of his parents with new eyes: "The Queen Mother [of the Ashanti] . . . invit[ed] me to her 'castle' for a drink. I accepted. Her 'castle' looked like a tenement on Chicago's South Side" (337). However, one senses that Wright is also expressing resentment at his exclusion by the Convention People's Party, which never allowed him access to its decision-making processes.

It's no wonder that the British-Ghanaian philosopher Kwame Anthony Appiah was irritated by all of this. Related to Ashanti royalty, he found *Black Power*'s open letter particularly offensive. Wright declares to his imagined Nkrumah: "The direction of [Africans'] lives, the duties that they must perform to overcome the stagnancy of tribalism . . . all of this must be placed under firm social discipline! . . . AFRICAN LIFE MUST BE MILITARIZED!" (*BP* 413–14, 415). As Appiah comments, "There is something simply mad in proposing from Paris . . . that Nkrumah—like Hitler and Mussolini?— needs the instruments of fascism if the trains of the Gold Coast are to run on time."[105] I agree that Wright's stance is misguided, but it seems to me that Appiah goes awry in his Europe-centered approach to Wright's thought. The Malian intellectual Manthia Diawara revealed the underlying Americanism of *Black Power* when he made a remarkable endorsement of Wright's open letter. Diawara explains that colonized Africans could only acquire a sense of national citizenship through military service. Hence, militarization signified "getting rid of tribal chiefs, eliminating corruption . . . In other words, . . . nationalism, with the masses as the basis of political power. . . . Even in America, the image of militarization can represent the discipline and mass mobilization needed for nation building. Franklin Roosevelt used the metaphor in his inaugural address of 1933."[106]

Indeed, whatever is compelling about Wright's open letter, instead of merely domineering, relates to his New Deal rhetoric of national solidarity. It is striking that of all the ways he could have ended *Black Power*, Wright chose thirteen lines from *Leaves of Grass*. As Sean McCann notes, "Wright's debt to Whitman highlights a rarely noted, yet central feature of his work—the frequency with which he, too, viewed national solidarity as the sine qua non of meaningful democracy."[107] When *Native Son* was published in 1940, Wright wrote in a letter to a colleague, "Paraphrasing Walt Whitman: 'Not until the sun excludes Bigger Thomas, will I exclude him.'"[108] *Black Power* uses the line from Whitman as an epigraph—"Not till the sun excludes you do I exclude you" (*BP* 7)—along with two stanzas from Countee Cullen's "Heritage" that end with "*What is Africa to me?*" Wright answered this question by transferring a 1930s sense of solidarity to African soil, and as Diawara indicates, Roosevelt is central to this effort. Wright uses Rooseveltian rhetoric when he stresses that African life must be militarized "not for war, but for peace; not for destruction, but for service; not for aggression, but for production." Nkrumah is usually discussed alongside figures like Nasser and Nehru, but

Wright also found in him an African FDR, since he urges Nkrumah to display the pragmatism associated with the New Deal and American philosophy
more generally. "Above all, feel free to *improvise!*" Wright exhorts Nkrumah:

> The political cat can be skinned in many fashions. . . . Kwame, the form
> of organization that you need will be dictated by the needs, emotional
> and material, of your people. . . . You have taken Marxism . . . but the mo-
> ment that that instrument ceases to shed meaning, drop it. Be on top of
> theory; don't let theory be on top of you. In short, be *free*. (414, 418–19)

Wright's exhortation is remarkably similar to Roosevelt's famous July 1932
speech at Chicago Stadium (Wright was living in Chicago at this time),
during which FDR first announced his New Deal program: "The country
needs and, unless I mistake its temper, the country demands bold, persistent
experimentation. . . . It is common sense to take a method and try it: If it fails,
admit it frankly and try another. But above all, try something."[109] Wright even
imagined forming a kind of brain trust for the postcolonial Ghanaian state:
accompanied by Padmore and C. L. R. James, he would settle in Accra to ad-
vise Nkrumah. "I can see radiating out from this land an organization devoted
full time to redeeming the blacks of this world," Wright wrote in his diary.[110]

Like *The Ugly American*'s professionals, Wright wants to be an organization man who transcends mere organizations. I think that he was sincere in
his desire for African independence, but this story has merged with his own
postwar story of individual liberation. "One's reaction to Africa is one's life,
one's ultimate sense of things," Wright claims (196–97). As Whatley Smith
remarks, "[Wright] becomes the travel text's subject, not the Africans . . . [he]
presents a unique, egocentric form of African American travel writing."[111]
Black Power might be read reflexively, as an account of how Wright's Protestant American background meshed with government support to produce
a globally mobile intellectual. Wright's emphasis throughout *Black Power* on
"firm social discipline" that will give "direction, meaning, and a sense of justification to [Africans'] lives" is a fair description of his grandmother's stern
regime for him in Jackson, Mississippi, which was constraining but fostered
ambition and resolve (414, 415). Meanwhile, in *Black Power*'s concluding vision for Ghana, Nkrumah is a stern parent as well as a political leader, creating
anew the activist state that empowered Wright in his adulthood. Yet it is difficult to see meaningful democracy in this vision: Wright's argument for racial
and class equality in the 1930s has now become a top-down model of social
change, as Wright himself might be said to embody Africa's Black New Deal.

By now, Wright was not enabled by the long-dissolved FWP, but rather by a strong dollar and an American passport. This helps to account for his betrayal of Nkrumah and other Pan-African leaders. On September 1, 1953, just before leaving the Gold Coast, Wright made a personal visit to the American consulate, informing them that Nkrumah slept with a portrait of Vladimir Lenin above his bed. His comments were relayed to the State Department in Washington, DC, in a four-page memo, which included very detailed information about the CPP's budget and methods of communication: "Padmore's letters to Nkrumah are generally sealed within envelope within envelope and addressed . . . in a barely legible scrawl to mislead government censorship," Wright claimed. (It is worth noting that Joe Appiah, Kwame Appiah's father, also communicated with the CPP in this way while residing in London.) Like Rostow in *The Stages of Economic Growth*, Wright wants Ghana to avoid what Rostow called a "disease of the transition," the temptation of the communist alternative on the path to modernity—although what is really at issue is national self-determination, free from American designs.[112]

We might argue that there is a distance between Wright's visit to the consulate and Edward Lansdale's bloody counterinsurgent techniques in the Philippines. However, when we set Wright's activity alongside Burroughs's hostility to Moroccan and Guatemalan nationalism, and Bishop's defense of a Brazilian dictatorship, we can see a marked investment in American control across a variety of identities. Wright's behavior was not anomalous but rather in keeping with his increasing involvement with overseas American institutions, especially the Congress for Cultural Freedom, whose journal *Encounter* printed four chapters from *Black Power*.[113] To use Gilroy's terms, Wright's Black Atlantic ship tacked rightward, in keeping with America's Cold War policies. However, the point here is not to discredit Wright, but instead to emphasize that American racial identities blur in a globalized postwar context, which is revealed by his understudied classic of travel literature, *Pagan Spain*.

Black Legends and White Negroes

I would like to conclude this chapter by following Wright's Citroën into the "Spanish frontier," which he visited three times from 1954 through 1955 (*PS* 3). The travel book that resulted might seem anomalous in a decade driven by Wright's concern for decolonizing Ghana and the Afro-Asian Conference in Bandung, Indonesia, but *Pagan Spain* was probably the most relevant for his mainstream American audience. As María DeGuzmán points out, mid-1950s

Spain was becoming one of middle-class America's favorite tourist destinations, in part because of the strength of the dollar vis-à-vis the peso.[114] Hollywood made a number of films set in Spain and sometimes produced there, including a film version of *The Sun Also Rises* (1957), starring Ava Gardner. Hemingway had won the Nobel Prize for literature in 1954, and *Pagan Spain*'s extended treatment of bullfighting responds to *Death in the Afternoon* (1932) as well as *The Sun Also Rises*.[115] "I can't understand why so many Americans want to come here. They're all over the place," a British woman complains in Bellow's short story "The Gonzaga Manuscripts" (1954).[116]

Wright's travel through Spain as a Black American involved a combination of othering and privilege. His skin color sometimes draws stares, and a bank clerk "quickly crossed herself" (*PS* 29), in episodes that parallel Frantz Fanon's famous anecdote about a white child pointing at him and shouting, "Look, a Negro! . . . I'm frightened!"[117] Yet Wright is also perceived as a wealthy American and a national ally, as when he falls for a tourist scam. A young boy badgers Wright into agreeing to have the boy wash his car, and the police then fine Wright for causing a public nuisance:

> "They're treating you with dignity," [Wright's friend] whispered.
>
> "Why?"
>
> "You're American. When they knew that you were American, I thought that they'd let you off. . . . Had you been French, they would have fined you more and made you pay on the spot. . . . You're our friend and ally." (43, 45)

Elsewhere Wright remarks of a Spanish village: "Undiluted ugliness was everywhere. The physical aspect of life made one feel that one was in the presence of an unnameable disease. The inhabitants were like vermin infesting the matted hair of a mangy dog."[118] Here Wright really is the Ugly American tourist, without any of the irony in Lederer and Burdick's account.

Accordingly, in the way that Brazilian scholarship has talked back to Bishop, recent essays have claimed that Wright othered Spain through the "Black Legend."[119] Although northern European countries had long thought their religion superior, in the nineteenth century, British and American Protestant writers claimed that "the institutions of Spanish Catholicism, especially the Inquisition, ossified Spain at its moment of greatest glory in the sixteenth century."[120] This stasis was a retribution for Spain's genocidal evils in the New World, which involved the ostensible blackness of the national character. My goal is not to redeem Wright from these critiques but rather to emphasize the postwar period, when he shifted from the Black Legend to "white Negroes," a specifically African American construction based upon the frontier and modernization theory (*PS* 162).

Pagan Spain is best read as a self-reflexive meditation on what makes for Wright's empowerment as a Black American traveler, able to analyze a country whose inhabitants are generally designated as white. Critics have paid attention to the extended bullfighting sequence that invites comparison with Hemingway, but more important is the final chapter in which Wright attends Santa Semana in Seville, a weeklong festival that pays homage to the Passion of Christ. At the beginning of the book, Gertrude Stein advises him to travel to Spain, saying: "You'll see the past there. You'll see what the Western world is made of. Spain is primitive, but lovely" (*PS* 4). For Wright, the Western world is made of racism and what Marx called primitive accumulation. His initial description of Seville calls it "the city whose cathedral held the body of Christopher Columbus," whose legacy Wright associates with "a long and bloody explosion" in which Europe "had hurled itself upon the masses of mankind in Asia and Africa and the then unknown Americas" (209, 191). Wright also claims to find in Seville the birthplace of the specific racial terror of his childhood:

> In almost all the shop windows of the city I saw tiny robed figures with tall, pointed hoods that gave me a creepy feeling, for these objects reminded me of the Ku Klux Klan of the Old American South. It must have been from here that the Ku Klux Klan regalia had been copied. (280)

As Charles Reagan Wilson observes, "the Klan's symbolism . . . came instead from the assumed mysteries of a Celtic religion. The Klan, in any event, would hardly have admitted to borrowing from Catholics."[121] But the truth of Wright's assertion seems less important than his reaction to Seville as a tourist attraction, one that is far more problematic for a Black American than the implicitly white sightseers of MacCannell's *The Tourist*. It is telling that Wright originally wanted to call his book *Pagan Spain: A Report of a Journey into the Past*, so as to parallel his memoir, *Black Boy: A Record of Childhood and Youth*.[122] *Black Boy* famously asks, "From where in this southern darkness had I caught a sense of freedom?"[123] Replacing the "southern darkness" of Jim Crow with centuries of colonial violence, *Pagan Spain* asks the same question at a global level.

In an earlier era focused on life in the United States, Wright answered his question by stressing autodidacticism and the Communist Party, although this book has called attention to an achievement-oriented family background and New Deal initiatives like the Writers' Project. In the 1950s, Wright's answer to this question as a global traveler is to extol the frontier, which is revealed by one of the two epigraphs for *Pagan Spain*, from "Prairie" in Carl Sandburg's Pulitzer Prize–winning collection *Cornhuskers* (1918). Since it is easy to overlook Wright's brief quotation—"I tell you the past is a bucket of ashes. / I tell you yesterday is a wind gone down, / a sun dropped in the west" (*PS* vii)—it is important to provide a longer excerpt:

> I have loved the prairie as a man with a heart shot full of
>   pain over love.
> Here I know I will hanker after nothing so much as one
>   more sunrise or a sky moon of fire doubled to a river
>   moon of water.
>
> I speak of new cities and new people.
> I tell you the past is a bucket of ashes.
> I tell you yesterday is a wind gone down, a sun dropped
>   in the west.
> I tell you there is nothing in the world only an ocean of
>   to-morrows, a sky of to-morrows.
>
> I am a brother of the cornhuskers who say at sundown:
>   To-morrow is a day.[124]

Wright's invocation of Sandburg recalls his New Deal days as a poet-activist working for the FWP. In "Prairie" we can also hear strains of the classic "For My People" (1937), written by his colleague Walker: "Let a new earth rise. Let another world be born . . . let a people loving freedom come to growth."[125] Walker's writing of the poem involved interracial progressive connections, since she received feedback from Nelson Algren, himself a friend of Wright as well as Sandburg.[126] In a New Deal context, Black writers were able to recruit Sandburg for a project of antiracist nationalism, yet in the postwar context of globalization, "Prairie" becomes the vehicle for an African American exceptionalism. As Wright put it on the book's jacket copy, "I found myself a man freed of traditions, uprooted from my racial heritage, looking at white people who were still caught in their age-old traditions. The white man had unknowingly freed me of my traditional, backward culture, but had clung fiercely to his own. This is the point of *Pagan Spain*."[127] Although Wright opposes himself to white men, he is one of those globalized middle-class Americans who understand themselves as the new people of the future.

As one of these new people, Wright has a paradoxical position: on one hand, *Pagan Spain* imagines a capacious selfhood. Stating that "Spain was geographically a part of Europe . . . [but] not the West," Wright concludes that Westernness "had come from one (and perhaps) unrepeatable historical accident that had been compounded in Rome from Greek science and love of the human personality, from Jewish notions of a One and Indivisible God, from Roman conceptions of law and order and property, and from a perhaps never-to-be-unraveled amalgamation of Eastern and African religions" (*PS* 228, 287). Elsewhere, Wright calls himself a "twentieth-century. . . . Western man of color"—"Am I ahead of or behind the West? My personal judgment is that I'm ahead."[128] If so, then the Black Atlantic is too small a container for his hybrid ambitions: he is a veritable Olympic gold medalist of ethnoscapes and ideoscapes, Third Spaces, and various postcolonial notions of selfhood. On the other hand, he is also at his most thoroughly middle-class and American, reading thinkers like Nietzsche and Weber through an affirmative sense of self-reliance. *Pagan Spain* marks Wright's final conversion from Marx to Weber, as in the following passage, which seems congruent with the latter's account of "worldly asceticism"[129]:

> Protestants had to make severe demands upon themselves; Catholics submitted to what had already been arranged. . . . The Protestant, therefore, could be dynamic, could project into his environment his sense of his dignity, could create his sense of God out of the worldliness of the world. Hence, the social systems of America, England, Switzerland, and large parts of Protestant Scandinavia had been transformed by Protestant pressure molding the environment; they had higher standards of living, more health, more literacy, more industry—all stemming from the Protestant's ability to handle the materials of reality. (*PS* 272)

To be sure, this is a Weber retrofitted for American Century triumphalism and the celebration of self-reliance in frontier mythology. Weber famously denounced the legacy of Puritan asceticism, calling the modern economic order an "iron cage," and declaring in Nietzschean fashion: "of the last stage of this cultural development, it might well be truly said: 'Specialists without spirit, sensualists without heart; this nullity imagines that it has attained a level of civilization never before achieved.'"[130] In contrast, *Pagan Spain*'s second epigraph, a quotation from Nietzsche—"How poor indeed is man . . ." (vii)—is taken quite literally, as Wright's explanation for Spain's economic backwardness celebrates Protestant initiative and identifies midcentury Spanish culture as the nullity. I think this American middle-class Weberianism leads to the ambiguity in Wright's analysis, which sometimes values Protestantism in itself vis-à-vis Catholicism, and sometimes values the secular attitudes that Protestantism inadvertently fostered. Insofar as *The Protestant Ethic and the Spirit of Capitalism* serves as a model for postwar development, Wright argues that, now that secular institutions have been created, it is better for supposedly traditional cultures to simply disappear, clearing the way for rapid modernization and the "rise of rational societies for the greater majority of mankind."[131] As with Lerner's *The Passing of Traditional Society*, Wright argues that "freedom of speech, the secular state, . . . [and] the autonomy of science" were only contingently Western in their emergence, and ultimately "not Western or Eastern, but human."[132]

Like other midcentury modernization theorists, Wright replaces Weber's iron cage with Turner's frontier. He certainly sounds grandiloquent, but I think it would be mistaken to view him as simply incorporated into a white and Eurocentric account of modernity.[133] Instead, inhabiting the postwar frontier, Wright throws racial identities into disarray. *Pagan Spain* might be viewed as a more extended form of the self-reflexivity found in *Black Power*'s open letter, since it retells the story of Wright's upbringing and implicitly celebrates his grandmother, who made Wright eat and breathe the Bible as a youth. In "Memories of My Grandmother," which was most likely written in the winter of 1941 through 1942 (Margaret Wilson died in 1935), Wright remarks: "I sometimes wonder—even though I've abandoned that faith [Seventh-Day Adventism]—if some of my present-day reactions are not derived, in whole or in part, from the extreme and profound effects of the emotional conditioning which I underwent at that period."[134]

Indeed, Wright's grandmother provides the basis for the African American exceptionalism, in which Black people lead the way to modernity instead of white people. Wright claims: "My grandmother was a rebel, as thorough a rebel as ever lived on this earth; she was at war, ceaselessly, militantly at war with every particle of reality she saw. In her way and according to her light, she strove to transform the world; she fought the world, she attacked it."[135] If we relate the "Memories" essay to Wright's account of Protestantism in *White Man, Listen!* and *Pagan Spain*, his grandmother becomes an oddly imperial figure, paralleling "Protestant rebel[s]" like Martin Luther and John Calvin[136]: "Determined to plant the religious impulse in each individual's heart, . . . Calvin and Luther blindly let loose mental and emotional forces which, in turn, caused a vast revolution . . . a revolution that finally negated their own racial attitudes! . . . A Church world was transformed into a worldly world, any man's world, a world in which even black, brown, and yellow men could have the possibility to live and breathe."[137] The idea that Calvin and Luther can be credited with the liberation of "black, brown, and yellow men" seems rather unlikely, but these were Wright's grandmother's missionary ideals: "Many times, when the Saturday evening sun was sinking—for Saturday was our Sabbath—she would call us children together and make us kneel; then she would pray for the Africans, the Japanese, the Chinese, and so forth. During weekdays she could be found standing upon street corners or going from door to door selling religious tracts dealing with the plight of the remote 'heathen.'"[138] I suggest that Wright's grandmother was the basis for his racially ecumenical ideals, which were based in the FWP and John Reed Clubs in the 1930s. Meanwhile, Wright's midcentury work rewrites the postwar text of modernization from a Black American perspective, thus creating a racial indeterminacy in which culture does not correspond to skin color. Although he endorses a globalized narrative of increasing rationality and progress, he challenges modernization theory's assumption that Euro-Americans embody this progress.

An example of such racial indeterminacy is the concept of "white Negroes," a term that Wright used several months before Norman Mailer published his famous essay "The White Negro" (1957). In Mailer's account, white, urban middle-class men can resist the control of the total society by adopting the behavior and mannerisms of the Black male underclass, who open themselves to raw experience and give free rein to their libidos. *Pagan Spain* turns Mailer's model of the white Negro inside out in the chapter "The Underground Christ" (*PS* 161–74). Here Wright tells the story of one of Spain's persecuted Protestants, a woman who has been imprisoned and subjected to state surveillance because of her faith. Wright says, "What drew my attention to the plight of Protestants in Spain were the undeniable and uncanny affinities that they had in common with American Negroes, Jews, and other oppressed minorities" (137). Wright critics have generally treated his affinity for Spanish

Protestants in terms of a structural parallel: Black people and other American minorities are oppressed, and Spanish Protestants are oppressed, which gives them a commonality.

However, given *Pagan Spain*'s total endorsement of the Protestant ethic against the norms of Catholicism, I think it is fair to read Wright's affinity for the Spanish Protestants in terms of the postwar Weberianism. Why refer to the Spanish Protestants specifically as "white Negroes," if not to suggest that they can only become modern by adopting Wright's own "deep non-Catholicness, [his] undeniable and inescapable Protestant background and conditioning, [his] irredeemably secular attitude"? (231) The Spanish Protestant woman's claim that she is "trying to save the children of the streets for God" suggests that she is not merely teaching the Bible but literacy itself, making her a figure for modernization (169). For Wright as for Mailer, the "white Negro" is a white person who has taken on cultural codes that the author has identified as Black. However, while for Mailer, to be Black is to be "a frontiersman in the Wild West of American night life" who exists for "Saturday night kicks," for Wright, to be Black is to "keep the children off the streets, . . . training and guiding them so that they could lead morally pure lives" (*PS* 165).[139] In short, Wright's use of the term "white Negroes" centers modern rationality and progress on African Americans.

Wright thus globalizes the imperial vision of *Black Power*'s open letter, and in so doing, imagines a reordering of the world's racial hierarchy. According to Wright, Franco had turned Spain into "a holy nation, a sacred State—a state as sacred and as irrational as the sacred State of the Akan in the African jungle. . . . *All was religion in Spain*" (*PS* 229). Relating *Pagan Spain* to works such as *Heart of Darkness*, DeGuzmán argues that Wright's "fear of Spain . . . may be viewed as a displacement of [his] anxieties as a hyphenated subject of empire burdened to prove his own contested identity as a 'modern' in every sense of that word."[140] But I think this misses Wright's reworking of modernization theory, which goes beyond anything contemplated by Conrad:

> The traditions of the Akan African were unwritten, were fragile, and had already been mortally jolted by the brutal and thoughtless impact of the Western world. The African, though thrashing about in a void, was free to create a future, but the pagan traditions of Spain had sustained no such mortal wound. Those traditions were intact today as never before. In fact, they were officially revered and honoured; they were the political

aims of the State. This was a fact that made me feel that the naked Afri-can in the bush would make greater progress during the next fifty years than the proud, tradition-bound Spaniard! (*PS* 229)

I doubt that Appiah, or any African intellectuals offended by *Black Power*, would be mollified by the above passage, in which Black people in Ghana come out ahead of white people in Spain in the race for modernization. How-ever, while we needn't set Wright up as a Nostradamus, he does seem prescient in foreseeing contemporary changes in the global order, when postcolonial African nations have often challenged Spain, as well as Portugal, in terms of development and economic influence. For better or for worse, *Pagan Spain* and Wright's other 1950s travel books universalize capitalist modernity and instrumental rationality, thereby anticipating the established Asian capital-ist nations of our own day, as well as emergent African ones. Not merely a "hyphenated subject of empire," Wright also challenges the racist assump-tions of *Pagan Spain*'s white Protestant American audience. In "Memories of My Grandmother," Wright says that his fiction is influenced by the "Christ legend," which involves "the brutal treatment of the superior man by his in-feriors."[141] For the Spanish, who from 1492 onward extolled whiteness and scorned the "biologically botched," pride goeth before a fall (*PS* 288). Even the phrase "naked African in the bush"—so horribly offensive when related to Conradian *Heart of Darkness* discourse—reads differently if one takes Wright to be overwriting the white supremacy that he finds at the heart of Seville's Santa Semana festival. In terms of Wright's residual Black Protestantism, the phrase recalls the baby Jesus in the manger (a box full of hay). "Thrashing about in a void" does not sound like an enviable condition for Africans, but when one reads the line alongside Sandburg's "threshing crews yelling in the chaff of a strawpile" in "Prairie," a "sky of to-morrows" is open to the new people of a decolonizing continent.[142]

   In my view, Wright's Black revision of postwar modernization discourse is more interesting than the work of his Nobel Prize-winning white compa-triots; indeed, *The Old Man and the Sea* (1952) is mind-numbing compared to Wright's story of Black Legends, white Negroes, imperial African Amer-ican grandmothers, and Ghanaians who accelerate into modernity while Hemingway's beloved Spain turns into a backwater. Nevertheless, Wright's antiracist modernization theory is American and middle-class in its orienta-tion, even if he imaginatively dethroned Euro-Americans, and white people more generally, as the exemplars of modernity. While Wright may have anticipated our multipolar capitalist world in some ways, his 1950s travel books share the limitations of conventional texts like *The Passing of Traditional Society* and *The Stages of Economic Growth*, since he advances a streamlined modernization-in-fast-forward paradigm and casts leaders like Nkrumah as technocratic elites. For Wright, as for Lerner and Rostow, modernization theory was a flight from class and race inequality in the US, instead of a globalization of New Deal aspirations. One wonders, then, if Wright's professional creativity was best put into the service of social reform in the United States. He admired Hemingway, after all, and the two were once allied in the days of the Spanish Civil War, when Hemingway—"looking in person like a retired Illinois business man," as Wright remarked—gave an inspiring talk promoting Loyalist Spain at the 1937 American Writers' Congress.[143] At this time, Spain was not only seen as an antifascist beacon, but as a social model for the US itself. On the draft title page of *Uncle Tom's Children*, Wright wrote, "To be sold only for the cause of Loyalist Spain 3/18/38," making it a part of a progressive literary movement that included *For Whom the Bell Tolls* (1940).

Reading *Pagan Spain* through Wright's 1930s commitments, some of the supposed departures do not appear so new: while the chapter "The Underground Christ" grants agency to a Spanish woman and might signal an emergent feminist sensibility, Wright had written about the political activism of Spanish women immigrants in Harlem in *The Daily Worker*.[144] Part of Wright's reason for visiting Spain was to see what had become of these earlier political ideals. As he says at the beginning of his book, "During the Spanish Civil War I had published, in no less than the New York *Daily Worker*, some harsh judgments concerning Franco; and the dive bombers and tanks of Hitler and Mussolini had brutally justified those judgments. The fate of Spain had hurt me, had haunted me; . . . How did one live after the death of the hope for freedom?" (*PS* 4). As globally mobile as he might be, Wright, too, has had certain freedoms curtailed and alliances fractured. Perhaps most significantly, the US developed a strong diplomatic link with Franco's regime at a time when the rest of Europe was still hostile to the Axis-fostered dictatorship. The 1953 Pact of Madrid guaranteed military and economic aid to Spain in return for America's building of naval and air bases on Spanish territory. Once upon a time, Wright might have openly contested Franco's dictatorship, its ties to the US, and the tourist industry that implicitly supported the fascist regime.

I think William Dow is right to note the "hybrid[,] . . . discontinuous, and multidisciplinary" writing of *Pagan Spain*, but for all of his racial revisions of modernization theory and criticisms of mainstream 1950s America, Wright's literary persona is nevertheless underwritten by these Cold War alliances.[145] Although his travel in the global frontier produced a fascinating body of work, it ultimately brings us full circle, back to the United States and its unfinished 1930s period of national renewal, stimulated by a sincere if incomplete attempt to address inequality.

Conclusion

....

The peculiarity of American institutions is, the fact that they have been
compelled to adapt themselves to the changes of an expanding people—to
the changes involved in crossing a continent. . . . Limiting our attention to
the Atlantic coast, we have the familiar phenomenon of the evolution of
institutions in a limited area, such as the rise of representative government.
. . . [But] American social development has been continually beginning over
again on the frontier. This perennial rebirth, this fluidity of American life,
this expansion westward with its new opportunities, its continuous touch
with the simplicity of primitive society, furnish the forces dominating
American character. The true point of view in the history of this nation is
not the Atlantic coast, it is the Great West.—Frederick Jackson Turner, "The
Significance of the Frontier in American History" (1893)

The frontier is a frontier of liberty. How hollow the rhetoric of the Federalists
would have been and how inadequate their own 'new political science' had
they not presupposed this vast and mobile threshold of the frontier! The
very idea of scarcity that—like the idea of war—had been at the center of
the European concept of modern sovereignty is a priori stripped away from
the constitutive processes of the American experience. Jefferson and Jackson
both understood the materiality of the frontier and recognized it as the basis
that supported the expansiveness of democracy. . . . From the Atlantic to the
Pacific extended a terrain of wealth and freedom, constantly open to new
lines of flight.—Michael Hardt and Antonio Negri, *Empire* (2000)

Although we associate the heterosexual white male with the Ugly
American stereotype, a wide variety of literary travelers sought
personal freedom and cultural enrichment outside their nation's
borders, including Black, female, and queer writers. Minorities as well as
straight white males went abroad to achieve autonomy and creativity, and
also were complicit in imperialism and the formation of global inequality. For

American writers, the price of incorporation into a transnational professional class was not only forswearing communism, but also rejecting 1930s social commitments and the concept of an interventionist state. Even Wright, who retained the collectivist sensibility of an earlier era, himself enjoyed the privilege of the American traveler, which gave an imperial aspect to his Black New Deal for Africa. I have tried to avoid demonizing the incipient neoliberalism of midcentury travel narratives, since globalization enabled creative expression for marginalized identities. Yet the ironic upshot of their personal liberation has been to highlight the importance of a progressive orientation toward state-based reform in the United States.

As various critics have suggested, after the Cold War ended in 1989, what we saw was not so much a new world order as the expansion of trends that had been developing since midcentury. Specifically, the transnational turn in the humanities and related developments, such as the celebration of diasporic sensibilities and cultural hybridity, were intimately related to postwar globalization. For example, Lawrence Buell's essay "American Literary Emergence as a Postcolonial Phenomenon" (1992) created a great deal of controversy, including the charge that he "coloniz[ed]" postcolonial theory.[1] In an analysis that merges Ralph Waldo Emerson with Homi Bhabha, Buell argues that while antebellum American writers were not dominated by Europe economically or politically, they dealt with feelings of cultural inferiority and marginalization. In particular, they felt stereotyped by travel narratives: "During what is now called our literary renaissance, America remained for many foreign commentators (especially the British) . . . the unvoiced 'other'—with the predictable connotations of exoticism, barbarism, and unstructuredness."[2] In response, writers like Thoreau and Whitman developed various forms of cultural affirmation such as hybridization, which involved "cross-cultural collages" and "composite persona."[3]

If we understand the frontier as a space of creativity and imagination coupled with geographic mobility, then Buell's essay might be read as another reformulation of Turner's Frontier Thesis, which extends the pioneer professional model to diasporic intellectuals from non-Western countries. Buell himself admits that "even mildly liberal academics will suspect the possible hypocrisy of an exercise in imagining America of the expansionist years as a postcolonial rather than proto-imperial power, as if to mystify modern America's increasingly interventionist role in world affairs."[4] But the issue is not one of hypocrisy or mystification; to borrow a term from Arjun Appadurai's

Modernity at Large (1996), Buell's meshing of postcolonial studies with American studies is enabled by his location in a global ethnoscape of cutting-edge scholars at Harvard.[5] A roughly contemporaneous book, Michael Hardt and Antonio Negri's *Empire* (2000), describes this culturally hybrid environment: "As a political discourse, postmodernism has a certain currency in Europe, Japan, and Latin America, but its primary site of application is within an elite segment of the U.S. intelligentsia. Similarly, the postcolonial theory that shares certain postmodernist tendencies has been developed primarily among a cosmopolitan set that moves among the metropolises and major universities of Europe and the United States."[6] Buell might indeed be read as trying to incorporate, if not colonize, certain elements of postmodern and postcolonial theory in order to retrofit authors like Emerson to changing times. But the alacrity with which he does so reveals that concepts such as cultural hybridization are not unique to late-twentieth-century postcolonial studies, but rather part of a larger literary history of postwar globalization. In this view, the major travel narrative of the late twentieth and early twenty-first century has not been otherness redeemed, but the extension of the privilege of mobility to a globalized professional middle class.

Although national culture and transnational culture should not be set in mortal opposition to each other, I suggest that an antistatist fantasy of the frontier has been embedded in the transnational turn, and this fantasy has been counterproductive.[7] For example, *Empire* incisively observes that Bhabha's thoughts on cultural hybridity are similar to the ethos of multinational business, which does "not operate simply by excluding the gendered and/or racialized Other. . . . The corporations seek to include difference within their realm and thus aim to maximize creativity, free play, and diversity in the corporate workplace" (*E* 153). Despite this critique of globalized professionalism, Hardt and Negri themselves codify the Frontier Thesis in a postmodern idiom, thereby revealing its limitations in confronting social inequality. They explain that modernity and its colonial hierarchies were based upon the ascendancy of the heterosexual white male:

> The world of modern sovereignty is a Manichaean world, divided by a series of binary oppositions that define Self and Other, white and black, inside and outside, ruler and ruled. Postmodernist thought challenges precisely this binary logic of modernity and in this respect provides important resources for those who are struggling to challenge modern

discourses of patriarchy, colonialism, and racism. In the context of post-modernist theories, the hybridity and ambivalences of our cultures and our senses of belonging seem to challenge the binary logic of Self and Other that stands behind modern colonialist, sexist, and racist construc-tions. (*E* 139)

Hardt and Negri argue that postrevolutionary America bypassed such colo-nial models with an ideology that stressed productive energy, hybridity, and self-governance. In their view, a "utopia of open spaces" was located not in the urbanizing Northeast or the plantation South, but rather in the West, which was "a terrain of wealth and freedom, constantly open to new lines of flight" (169). *Empire* is strictly faithful to Turner's model of the pioneer spirit when it claims "The frontier is a frontier of liberty. . . . Across the great open spaces the constituent tendency wins out over the constitutional decree, the tendency of the immanence of the principle over regulative reflection, and the initiative of the multitude over the centralization of power" (169). This is the flight that I associate with the frontier, and while it is individualistic in Turner's con-ception and ostensibly communal in Hardt and Negri's, all of them valorize professional creativity coupled with geographic mobility.

Limerick remarks that since its publication, "Turner's Frontier Thesis [has] existed in its own bewitched historiographical space, a zone in which critiques and contradictory evidence instantly lost power and force. Fighting the thesis was like fighting the Pillsbury Dough Boy; it bent momentarily to absorb challenges and then instantly resumed its previous shape."[8] It is not clear that Hardt and Negri come off any better in the fight. To be sure, *Em-pire* criticizes near-genocide against Native Americans and the enslavement of African Americans, and also gestures toward a critique of frontier discourse in terms of global class structures: "Certainly from the standpoint of many around the world, hybridity, mobility, and difference do not immediately ap-pear as liberatory in themselves" (154). However, in the final pages of their book, Hardt and Negri return to Western imagery, developing the notion of a "postmodern posse" that they connect to "Wild West lore, the rough group of armed men who were constantly prepared to be authorized by the sheriff to hunt down outlaws" (*E* 411, 408). Despite the Marxism of the authors, the "creative imagination of the multitude" once more has a striking connection to the Turnerian frontier ideal: "the postmodern multitude takes away from the U.S. Constitution what allowed it to become . . . an imperial constitution:

its notion of a boundless frontier of freedom and its definition of an open spatiality and temporality" (406). Like Turner's essays, *Empire* is arguably professional New Class allegory; when the authors make an admiring paean to Charlie Chaplin and reference the film *Modern Times* (1936), it is Chaplin's creativity that they valorize and identify with, not the anonymous labor of the rather mysterious multitude (159).

In this view, the central dilemma in *Empire* parallels that in Turner's work: how can one reconcile professional autonomy and creativity with an activist state? *Empire* begins by claiming that "capitalism only triumphs when it becomes identified with the state, when it is the state."[9] Hardt and Negri are prepared to do away with government altogether. "Big Government Is Over!" they cry (*E* 348):

> It is our turn to cry "Big government is over!" Why should that slogan be the exclusive property of the conservatives? Certainly, having been educated in class struggle, we know well that big government has also been an instrument for the redistribution of social wealth and that, under the pressure of working-class struggle, it has served in the fight for equality and democracy. Today, however, those times are over. In imperial postmodernity big government has become merely the despotic means of domination and the totalitarian production of subjectivity. Big government conducts the great orchestra of subjectivities reduced to commodities. (349)

If progressive government has come to an end, it would seem that Hardt and Negri are under some obligation to provide an alternative model of how society should work. However, "the task for the multitude . . . remains rather abstract": "What specific and concrete practices will animate this political project? We cannot say at this point" (399–400). Later they candidly admit that, awaiting "the political development of the posse," "We do not have any models to offer for this event" (411). The major concrete suggestion for political reform in *Empire*'s conclusion is "Residency papers for everyone . . . all should have the full rights of citizenship in the country where they live and work" (400). The frontier-pursuing creative people have now become oddly sessile and nation-bound in their roles as citizens.

It would seem that as we steered into the transnational turn, we were actually boats against the current, borne back ceaselessly into the past: toward the welfare state that replaced the excesses of the Roaring Twenties and made an attempt, however rough and incomplete, to deal with social inequality. With the first chapter in mind, the problem for literature scholars is that this welfare state has been diminished by postwar Ugly American discourse, a legacy that has stuck with us and diminishes the political impact of our work. I have drawn on a number of recent books that, while taking a transnational approach to American literature, might be said to descend from *The Cultural Cold War* instead of *Empire* and do not celebrate the transnational as a source of liberation: Maxwell's *F.B. Eyes* (2015); Bennett's *Workshops of Empire* (2015); Emre's *Paraliterary* (2017); Spahr's *Du Bois's Telegram* (2018). However, I think the writers' criticism would be more effective if they provided accounts of alternative institutions that they did actually endorse. Meanwhile, they overlook, or actively discredit, the activist state that I have cast as the alternative to the escapist frontier paradigm—as indicated by the subtitle of Spahr's book, which is *Literary Resistance and State Containment*. I think we need to move beyond a paradigm in which the state merely contains resistant energies.

Can our contemporary cultural diversity, our plethora of identities, be refocused on a progressive nationalism? Although Said himself did not experience the 1930s in America, his commencement speech at the Northfield Mount Hermon School in 2002 emphasizes "our life as a republic," and I would like to return to this important text.[10] This is not to make Said play the role of FDR, which might be too much cultural hybridity for any book. All the same, when he addressed future professionals who will play a leading role in America, Said made an appeal to national solidarity as well as economic justice, one that contrasts with the more individualistic fantasy of his "Jungle Calling" essay. Since Said was ill with leukemia at this time, his son Wadie Said read the following passage:

> [D]espite the great self-sufficiency of our country, its enormous power, geographic range, the variety of its people and history, we must never forget that its real essence is that it remains a heterogeneous society of former immigrants, not the home of a homogenous master race. Being American means being a hundred other things as well since the world has come here, left its marks bad as in the events of 9/11, good as in contributions of immigrants like Einstein and Charlie Chaplin, as well as children of transported slaves like Toni Morrison and W. E. B. Du Bois and stamped our society with their traces. No identity is pure . . . We are all Others in the final analysis. This is what makes America unique.[11]

Like Hollinger, Said asks "How wide the circle of the 'we'?" and finds that circle very wide indeed, centered on a shared national fate.[12] Although Said claims that "America is the best vantage point to actually see history being made," it would not be fair to call this American exceptionalism, since he emphasizes that "we still have a very long way to go ... toward emancipation and enlightenment" (8–9). In a word, the speech strikes me as being the reverse of postwar rearticulations of the Frontier Thesis, including the transnational turn.

Like Said at the end of his life, we need to return to nation-based thinking in our own time of climate crisis and continual health crises. Recently the historian Jefferson Cowie has written an epitaph for the New Deal in his *The Great Exception* (2016): "Out of the historic fault lines of American political culture—individualism, anti-statism, cultural conflicts, and racial and ethnic divisions—emerged the sociological foundation for a rare period of political unity that contrasted with much of American history."[13] Cowie argues that these fault lines have dominated the past few decades, making demands for a "new New Deal" or a "global New Deal" akin to "chasing ghosts."[14] I agree that nostalgia for the New Deal era can be its own form of American exceptionalism. Yet I would problematize Cowie's account of his intellectual stance: "The ideas here come from wading into the muddy tributaries of skepticism fed by Melville rather than walking the sunny fields of Whitman; its sentiments are more allied with the sparks in the twilight of Eugene O'Neill rather than the intense fires of brotherhood of Clifford Odets; its kinship is with the burdens of the past carved into Lincoln's visage rather than the indefatigable smile of FDR."[15] At the moment of this writing, the presidency seems to be dominated by a white male gerontocracy, but Congress is more diverse than ever before. While Odets's play *Waiting for Lefty* was important for the 1930s, writers like Bellow, Bishop, and Wright also provided the literary foundation for this rare period of political unity. Instead of relics of the past, were they ahead of their time? In any case, an urgent task for contemporary writers is the reimagination of reformist government and national solidarity instead of the freedom of travel, now that a major period of American history, that of the global frontier, has closed.

Notes

Introduction

1. Dean MacCannell, *The Tourist* (1976; Berkeley: University of California Press, 2013), 160.
2. Christina Klein, *Cold War Orientalism* (Berkeley: University of California Press, 2003), 107.
3. See Thomas Hill Schaub, *American Fiction in the Cold War* (Madison: University of Wisconsin Press, 1991); Alan Nadel, *Containment Culture* (Durham, NC: Duke University Press, 1995); Lawrence P. Jackson, *The Indignant Generation* (Princeton, NJ: Princeton University Press, 2011); Stephen Schryer, *Fantasies of the New Class* (New York: Columbia University Press, 2011); Mark Greif, *The Age of the Crisis of Man* (Princeton, NJ: Princeton University Press, 2015). Meanwhile, Catherine Jurca's use of the term "diaspora" in *White Diaspora* (Princeton, NJ: Princeton University Press, 2001) is entirely sarcastic, since she criticizes "the excesses of self-pity" in novels about suburban life by white males (18).
4. Morris Dickstein, *Leopards in the Temple* (Cambridge, MA: Harvard University Press, 2002).
5. See Myka Tucker-Abramson, *Novel Shocks* (New York: Fordham University Press, 2019).
6. Edward W. Said, *Culture and Imperialism* (New York: Alfred A. Knopf, 1993), xxiii.
7. Klein, 103.
8. Klein, 16.
9. Klein, 9.
10. Richard Slotkin, *The Fatal Environment* (Norman: University of Oklahoma Press, 1994), xv.
11. Slotkin, *The Fatal Environment*, 12. Richard Drinnon makes a similar analysis in *Facing West* (Norman: University of Oklahoma Press, 1980).
12. Patricia Nelson Limerick, "The Adventures of the Frontier in the Twentieth Century," in *The Frontier in American Culture*, ed. James R. Grossman (Berkeley: University of California Press, 1994), 88.
13. Limerick, "Adventures," 94.
14. Limerick, "Adventures," 94.
15. Frederick Jackson Turner, "The Significance of the Frontier in American

History," in *Rereading Frederick Jackson Turner*, ed. John Mack Faragher (New Haven, CT: Yale University Press, 1998), 31. Hereafter cited parenthetically as *FJT*.

16. Slotkin, *Gunfighter Nation* (Norman: University of Oklahoma Press, 1992), 34, 59. See also Amy Kaplan, *The Anarchy of Empire in the Making of U.S. Culture* (Cambridge, MA: Harvard University Press, 2002), 121–45.

17. See Amy Kaplan and Donald E. Pease, eds., *Cultures of United States Imperialism* (Durham, NC: Duke University Press, 1993).

18. Limerick, for example, acknowledges that her own role as an autonomous professional is based on the Turnerian model of academic success; see Limerick, "Turnerians All," *American Historical Review* 100, no. 3 (1995): 697–716.

19. Lee Benson, "The Historical Background of Turner's Frontier Essay," *Agricultural History* 25, no. 2 (1951): 59, 60.

20. For classic works on the subject, see Burton J. Bledstein, *The Culture of Professionalism* (New York: W. W. Norton, 1976); Barbara and John Ehrenreich, "The Professional-Managerial Class," *Between Labor and Capital*, ed. Pat Walker (Boston: South End Press, 1979): 5–45.

21. Ray Allen Billington, *Frederick Jackson Turner* (New York: Oxford University Press, 1973), 12.

22. For a comprehensive account of Turner's reception and the legacy of his frontier thesis, see Gerald D. Nash, *Creating the West* (Albuquerque: University of New Mexico Press, 1991). In *The End of American Exceptionalism* (Lawrence: University Press of Kansas, 1993), David M. Wrobel brackets the truth of the thesis— viz., whether or not the frontier actually closed in 1890—and discusses "frontier anxiety," the perception that it had closed and the social anxieties thereby raised. In this view, the underlying issue is really class conflict and how professionals and intellectuals like Turner himself should address it.

23. Richard Hofstadter, *The Progressive Historians* (New York: Alfred A. Knopf, 1969), 110.

24. Billington, 442.

25. Billington, 442–43.

26. Warren I. Susman, "The Frontier Thesis and the American Intellectual," in *Culture as History* (New York: Pantheon, 1984), 30, 31.

27. Susman, 37.

28. Roosevelt quoted in Wrobel, 137.

29. See Michael Denning, *The Cultural Front* (New York: Verso, 1997).

30. Michael Szalay, "'Nothing More Than Feelings': Generational Politics and the Authenticity of Alternative Culture," *Michigan Quarterly Review* 37, no. 4 (1998): 855, 857.

31. David Levering Lewis, *W. E. B. Du Bois: The Fight for Equality and the American Century, 1919–1963* (New York: Henry Holt, 2000), 464, 465.

32. Michael Berkowitz, "A 'New Deal' for Leisure: Making Mass Tourism during

the Great Depression," in *Being Elsewhere*, ed. Shelley Baranowski and Ellen Furlough (Ann Arbor: University of Michigan Press, 2001), 187.

33. Berkowitz, 199.

34. Brian Dolinar, "Editor's Introduction," *The Negro in Illinois* (Urbana: University of Illinois Press, 2013), x.

35. Jerrold Hirsch, *Portrait of America* (Chapel Hill: University of North Carolina Press, 2003), 64.

36. Paul Fussell, *Abroad* (New York: Oxford University Press, 1980), 62.

37. Fussell, *Abroad*, 26.

38. Fussell, *Abroad*, 30.

39. Scott Borchert, *Republic of Detours* (New York: Farrar, Straus and Giroux, 2021), 4.

40. Wendy Griswold, *American Guides* (Chicago: University of Chicago Press, 2016), 4.

41. Griswold, 4, xiii.

42. Griswold, 251.

43. Quoted in Daniel S. Gross, "The American Guide Series," *Arizona Quarterly* 62, no. 1 (2006): 92.

44. Richard Wright, "Transcontinental," in Michel Fabre, *The World of Richard Wright* (New York: University of Mississippi Press, 1985), 246.

45. Wright, "Transcontinental," 243, 244.

46. Wright, "Transcontinental," 244–45.

47. Wright, "Transcontinental," 242, 243, 245.

48. See Nathaniel Mills, *Ragged Revolutionaries* (Amherst: University of Massachusetts Press, 2017), 56–57.

49. Jerre Mangione, *The Dream and the Deal* (Syracuse, NY: Syracuse University Press, 1973), 88.

50. Susan Rubenstein DeMasi, *Henry Alsberg* (Jefferson, NC: McFarland, 2016), 95.

51. Maryemma Graham quoted in Kevin Nance, "Roosevelt's Writers," *Poets & Writers*, July 1, 2010, par. 6; Thadious M. Davis, "Becoming Richard Wright," in *Richard Wright*, ed. Alice Mikal Craven and William E. Dow (New York: Palgrave Macmillan, 2011), 83–100. For a valuable study of how the FWP enabled later novels like Ralph Ellison's *Invisible Man* (1950) and Margaret Walker's *Jubilee* (1966), see Sara Rutkowski, *Literary Legacies of the Federal Writers' Project* (New York: Palgrave Macmillan, 2017).

52. See Christine Bold, *The WPA Guides* (Jackson: University of Mississippi Press, 1999).

53. For an account of Sterling Brown and the FWP, see Evan Kindley, *Poet-Critics and the Administration of Culture* (Cambridge, MA: Harvard University Press, 2017), 85–108.

54. Mindy J. Morgan, "Native American Communities and the Federal Writers' Project, 1935–1941," *American Indian Quarterly* 29, no. 1–2 (2005): 62.

55. Morgan, 77.

56. David Hollinger, *Postethnic America*, revised edition (New York: Basic Books, 2006), 94.

57. Hollinger, 116.

58. See Slavoj Žižek, "Multiculturalism, or, the Cultural Logic of Multinational Capitalism," *New Left Review* 225 (1997), 28–51; Jodi Melamed, "The Spirit of Neoliberalism: From Racial Liberalism to Neoliberal Multiculturalism," *Social Text* 24, no. 4 (2006): 1–24; Nikhil Pal Singh, "Culture/Wars," *American Quarterly* 50, no. 3 (1998): 471–522.

59. Quoted in James T. Kloppenberg, *The Virtues of Liberalism* (New York: Oxford University Press, 1998), 141.

60. Kloppenberg, 117.

61. Michel Fabre, *The Unfinished Quest of Richard Wright* (Urbana: University of Illinois Press, 1993), 223.

62. W. E. B. Du Bois, *Worlds of Color* (1961; New York: Oxford University Press, 2007), 117.

63. Du Bois, 142.

64. Du Bois, 113.

65. Du Bois, 144.

66. Du Bois quotes from this campaign speech in *The Autobiography of W. E. B. Du Bois* (1968; New York: Oxford University Press, 2007), 244. For more on this topic, see my "Du Bois's *Dark Princess*, Kautilya's *Arthashastra*, and the Welfare State," *PMLA* 136, no. 1 (2021): 72–87.

67. Doug Rossinow, *Visions of Progress* (Philadelphia: University of Pennsylvania Press, 2008), 103–104.

68. Kloppenberg, 116.

69. Mailer quoted in Schaub, 50.

70. Henry R. Luce, "The American Century," *Life* (January 17, 1941): 62.

71. Luce, 64, 65.

72. Luce, 65.

73. My reading of Turner runs counter to that of Brook Thomas, who draws on the concept of the melting pot to argue that "the frontier allowed for an organic synthesis of a diverse [national] population": "in Turner's imagination, the liminal space of the frontier enables a narrative in which a common human community overcoming cultural differences can be constructed through the progress of history," making for a "space of consensus" ("Turner's 'Frontier Thesis' as a Narrative of Reconstruction," in *Centuries' Ends, Narrative Means*, ed. Robert Newman [Stanford, CA: Stanford University Press, 1996], 125, 127–28, 132).

74. William Appleman Williams, "The Frontier Thesis and American Foreign Policy" (1955), in *A William Appleman Williams Reader*, ed. Henry W. Berger (Chicago: Ivan R. Dee, 1992), 90–91. See also Williams, *The Tragedy of American*

Diplomacy (1959; New York: W. W. Norton, 2009), and Walter LaFeber, *The New Empire* (Ithaca, NY: Cornell University Press, 1963).

75. Williams, "The Frontier Thesis," 90. In this book, I give more weight than Williams does to the reform and regulation of the New Deal, although Williams, too, identifies this as an interruption and complication of America's frontier mentality (98–99).

76. Martin Ridge, "Ray Allen Billington, Western History, and American Exceptionalism," *Pacific Historical Review* 56, no. 4 (1987): 499.

77. Billington quoted in Ridge, 504.

78. Henry Nash Smith, *Virgin Land* (Cambridge, MA: Harvard University Press, 1950), 260.

79. Slotkin, *The Fatal Environment*, xv.

80. Said, *Orientalism* (1978; New York: Vintage, 1994), 351.

81. Tony Tanner, *City of Words: American Fiction 1950–1970* (New York: Harper and Row, 1971), 417.

82. Williams, "The Frontier Thesis," 91.

83. Michael E. Latham, *Modernization as Ideology* (Chapel Hill: University of North Carolina Press, 2000), 4.

84. Jonathan Nashel, "Modernization Theory in Fact and Fiction," in *Cold War Constructions*, ed. Christian G. Appy (Amherst: University of Massachusetts Press, 2000), 153.

85. Daniel Lerner, "The Grocer and the Chief," *Harper's Magazine* (September 1955), 47–56.

86. For Rostow's relationship to Kennedy and the Vietnam War, see David Milne, *America's Rasputin: Walt Rostow and the Vietnam War* (New York: Hill and Wang, 2008).

87. Guy Reynolds, *Apostles of Modernity* (Lincoln: University of Nebraska Press, 2008), 20.

88. John Carlos Rowe, "Edward Said and American Studies," *American Quarterly* 56, no. 1 (2004): 42.

89. Rowe, 40.

90. Said, *Reflections on Exile and Other Essays* (Cambridge, MA: Harvard University Press, 2002), xiii.

91. See Frances Stonor Saunders, *The Cultural Cold War: The CIA and the World of Arts and Letters* (New York: New Press, 1999).

92. Timothy Brennan, *Places of Mind: A Life of Edward Said* (New York: Farrar, Straus and Giroux, 2021), 63.

93. Dickstein, 7.

94. See Arif Dirlik, "Race Talk, Race, and Contemporary Racism," *PMLA* 123, no. 5 (2008): 1363–1379.

95. Said, *Out of Place* (New York: Alfred A. Knopf, 1999), 8.

96. Said, *Out of Place*, 10–11.
97. Said, *Out of Place*, 10.
98. Brennan, *Places*, 24.
99. See David Potter, *People of Plenty* (Chicago: University of Chicago Press, 1954).
100. Said, *Out of Place*, 22–23.
101. Brennan, *Places*, 66.
102. Brennan, *Places*, 65.
103. Said, *Reflections*, 329.
104. Said, *Reflections*, 334.
105. Said, *Reflections*, 336.
106. Said, *Orientalism*, 204.
107. Said, *Orientalism*, 290.
108. Said, *Orientalism*, 301–302, 307.
109. Said, *Orientalism*, 324, 323.
110. Said, *Orientalism*, 336.
111. Said, *Orientalism*, 339.
112. Said, *Reflections*, xi.
113. Said, "Mount Hermon Commencement Speech" (June 2002), 9. The text of this speech was generously shared with me by Timothy Brennan and the Said family. I will return to this important document in the conclusion.
114. For a defense of progressive nationalism in the developing world, see Brennan, "Cosmopolitanism and Internationalism," *New Left Review* 7 (2001): 75–84.
115. Dickstein, 4, 2.
116. Mark McGurl, *The Program Era: Postwar Fiction and the Rise of Creative Writing* (Cambridge, MA: Harvard University Press, 2009), 75.
117. Richard Wright, *Pagan Spain* (1957; New York: Harper Perennial, 2008), 162. Wright uses this significant term only once, in italics.

Chapter One. Ugly Americans

1. John Hellmann, *American Myth and the Legacy of Vietnam* (New York: Columbia University Press, 1986), 36.
2. Quoted in Fabre, *Richard Wright: Books and Writers* (Jackson: University Press of Mississippi, 1990), 93.
3. McGurl, 1; James Angleton quoted in Duncan White, *Cold Warriors* (New York: HarperCollins, 2019), 486.
4. Reynolds, 180, 182.
5. Eugene Burdick, "The Democratic Party," *Holiday* (June 1960): 129.
6. Chris Smith, "Intellectual Action Hero," *California* (June 19, 2010): par. 3.
7. Burdick, "Political Theory and the Voting Studies," in *American Voting Behavior*, ed. Burdick and Arthur J. Brodbeck (New York: Free Press, 1959), 141.

8. Rupert Wilkinson, "Connections with Toughness: The Novels of Eugene Burdick," *Journal of American Studies* 11, no. 2 (1977): 223.

9. Hellmann, 26.

10. C. Wright Mills, *White Collar: The American Middle Classes* (New York: Oxford University Press, 1951), 11.

11. Mills, 12.

12. Mills, 233.

13. David Riesman, "Preface to the 1961 edition," in *The Lonely Crowd: A Study of the Changing American Character* by Riesman, Nathan Glazer, and Reuel Denney (1961; New Haven, CT: Yale University Press, 2001), xlii.

14. Riesman, "Preface," xliii.

15. Riesman, "Preface," lxvi.

16. Riesman, *The Lonely Crowd*, 290–91.

17. Riesman, *The Lonely Crowd*, 300.

18. William J. Lederer and Eugene Burdick, "Salute to Deeds of Non-Ugly Americans," *Life*, December 7, 1959: 148.

19. Quoted in Chris Smith, par. 10.

20. Academic Senate, "Eugene Leonard Burdick, Political Science: Berkeley," *1967, University of California: In Memoriam* (June 1967), par. 9. Web.

21. Lederer, "The Western Pacific," *Saturday Review* (October 17, 1959): 42.

22. Lederer, "The Western Pacific," 57.

23. Klein, 104.

24. Klein, 71.

25. Lederer and Eugene Burdick, *The Ugly American* (1958; New York: W. W. Norton, 1999), 11. Hereafter cited parenthetically as *UA*.

26. Said, *Orientalism*, 325.

27. See William E. Leuchtenburg, "Roosevelt, Norris and the 'Seven Little TVAs,'" *The Journal of Politics* 14, no. 3 (1952): 418–41.

28. David Ekbladh, *The Great American Mission: Modernization and the Construction of an American World Order* (Princeton, NJ: Princeton University Press, 2010), 72.

29. Ekbladh, 59–60.

30. Dwight D. Eisenhower quoted in Robert Rook, "Race, Water, and Foreign Policy: The Tennessee Valley Authority's Global Agenda Meets 'Jim Crow,'" *Diplomatic History* 28, no. 1 (2004), 66.

31. David E. Lilienthal quoted in Rook, 65; Gordon R. Clapp quoted in Rook, 65.

32. Rook, 75.

33. Hellmann, 35.

34. Daniel Immerwahr, "*The Ugly American*: Peeling the Onion of an Iconic Cold War Text," *Journal of American-East Asian Relations* 26 (2019): 10.

35. Joseph Buttinger, "Fact and Fiction on Foreign Aid: A Critique of *The Ugly American*," *Dissent* 6, no. 3 (1959): 347.

36. Irving Howe, "Introduction" to *Beyond the Welfare State*, ed. Howe (New York: Schocken, 1982), 12.

37. Buttinger, 338–39.

38. For a brief account of the New Left and Buttinger, see Todd Gitlin, *The Sixties* (New York: Bantam Books, 1993).

39. McGurl, 186.

40. Immerwahr, 7–8.

41. Immerwahr, 18 n. 13. Lederer's quotation is from James T. Fisher, *Dr. America: The Lives of Thomas A. Dooley, 1927–1961* (Amherst: University of Massachusetts Press, 1997), who provides the information about Dooley that follows.

42. McGurl, 34.

43. McGurl, 4.

44. McGurl, 4.

45. McGurl, 81.

46. McGurl, 15.

47. McGurl, 16, 14.

48. McGurl, 74.

49. McGurl, 408. Greg Barnhisel also says that *The Program Era* endorses Cold War liberalism, but his claim that McGurl partakes in "the defanging of the once-radical modernist movement" is a bit vague ("Modernism and the MFA," *After the Program Era*, ed. Loren Glass [Iowa City: University of Iowa Press, 2016], 56). There were different kinds of interwar modernism, after all, not all of them politically radical.

50. McGurl, 411.

51. Vladimir Nabokov, *Lolita* (1955; New York: Penguin, 2000), 95, 101.

52. John Steinbeck, *Travels with Charley in Search of America* (1962; New York: Penguin Classics, 2000), 103–104.

53. See Benjamin Mangrum, *Land of Tomorrow* (New York: Oxford University Press, 2018).

54. Eric Bennett, "How Iowa Flattened Literature," *Chronicle of Higher Education* (February 10, 2014), 4. Bennett goes into more detail about the Program Era's international influence in "How America Taught the World to Write Small," *Chronicle of Higher Education* (September 28, 2020).

55. Fred Landis, "The CIA and *Reader's Digest*," *Covert Action Information Bulletin* 29 (1988): 41.

56. John Heidenry, *Theirs Was the Kingdom* (New York: W. W. Norton, 1993), 471.

57. Landis, 47.

58. McGurl, 81.

59. Klein, 89.

60. Bennett, *Workshops of Empire: Stegner, Engle, and American Creative Writing during the Cold War* (Iowa City: University of Iowa Press, 2015), 7, 12.

61. Bennett, *Workshops*, 150.

62. Bennett, *Workshops*, 150, 151.

63. Bennett, *Workshops*, 151. I do not think that Hemingway was ever a progressive writer, although he associated with the Left in the later 1930s during the Spanish Civil War (see Milton A. Cohen, "Beleaguered Modernists: Hemingway, Stevens, and the Left," *Key West Hemingway*, ed. Kirk Curnutt and Gail Sinclair [Gainesville: University Press of Florida, 2009], 77–90). In any case, although postwar MFA programs may have routinized his style and caricatured his worldview, Hemingway himself took a Cold War turn, writing a novella that would bore to death many generations of high school students, *The Old Man and the Sea* (1952), as well as becoming a celebrity sponsor for Pan American Airlines, the Parker 51 pen, and the Ringling Bros. and Barnum & Bailey Circus, as well as Burdick's favorite beer, Ballantine Ale. For Hemingway's Cold War ideological turn, see Greif, 122–25; for his endorsements, see Paul Devlin, "For Whom the Shill Toils," *Slate* (October 13, 2006).

64. Fisher, 178.

65. Buttinger, 361, 362.

66. See Noam Chomsky, *Deterring Democracy* (New York: Hill and Wang, 1992).

67. Juliana Spahr, *Du Bois's Telegram* (Cambridge, MA: Harvard University Press, 2018), 85.

68. Denning, *Culture in the Age of Three Worlds* (New York: Verso, 2004), 52.

69. Bennett, "How," 17.

70. Vijay Prashad, foreword to *AfroAsian Encounters,* ed. Heike Raphael-Hernandez and Shannon Steen (New York: New York University Press, 2006), xi.

71. See *Indonesian Notebook: A Sourcebook on Richard Wright and the Bandung Conference*, ed. Brian Russell Roberts and Keith Foulcher (Durham, NC: Duke University Press, 2016).

72. Wright, *The Color Curtain* (1956), in *Three Books from Exile* (New York: Harper-Collins, 2008), 599.

73. Borchert, 294.

74. Stegner quoted in Joseph Darda, *How White Men Won the Culture Wars* (Berkeley: University of California Press, 2021), 71.

75. Maria Damon, "Beat Poetry," in *The Cambridge Companion to Modern American Poetry*, ed. Walter Kalaidjian (New York: Cambridge University Press, 2015), 169.

76. Nancy Grace, "The Beats and Literary History," in *The Cambridge Companion to the Beats*, ed. Steven Belletto (New York: Cambridge University Press, 2017), 68.

77. Jack Kerouac, *On the Road* (1957; New York: Penguin, 2000), 116–17. Hereafter cited parenthetically as *OTR*.

78. See Gerald Nicosia, *Memory Babe* (Berkeley: University of California Press, 1994).

79. Griswold, 113.

80. Hirsch, "Federal Writers' Project," in *American Literature in Transition, 1930–1940*, ed. Ichiro Takayoshi (New York: Cambridge University Press, 2018), 366.

81. Hirsch, "Folklore in the Making: B. A. Botkin," *Journal of American Folklore* 100, no. 395 (1987): 15.

82. Hirsch, *Portrait*, 102.

83. Dickstein, 8.

84. Thomas Frank, "Why Johnny Can't Dissent," in *Commodify Your Dissent: Salvos from The Baffler*, ed. Frank and Matt Weiland (New York: W. W. Norton, 1997), 33.

85. Frank, "Why," 34.

86. Darda, 63.

87. Allen Ginsberg, *Howl and Other Poems* (San Francisco: City Lights Books, 1956), 18.

88. Jason Spangler, "Steinbeck, Kerouac, and the Legacy of the Great Depression," *Studies in the Novel* 40, no. 3 (2008): 310, 308.

89. See Roger Bill, "Traveler or Tourist? Jack Kerouac and the Commodification of Culture," *Dialectical Anthropology* 34, no. 3 (2010): 395–417.

90. For essays that generally take a more positive view of Beat transnationalism, see *The Transnational Beat Generation*, ed. Grace and Jennie Skerl (New York: Palgrave Macmillan, 2012).

91. McGurl, 188.

92. Burdick, "The Politics of the Beat Generation," *Western Political Quarterly* 12, no. 2 (1959): 554.

93. See Sean DiLeonardi, "Improbable Realism: The Postwar American Novel and the Digital Aesthetic" (PhD diss., University of North Carolina, 2021), for a discussion of *The 480*, a novel that criticizes "political machines [that] reduced private citizens to statistical groups" (97).

94. Burdick, "Beat Generation," 555.

95. Max Boot, *The Road Not Taken* (New York: Liveright, 2018), xlvi–xlvii, xlv. Boot is admiring of Lansdale, going on to remark that "Lansdale was a master of political warfare and propaganda whose tactics in fighting global communism could, I propose, usefully be studied by officials today fighting global jihadism" (xlv).

96. Immerwahr, 15.

97. Not only did this conflate two very different countries, but Lansdale may have overestimated his influence on Magsaysay, who owed his position to various local and transnational patronage ties; see Nick Cullather, *Illusions of Influence* (Stanford, CA: Stanford University Press, 1994).

98. Graham Greene, *The Quiet American* (1955; New York: Penguin, 2004), 17.

99. Robert Stone, introduction to Greene, vii–viii.

100. See Kevin Ruane, "The Hidden History of Graham Greene's Vietnam War," *History* 97 (2012): 431–52; White, *Cold Warriors*, 161–78.
101. Robert D. Dean, *Imperial Brotherhood* (Amherst: University of Massachusetts Press, 2001), 173.
102. Greene, 23.
103. Dean, 174.
104. Drinnon, 378.
105. Boot, xliv.
106. Elizabeth Cobbs Hoffman, *All You Need Is Love: The Peace Corps and the Spirit of the 1960s* (Cambridge, MA: Harvard University Press, 2009).
107. Latham, 120.
108. Quoted in Molly Geidel, *Peace Corps Fantasies* (Minneapolis: University of Minnesota Press, 2015), 35.
109. Geidel, 35, 41.
110. Merve Emre, *Paraliterary: The Making of Bad Readers in Postwar America* (Chicago: University of Chicago Press, 2017), 204.
111. Emre, 206.
112. Bishop, *One Art: Letters*, ed. Robert Giroux (New York: Farrar, Straus and Giroux, 1994), 320.

Chapter Two. The Last Frontier

1. Timothy S. Murphy, *Wising Up the Marks: The Amodern William S. Burroughs* (Berkeley: University of California Press, 1997), 4.
2. Dennis McDaniel, "New World Ordure: Burroughs, Globalization and the Grotesque," in *Retaking the Universe: William S. Burroughs in the Age of Globalization*, ed. Davis Schneiderman and Philip Walsh (Sterling, VA: Pluto Press, 2004), 134.
3. Oliver Harris, introduction to *The Yage Letters Redux* by Burroughs and Allen Ginsberg (San Francisco: City Lights Books, 2006), xxx, xxviii.
4. Brian T. Edwards, *Morocco Bound* (Durham, NC: Duke University Press, 2005), 172.
5. William S. Burroughs, *The Letters of William S. Burroughs, 1945–1959*, ed. Harris (New York: Viking, 1993), 63, 103, 196. Hereafter cited parenthetically as *L*.
6. Harris, introduction, xxviii.
7. Edwards, 181, 182.
8. See Brennan, *At Home in the World* (Cambridge, MA: Harvard University Press, 1997).
9. Schneiderman and Walsh, Introduction to *Retaking the Universe*, 2.
10. Burroughs, *The Job*, ed. Daniel Odier (New York: Grove Press, 1969), 7. Here I diverge from Murphy's important study *Wising Up the Marks*, which divides

Burroughs's career into a *modern* phase, in which he criticized state control and
mass culture in Adornoesque fashion; a *postmodern* phase, characterized by
the linguistic experimentation of the cut-up trilogy; and a late *amodern* phase,
which hearkens back to Burroughs's early novel *Queer* (unpublished until 1985)
in its imagination of revolutionary communities. I am unconvinced by the claim
that Burroughs's social critique can be likened to Marxist thought; instead, I
think he is best seen as a radical individualist who was creatively engaged with
global capitalism instead of opposed to it. Perhaps we could say that in his late
work, Burroughs replaced the individualists of his early fiction with teams of
like-minded creative thinkers, artists, and technicians, enjoying a kind of professional liberation outside state regulation. As Burroughs writes of the pirates'
alternative society in the introduction to *Cities of the Red Night* (New York:
Henry Holt, 1981): "Imagine such a movement on a world-wide scale [in the
1700s]. . . . Any man would have the right to settle in any area of his choosing.
The land would belong to those who used it. No white-man boss, no Pukka
Sahib, no Patrons, no colonists. The escalation of mass production and concen-
tration of population in urban areas would be halted, for who would work in
their factories and buy their products when he could live from the fields and the
sea and the lakes and the rivers in areas of unbelievable plenty?" (xiv). This is not
Marxism but rather the "safety valve" theory, an American theory much older
than Turner, which Burroughs pitches at a global level.

11. Robin Lydenberg, *Word Cultures* (Urbana: University of Illinois Press, 1987), 52;
Tanner, 140.

12. Mary McCarthy, *The Writing on the Wall and Other Literary Essays* (New York:
Harcourt, 1970), 42.

13. Fussell, *Abroad*, 39.

14. Ginsberg, *The Yage Letters Redux*, 101, 105.

15. Burroughs, *The Yage Letters Redux*, 50, 52.

16. Kerouac, 144.

17. Quoted in Barry Miles, *Call Me Burroughs: A Life* (New York: Hachette, 2013),
52. Burroughs later mocked the New Deal in his short story "Roosevelt after
Inauguration" (1953), in which Roosevelt "appeared on the White House balcony
dressed in the purple robes of a Roman emperor" and proceeds to appoint
"hoodlums and riff raff of the vilest calibre" to "the highest offices of the land"
(*Roosevelt after Inauguration* [New York: Fuck You Press, 1964], 4, 5–6). When
the Supreme Court opposes his legislation, Roosevelt "forced that august body
. . . to submit to intercourse with a purple assed baboon, so that venerable, honored men surrendered themselves to the embraces of a lecherous snarling simian,
while Roosevelt and his strumpet wife and the venerable brown nose Harry
Hopkins, smoking a communal hookah of hashish, watch the lamentable sight
with cackles of obscene laughter" (8). As the story goes on, Roosevelt seems to

become one of Burroughs's antiheroes, somewhat like Benway—an agent of disruption instead of a force of order. Although obviously meant to be comical, the story has disturbing undertones, serving as an obscene counterpoint to Du Bois's endorsement of Roosevelt, Hopkins, and the New Deal in *Worlds of Color*.

18. Rob Johnson, *The Lost Years of William S. Burroughs* (College Station: Texas A&M University Press, 2006), 61, 78.

19. Johnson, 103–104, 107–108.

20. Burroughs, *Naked Lunch* (1957; New York: Grove Press, 1992), 121–22. Hereafter cited parenthetically as *NL*.

21. Johnson, 17.

22. Johnson, 162.

23. Fussell, *Abroad*, 42.

24. Ted Morgan, *Literary Outlaw* (1988; New York: W. W. Norton, 2012), 65.

25. Morgan, 237.

26. Burroughs, *Queer* (New York: Viking, 1985), 131–32.

27. Morgan, 262, 253.

28. McCarthy, 42.

29. Harris, *William Burroughs and the Secret of Fascination* (Carbondale: Southern Illinois University Press, 2003), 19.

30. Murphy, 73.

31. Lydenberg, 69; Murphy, 4.

32. Seán Burke, introduction to *Authorship: From Plato to the Postmodern*, ed. Burke (Edinburgh: Edinburgh University Press, 1995), xix.

33. MacCannell, *The Tourist*, 155. Hereafter cited parenthetically as *T*.

34. Jonathan Culler, "The Semiotics of Tourism," in *Framing the Sign* (Oxford: Blackwell, 1988), 155.

35. See Ferdinand de Saussure, *Course in General Linguistics*, trans. Wade Baskin (New York: McGraw-Hill, 1959), 7–20.

36. Michael Clune, *American Literature and the Free Market, 1945–2000* (New York: Cambridge University Press, 2010), 96.

37. Burroughs, "My Purpose Is to Write for the Space Age," in *William S. Burroughs at the Front*, ed. Jennie Skerl and Robin Lydenberg (Carbondale: Southern Illinois University Press, 1991), 266.

38. Clune, 102.

39. Clune, 102, 96.

40. See Roland Barthes, *Mythologies* (1957), trans. Annette Lavers (London: Paladin, 1972).

41. Burroughs, "The Art of Fiction XXXVI," *Paris Review* 35 (1965), 30.

42. Timothy Melley, *Empire of Conspiracy* (Ithaca, NY: Cornell University Press, 2000), 4.

43. Burroughs, "The Art," 28.

44. See Melley, 7–16.
45. Homi Bhabha, *The Location of Culture* (New York: Routledge, 2004), 54, 55.
46. Burroughs, "My Purpose," 266.
47. Burroughs, *The Yage Letters*, 50.
48. Murphy discusses Burroughs's relation to this movement in "William S. Burroughs among the Situationists" in Schneiderman and Walsh, 29–57.
49. Guy Debord, *The Society of the Spectacle*, trans. Donald Nicholson-Smith (New York: Zone, 1994), 24.
50. Benway performed this subversive role throughout his career, which extends from "Twilight's Last Gleaming," where he performs surgery while smoking a cigarette (this story was written in 1938, although not published until 1964 in *Nova Express*), to his anachronistic advisory visit to the pirate-frontiersmen in *Cities of the Red Night* (104).
51. Morgan, 268.
52. Culler, 155.
53. Edwards, 171; Luce quoted in Edwards, 3.
54. Edwards, 179.
55. Limerick, *The Legacy of Conquest* (New York: W. W. Norton, 1987), 44–45.
56. Burroughs, *The Soft Machine* (1961), restored edition, ed. Harris (New York: Grove Press, 2014). Hereafter cited parenthetically as *SM*.
57. Greg A. Mullins, *Colonial Affairs: Bowles, Burroughs, and Chester Write Tangier* (Madison: University of Wisconsin Press, 2002), 69.
58. Pratt, *Imperial Eyes*, 7.
59. Said, *Culture and Imperialism*, 54.
60. Frantz Fanon, *The Wretched of the Earth*, trans. Richard Philcox (1961; New York: Grove Press, 2004), 144.
61. Burroughs, *The Job*, 28.
62. Burroughs, "The Art," 35.
63. Burroughs, *Nova Express* (New York: Grove Press, 1964), 22. Hereafter cited parenthetically.
64. Lydenberg, *Word Cultures* 113; Fernand Braudel quoted in Thomas J. McCormick, *America's Half-Century* (Baltimore: Johns Hopkins University Press, 1995), 1.
65. Loren Glass, "Still Dirty after All These Years," *Naked Lunch @ 50: Anniversary Essays*, ed. Oliver Harris and Ian MacFadyen (Carbondale: Southern Illinois University Press, 2009), 179.
66. David Harvey, *The Condition of Postmodernity* (Oxford: Blackwell, 1990), 156.
67. Frederic Jameson, *Postmodernism* (Durham: Duke University Press, 1991), 298.
68. Jameson, 298.
69. Jameson, 298–99.
70. Jameson, 5.
71. Burroughs, "The Art," 29.

72. Quoted in David Banash, "From Advertising to the Avant-Garde," *Postmodern Culture* 14, no. 2 (2004): par. 30.

73. Belletto, *The Beats* (New York: Cambridge University Press, 2020), 84–85.

Chapter Three. To Jerusalem and Back with Huckleberry Finn

1. Saul Bellow quoted in James Atlas, "Chicago's Grumpy Guru," *New York Times Magazine*, January 3, 1988.

2. Carol R. Smith, "The Jewish Atlantic—The Deployment of Blackness in Saul Bellow," *Saul Bellow Journal* 16.2–17.2 (2000): 256.

3. Lee Siegel quoted in David Brauner, "Bellow's Short Fiction," in *The Cambridge Companion to Saul Bellow*, ed. Victoria Aarons (New York: Cambridge University Press, 2017), 159.

4. James Clifford, "Traveling Cultures," in *Cultural Studies*, ed. Lawrence Grossberg, Cary Nelson, and Paula A. Treichler (New York: Routledge, 1992), 97.

5. Saul Bellow, *Henderson the Rain King* (New York: Viking, 1959), 281. Hereafter cited parenthetically as *H*.

6. Bellow, "Looking for Mr. Green," in *Mosby's Memoirs and Other Stories* (New York: Viking, 1968), 90. Hereafter cited parenthetically.

7. Greif, 164.

8. Quoted in Zachary Leader, *The Life of Saul Bellow: 1915–1964* (New York: Alfred A. Knopf, 2015), 200.

9. Isaac Rosenfeld and Bellow, "Der shir hashirim fun Mendl Pumshtok," trans. Barbara Mann, *The Princeton University Library Chronicle* 63, no. 1–2 (2002), 24, 25.

10. Quoted in Judie Newman, "Trotskyism in the Early Work of Saul Bellow," in *A Political Companion to Saul Bellow*, ed. Gloria L. Cronin and Lee Trepanier (Lexington: University Press of Kentucky, 2013), 10.

11. Quoted in Mangione, 95.

12. Atlas, *Bellow* (New York: Modern Library, 2000), 66.

13. Bellow, "In the Days of Mr. Roosevelt," in *It All Adds Up* (New York: Viking, 1994), 28–29.

14. Quoted in David Taylor, 199.

15. See Leader, 231–32.

16. Atlas, *Bellow*, 76.

17. Atlas, *Bellow*, 79.

18. Bellow, *Dangling Man* (1944; New York: Penguin, 1996), 159.

19. Bellow, *The Adventures of Augie March* (1953; New York: Penguin, 2001), 338.

20. Bellow, *Augie*, 569.

21. Hitchens, "The Great American Augie," in Bellow, *Augie*, xvi–xvii.

22. Bellow, "Papuans and Zulus" (1994), in *There Is Simply Too Much to Think About*, ed. Benjamin Taylor (New York: Viking, 2015), 408.

23. See John Cullen Gruesser, *White on Black: Contemporary Literature about*

Africa (Urbana: University of Illinois Press, 1992), and Daniel Lamont, "'A Dark and Empty Continent': The Representation of Africa in Saul Bellow's *Henderson the Rain King*," *Saul Bellow Journal* 16.2–17.2 (2000): 129–49.

24. Newman discusses Bellow's later short story "Cousins" in relation to Franz Boas in "Saul Bellow and Social Anthropology," in *Saul Bellow at Seventy-five*, ed. Gerhard Bach (Tübingen: Gunter Narr Verlag, 1991), 137–49.

25. See Eusebio Rodrigues, "Bellow's Africa," *American Literature* 43, no. 2 (1971): 242–56.

26. Said, "Representing the Colonized: Anthropology's Interlocutors," in *Reflections on Exile*, 307–308.

27. See Robert J. C. Young, *Colonial Desire* (New York: Routledge, 1995), 45–50.

28. Chinua Achebe, "An Image of Africa: Racism in Conrad's *Heart of Darkness*," in Joseph Conrad, *Heart of Darkness*, ed. Paul B. Armstrong (New York: Norton, 2006), 338.

29. See Peter Edgerly Firchow, "Race, Ethnicity, Nationality, Empire," in *Heart of Darkness*, 233–41.

30. As Herskovits wrote in an intellectual biography of his mentor, "Evolutionism arose with the expanding universe of knowledge in Europe, when the conquest of the nonliterate world afforded what was accepted as proof positive of the cultural superiority of the peoples who had devised the means to impose their rule on the diverse societies that the voyages of the preceding four centuries had discovered" (*Franz Boas* [New York: Scribner's, 1953], 51).

31. Herskovits, *Franz Boas*, 57.

32. See Herskovits, *The Myth of the Negro Past* (New York: Harper and Brothers, 1941).

33. See Jerry Gershenhorn's intellectual biography *Melville J. Herskovits and the Racial Politics of Knowledge* (Lincoln: University of Nebraska Press, 2004), 201–29. As Gershenhorn notes, "Herskovits supported American aid for African economic development but with the important proviso that African development should be based on African values with African involvement in decision-making" (219).

34. William G. Martin and Michael O. West, "The Ascent, Triumph, and Disintegration of the Africanist Enterprise, USA," in *Out of One, Many Africas*, ed. Martin and West (Urbana: University of Illinois Press, 1999), 85.

35. See Henry Louis Gates Jr., *The Signifying Monkey: A Theory of African-American Literary Criticism* (New York: Oxford University Press, 1988), xxiii, 15, 26–28, 259–62.

36. See Herskovits, *Cultural Relativism* (New York: Random House, 1972), xxiv.

37. Quoted in Atlas, *Bellow*, 49.

38. Atlas, *Bellow*, 50.

39. Sukhbir Singh, "The Political Satire in *Henderson the Rain King*," *Saul Bellow Journal* 18, no. 2 (2002): 25.

40. Herskovits, *Cultural Relativism*, 56.

41. Conrad, 48.

42. See Ruth Miller, *Saul Bellow: A Biography of the Imagination* (New York: St. Martin's Press, 1991), 107.

43. Bellow, "The Future of Fiction," in *To the Young Writer: Hopwood Lectures*, ed. A. L. Bader (Ann Arbor: University of Michigan Press, 1965), 137.

44. See Jurca.

45. Leader, 488.

46. Bellow quoted in Leader, 762 n. 9.

47. Bellow, "Leaving the Yellow House," in *Mosby's Memoirs*, 25.

48. Atlas, 273.

49. Quoted in Rodrigues, "Bellow's Africa," 243.

50. Toni Morrison, *Playing in the Dark* (Cambridge, MA: Harvard University Press, 1992), 57, 56.

51. Morrison, 59.

52. Steven Gould Axelrod, "The Jewishness of Bellow's Henderson," *American Literature* 47, no. 3 (1975): 441.

53. Daniel Fuchs, *Saul Bellow: Vision and Revision* (Durham, NC: Duke University Press, 1984), 117.

54. Bellow quoted in Leader, 484.

55. Bellow, "Illinois Journey," in *It All Adds Up*, 203.

56. Bellow, "Illinois Journey," 203–204.

57. Bellow, "Illinois Journey," 204–205.

58. Bellow, "Illinois Journey," 205.

59. Leslie Fiedler, "Come Back to the Raft Ag'in, Huck Honey!," *Partisan Review* 15, no. 6 (1948), 667.

60. Fiedler, 665, 667.

61. Fiedler, 670.

62. Fiedler, 671.

63. See Rodrigues, "Reichianism in *Henderson the Rain King*," *Criticism* 15, no. 3 (1973): 212–33. For readings of Dahfu that follow that of Rodrigues, see Newman, *Saul Bellow and History* (New York: St. Martin's Press, 1984), 69–94, and Cronin, "*Henderson the Rain King*," in *Saul Bellow in the 1980s*, ed. Cronin and L. H. Goldman (East Lansing: Michigan State University Press, 1989), 191–99. Atlas calls Dahfu a fictional rendering of Chester Raphael, a Reichian who trained Bellow in the 1940s; see *Bellow*, 272.

64. Atlas, *Bellow*, 162.

65. Atlas, *Bellow*, 88.

66. Quoted in Atlas, *Bellow*, 301.

67. Leader, 488.

68. Clifford, "Traveling Cultures," 106.

69. Fuchs, 111.

70. Bellow, "Deep Readers of the World, Beware!" (1959), in *There Is Simply Too Much to Think About*, 95.
71. Miller, 105.
72. Sean Homer, *Jacques Lacan* (New York: Routledge, 2005), 65.
73. Bhabha, 60, 252.
74. Kaplan, "Left Alone with America," 17.
75. Axelrod, 443.
76. Eberhard Alsen, *Romantic Postmodernism in American Fiction* (Atlanta: Rodopi, 1996), 49.
77. See Foley, *Wrestling with the Left* (Durham, NC: Duke University Press, 2010).
78. Brennan, *At Home in the World*, 17.
79. Frank D. McConnell, *Four Postwar American Novelists* (Chicago: University of Chicago Press, 1977), 35.
80. Jonathan Freedman, *The Temple of Culture: Assimilation and Anti-Semitism in Literary Anglo-America* (New York: Oxford University Press, 2000), 220, 218.
81. Terry A. Cooney, *The Rise of the New York Intellectuals:* Partisan Review *and Its Circle* (Madison: University of Wisconsin Press, 1986), 7, 8.
82. McConnell, 7.
83. Smith, 266.
84. Smith, 275.
85. Smith, 275; Alan L. Berger, "Bellow's Post-War America and the American Jewish Diaspora," in Aarons, *Cambridge Companion*, 82.
86. Bellow, *Mr. Sammler's Planet* (New York: Viking, 1970), 81–82. Hereafter cited parenthetically.
87. Emily Miller Budick, "The Place of Israel in American Writing: Reflections on Saul Bellow's *To Jerusalem and Back*," *South Central Review* 8, no. 1 (1991): 59.
88. Bellow, *To Jerusalem and Back* (New York: Viking, 1976), 89.
89. Bellow, *To Jerusalem*, 135–36.
90. Bellow, *To Jerusalem*, 146.
91. Bellow, *To Jerusalem*, 46.
92. Bellow, *To Jerusalem*, 46.
93. Leader, *The Life of Saul Bellow, 1965–2005* (New York: Alfred A. Knopf, 2018), 224.
94. Bellow, "The Six-Day War," in *It All Adds Up*, 215.
95. Bellow, "The Six-Day War," 209.
96. Quoted in Atlas, 411.

Chapter Four. The Imperial Eyes of the Outsider

1. Adrienne Rich, "The Eye of the Outsider," in *Blood, Bread, and Poetry* (New York: W. W. Norton, 1986), 127.
2. Langdon Hammer, "The New Elizabeth Bishop," *Yale Review* 82, no. 1 (1994): 135.

3. Gillian White, "Words in Air and 'Space' in Art," *Elizabeth Bishop in the 21st Century*, ed. Angus Cleghorn, Bethany Hicok, and Thomas Travisano (Charlottesville: University of Virginia Press, 2012), 261; Siobhan Phillips, "Bishop's Correspondence," *The Cambridge Companion to Elizabeth Bishop*, ed. Cleghorn and Jonathan Ellis (New York: Cambridge University Press, 2014), 166; Cleghorn, "The Politics of Editing Bishop's 1962 *Brazil* Volume for Life World Library," *Berfrois* (September 20, 2011): par. 4 (web).

4. Hicok, *Elizabeth Bishop's Brazil* (Charlottesville: University of Virginia Press, 2016), 113, 49.

5. As Travisano notes, the material "has vastly expanded her published oeuvre and established Bishop not only as a surprisingly wide-ranging and prolific poet, and as a deft and original prose writer, but also as one of the most brilliant and entertaining letter writers in the Language" ("Bishop and Biography," *Cambridge Companion*, 24). Indeed, instead of a poet who was reticent and shy, we have one who is confident and verbose, yet this allows us to provide a more complex account of Bishop's relationship to global power structures.

6. Brett C. Millier, "The Drafts of Elizabeth Bishop's 'One Art,'" *Elizabeth Bishop: The Geography of Gender*, ed. Marilyn May Lombardi (Charlottesville: University Press of Virginia, 1993), 241.

7. Elizabeth Bishop, *Poems, Prose, and Letters*, ed. Robert Giroux and Lloyd Schwartz (New York: Library of America, 2008), 167. Hereafter cited parenthetically as *PPL*.

8. Jeffrey Gray, *Mastery's End: Travel and Postwar American Poetry* (Athens: University of Georgia Press, 2005), 24–25.

9. Helen Vendler, "The Poems of Elizabeth Bishop," *Critical Inquiry* 13 (Summer 1987): 829.

10. In an essay on Bishop's "lesbian poetics," David R. Jarraway points to "the positive effects of mother loss, especially to the strong sense of independence, mobility, and freedom such separation can instill in the young child" ("'O Canada!': The Spectral Lesbian Poetics of Elizabeth Bishop," *PMLA* 113, no. 2 [1998]: 246).

11. Axelrod, "Bishop, History, and Politics," *Cambridge Companion*, 45–46.

12. John Lowney provides detail regarding Bishop's New Deal context in Key West, but he sees this context as a backdrop for her "fables of the margins," instead of something that directly influenced her writing (*History, Memory, and the Literary Left* [Iowa City: University of Iowa Press, 2006]: 30).

13. Bishop and Robert Lowell, *Words in Air*, ed. Travisano with Saskia Hamilton (New York: Farrar, Straus and Giroux, 2008), 172. Hereafter cited parenthetically as *WIA*.

14. Betsy Erkkila, "Elizabeth Bishop, Modernism, and the Left," *American Literary History* 8, no. 2 (1996): 285.

15. Michael Warner, Introduction to *Fear of a Queer Planet*, ed. Warner (Minneapolis: University of Minnesota Press, 1993), vii.

16. Barbara Page, "The Key West Notebooks of Elizabeth Bishop," in Lombardi, 197, 201–202.

17. Stephen G. Noll, "When Government Really Mattered," H-Florida, H-Net Reviews (November 2008), par. 1.

18. Elmer Davis, "New World Symphony, with a Few Sour Notes," *Harper's* 170 (May 1935), 649.

19. Cleghorn, "Bishop's 'Wiring Fused,'" in Cleghorn, Hicok, and Travisano, 80.

20. Bishop, *One Art*, 89. Hereafter cited parenthetically as *OA*.

21. Durward Long, "Key West and the New Deal, 1934–1936," *The Florida Historical Quarterly* 46, no. 3 (1968), 212.

22. "New Deal Awakens Key West," *The New York Times* 2 May 1937, pg. II_R02.

23. Long, 215.

24. Bishop quoted in Ashley Brown, "An Interview with Elizabeth Bishop" (1966), in Lloyd Schwartz and Sybil P. Estess, eds., *Elizabeth Bishop and Her Art* (Ann Arbor: University of Michigan Press, 1983), 299.

25. Eleanor Cook, *Elizabeth Bishop at Work* (Cambridge, MA: Harvard University Press, 2016), 78, 76.

26. Millier, *Elizabeth Bishop: Life and the Memory of It* (Berkeley: University of California Press, 1993), 114. Hereafter cited parenthetically as *M*.

27. Nick Taylor, *American-Made* (New York: Bantam Books, 2008), 292. This is not to say that Moore's politics were directly equivalent to Bishop's, since Moore had a generally negative attitude toward the WPA and Roosevelt. I suggest that a subtle conflict between Bishop and Moore was long in the making before it broke out openly over "Roosters."

28. Susannah L. Hollister, "Elizabeth Bishop's Geographic Feeling," *Twentieth-Century Literature* 58, no. 3 (2012), 399.

29. Davis, 646.

30. Here I refer to a progressive social Keynesianism that can be allied with substantial reform, as opposed to the postwar Keynesian macroeconomic policy that evaded such reform (see Kloppenberg 116, 141).

31. Quoted in Dan Monroe, "Hemingway, the Left, and Key West," in Curnutt and Sinclair, 95.

32. E. Stone Shiflet and Curnutt, "Letters and Literary Tourism," in Curnutt and Sinclair, 227.

33. Monroe, 96.

34. Maureen Ogle, *Key West* (University of Florida Press, 2003), 152–53.

35. Ogle, 186.

36. David Kurnick, "Is There a Gay Literature of Poverty?" *Politics/Letters* (March 2, 2018): par. 5 (web).

37. For more detail on this relationship, see my "Elizabeth Bishop and the New Deal: Queer Poetics and the Welfare State in Key West," *Twentieth-Century Literature* 68, no. 2 (2022): 199–224.

38. Betty Friedan, *The Feminine Mystique* (New York: W. W. Norton, 2013), 337.

39. Bishop, *Prose*, ed. Schwartz (New York: Farrar, Straus and Giroux, 2011), 54. Hereafter cited parenthetically as *Pr*.

40. Judith Butler, *Gender Trouble* (New York: Routledge, 2014), 44.

41. White, 256, 257.

42. For the New York Intellectuals, see Andrew Ross, *No Respect: Intellectuals and Popular Culture* (New York: Routledge, 1989). Hicok has shown that in a Brazilian context, Bishop had an "almost obsessional interest in the car and the road," and even compares her to Jack Kerouac (*Brazil*, 40).

43. Qtd. in Lombardi, Prologue, *The Geography of Gender*: 1.

44. Hicok, "Elizabeth Bishop's 'Queer Birds': Vassar, *Con Spirito*, and the Romance of Female Community," *Contemporary Literature* 40, no. 2 (1999): 287, 307–308.

45. Hicok, "Queer Birds," 299.

46. Fiona Green, "Elizabeth Bishop in Brazil and the *New Yorker*," *Journal of American Studies* 46, no. 4 (2012): 813.

47. Hicok, *Brazil*, 68.

48. Maria Teresa Machado, "Elizabeth Bishop's Translation of *The Diary of 'Helena Morley,'*" in *The Art of Elizabeth Bishop*, ed. Sandra Regina Goulart Almeida, Glaucia Renate Goncalves, and Eliana Lourenco de Lima Reis (Belo Horizonte: Editora UFMG, 2002), 125.

49. Jonathan Arac, Huckleberry Finn *as Idol and Target* (Madison: University of Wisconsin Press, 1997), 21.

50. Arac, 21.

51. Fiedler, 667.

52. Fiedler, 671; Hicok, *Brazil*, 70.

53. Fiedler, 666.

54. Thomas E. Skidmore, *Politics in Brazil, 1930–1964* (New York: Oxford University Press, 1967), 184.

55. Cleghorn, Hicok, and Travisano, "Introduction," *Elizabeth Bishop in the 21st Century*, 2.

56. Raul Brunini qtd. in Bryan McCann, "Carlos Lacerda: The Rise and Fall of a Middle-Class Populist in 1950s Brazil," *Hispanic American Historical Review* 83, no. 4 (2003): 681.

57. McCann, 668, 666.

58. McCann, 662.

59. Skidmore, *Politics*, 87.

60. McCann, 682.

61. McCann, 675, 683–84.

62. Bishop, *Elizabeth Bishop and* The New Yorker: *The Complete Correspondence*, ed. Joelle Biele (New York: Farrar, Straus and Giroux, 2011), 123.

63. Skidmore, *Politics*, 87–88.

64. Robert M. Levine, *Father of the Poor?: Vargas and His Era* (New York: Cambridge University Press, 1998), 89, 88.

65. Axelrod, "Bishop, History, and Politics," 45–46.

66. See Victoria Harrison, *Elizabeth Bishop's Poetics of Intimacy* (New York: Cambridge University Press, 1993), 145.

67. McCann, 688.

68. Quoted in McCann, 690.

69. McCann, 690.

70. James C. Scott, *Seeing Like a State: How Certain Schemes to Improve the Human Condition Have Failed* (New Haven, CT: Yale University Press, 1998). Hereafter cited parenthetically.

71. Axelrod, "Elizabeth Bishop and Containment Policy," *American Literature* 75, no. 4 (2003): 857.

72. Axelrod, "Containment," 858.

73. Axelrod, "Containment," 853, 856.

74. Axelrod, "Containment," 856.

75. John DeWitt, "The Alliance for Progress: Economic Warfare in Brazil (1962–1964)," *Journal of Third World Studies* 26, no. 1 (2009).

76. Saunders, 292.

77. Latham, 74, 75.

78. Latham, 99.

79. See Michael Augspurger, "Archibald MacLeish and Professional Leadership," *College Literature* 36, no. 4 (2009): 1–24.

80. Phillips, "Bishop's Correspondence," 166.

81. Phillips, 166.

82. Hicok, *Brazil*, 117.

83. After the resignation of his predecessor in 1961, Goulart took office under a parliamentary system, but held a plebiscite in 1963 in which he was overwhelmingly given presidential powers.

84. Skidmore, *The Politics of Military Rule in Brazil, 1964–85* (New York: Oxford University Press, 1988), 24, 25.

85. In 2013, Goulart's remains were exhumed to find out if he had been poisoned or died of natural causes; see Vincent Bevins, "Brazil Exhumes Remains of Leftist President Deposed in 1964 Coup," *Los Angeles Times*, November 14, 2013.

86. See Phyllis R. Parker, *Brazil and the Quiet Intervention, 1964* (Austin: University of Texas Press, 1979).

87. Rich, 133.

88. Rich, 127.

89. Caetano Veloso, *Tropical Truth*, trans. Isabel de Sena (New York: Alfred A. Knopf, 2002), 309. Hereafter cited parenthetically.

90. Cleghorn, "The Politics of Editing Bishop's 1962 *Brazil* Volume for Life World Library," *Berfrois* (September 20, 2011): par. 4 (web).

91. Cleghorn, par. 3, 6.

92. Latham, 91.

93. Carmen L. Oliveira, *Rare and Commonplace Flowers*, trans. Neil K. Besner (New Brunswick, NJ: Rutgers University Press, 2003), 128.

94. Jacqueline Vaught Brogan's insightful analysis of "The Burglar of Babylon" is a case in point. The poem may indeed be trying to show that "society and its scripting of situations . . . is the actual 'criminal,'" as she says in "Naming the Thief in 'Babylon,'" *Contemporary Literature* 42, no. 3 (2001): 522. But the poem is best read as another attack upon "the old dictator gang" in its focus on the *favelas* (slums) that expanded on the hills of Rio during Vargas's initial tenure (*WIA* 172). "Burglar" thus encourages readers to look beyond tourist brochures, raising awareness of Brazil's vast social inequality, yet it is difficult to see why the poem would criticize the speaker/observer as "a participant in a capitalist structure [Bishop] clearly deplores" (Brogan, 532).

Chapter Five. A Native Son on the Global Frontier

1. Gruesser, *Black on Black: Twentieth-Century African American Writing about Africa* (Lexington: University Press of Kentucky, 2000), 138.

2. Houston A. Baker Jr., *Long Black Song* (Charlottesville: University of Virginia Press, 1972), 2–4.

3. See William Loren Katz, *The Black West* (1971; Golden, Colorado: Fulcrum, 2019); Margaret Washington, "African American History and the Frontier Thesis," *Journal of the Early Republic* 13, no. 2 (1993): 230–41.

4. Wright, *Pagan Spain* (1957; New York: HarperCollins, 1995), 21. Hereafter cited parenthetically as *PS*.

5. McGurl, 411.

6. Walter Prescott Webb, "Ended: 400 Year Boom," *Harper's Magazine* (October 1951): 26. See also *The Great Frontier* (1951; Lincoln: University of Nebraska Press, 1986).

7. Wright, *Black Boy (American Hunger)* (New York: Library of America, 1991), 352.

8. Fabre, *Quest*, 529.

9. Quoted in Hazel Rowley, *Richard Wright* (Chicago: University of Chicago Press, 2001), 17.

10. Fabre, *Quest*, 6.

11. Wright, "Memories of My Grandmother," in *The Man Who Lived Underground* (New York: Library of America, 2021), 171.

12. Ralph Ellison, *Shadow and Act* (New York: Vintage, 1995), 135.

13. Wright, *Black Boy*, 241.

14. Wright, "Blueprint for Negro Writing," in *Richard Wright Reader*, ed. Ellen Wright and Fabre (New York: Da Capo Press, 1978), 47–48. Hereafter cited parenthetically.

15. Kindley, 2–3.

16. In Fabre, *The World of Richard Wright*, 245. Hereafter cited parenthetically as *W*.

17. Rowley, 108, 109.

18. Langston Hughes, *The Big Sea* (New York: Hill and Wang, 1993), 223.

19. See "The Illinois Writers' Project Essays," with an introduction by Dolinar (*Southern Quarterly* 46, no. 2 [2009]: 84–128). The fullest account of Wright's relationship to the FWP is in Margaret Walker, *Richard Wright, Daemonic Genius* (New York: Warner Books, 1988), 68–85. See also Thadious M. Davis, "Becoming Richard Wright."

20. Federal Writers' Project, *New York Panorama* (New York: Random House, 1938), 142, 143, 146.

21. Fabre, *Quest*, 166.

22. Federal Writers' Project, *New York Panorama*, 142–43.

23. See Wright, *Byline, Richard Wright*, ed. Earle V. Bryant (Columbia: University of Missouri Press, 2015).

24. See Vaughn Rasberry, *Race and the Totalitarian Century* (Cambridge, MA: Harvard University Press, 2016), 79–92.

25. Greif, 13. Greif discusses Wright's *The Outsider* (1953) as an example of the discourse (103).

26. Mangione, 245.

27. Jackson, 54.

28. Quoted in Ira Katznelson, *Fear Itself: The New Deal and the Origins of Our Time* (New York: Liveright, 2013), 329.

29. Mangione, 4, 290.

30. DeMasi, 215.

31. McGurl, 21.

32. McGurl, 19.

33. Valerie Smith notes that both Wright in his memoirs, and Bigger in *Native Son*, "rely on their ability to manipulate language and its assumptions—to tell their own stories—as a means of liberating themselves from the plots others impose upon them" (*Self-Discovery and Authority in Afro-American Narrative* [Cambridge, MA: Harvard University Press, 1987], 70).

34. Ellison, 114.

35. Quoted in Jackson, 3.

36. Arnold Rampersad, Introduction to *Native Son*, xi.

37. Wright, *Native Son* (New York: HarperCollins, 2005), 245, 341. Hereafter cited parenthetically by page number as *NS*.

38. Smith, 80.

39. Wright, "Illinois Writer's Project," 92–93.

40. Wright, "Blueprint," 40.

41. James Baldwin, *Collected Essays* (New York: Library of America, 1998), 31. Hereafter cited parenthetically as *B*.

42. Katznelson, *Fear Itself*, 177–78.

43. Quoted in Katznelson, *Fear Itself*, 177.

44. Virginia Whatley Smith, "Down South/Up North: Bigger Thomas's Carceral Societies in *Native Son*," in Virginia Whatley Smith, ed., *Richard Wright: Writing America at Home and from Abroad* (Jackson: University of Mississippi Press, 2016), 37.

45. Virginia Whatley Smith, "Down South," 41.

46. Horace R. Cayton, *Long Old Road* (1965; New York: Routledge, 2017), 183.

47. Cayton, "*12 Million Black Voices* (1941)," in *Richard Wright: Critical Perspectives, Past and Present*. ed. Gates and K. A. Appiah (New York: Amistad, 1993), 26.

48. As Bruce Robbins emphasizes in *Upward Mobility and the Common Good: Toward a Literary History of the Welfare State*, "it is theoretically possible . . . to reconcile the desire for individual success and achievement with sympathy for and from others, with an achievement that somehow touches their welfare as well as one's own" (Princeton, NJ: Princeton University Press, 2007), 34.

49. Szalay, *New Deal Modernism* (Durham, NC: Duke University Press, 2000), 218.

50. See Bennett's *Workshops of Empire*.

51. Alsberg quoted in DeMasi, 146.

52. DeMasi, 192.

53. DeMasi, 215.

54. Quoted in Borchert, 243.

55. Fabre, *Quest*, 223.

56. Quoted in Mangione, 159.

57. Quoted in Rowley, 313.

58. Wright, "Not My People's War," *New Masses* (July 17, 1941): 9.

59. Franklin Roosevelt quoted in Alan Brinkley, *The End of Reform* (New York: Vintage, 1995), 144.

60. Fabre, *Quest*, 245–46.

61. Fabre, *Quest*, 576, 277. This latter effort was foiled by the CP, which had declared Wright persona non grata.

62. William J. Maxwell, *F.B. Eyes* (Princeton, NJ: Princeton University Press, 2015), 17.

63. Quoted in Maxwell, vii.

64. Maxwell, 217.

65. Denning, *Cultural Front*, 398.

66. Denning, *Cultural Front*, 399.

67. Fabre, *Quest*, 337.

68. Walker, *Richard Wright*, 224; Baldwin, "Alas," 262.

69. Ellen Scott, "Blacker than Noir: The Making and Unmaking of Richard Wright's 'Ugly' *Native Son* (1951)," *Adaptation* 6, no. 1 (2012): 93.

70. Scott, 94.

71. Edgardo C. Krebs, "*Native Son*, Lost and Found," *Film Comment*, September–October 2012 (www.filmcomment.com/issue/september-october-2012).

72. *Native Son*, directed by Pierre Chenal (Sono Film, 1951). https://www.kinolorber.com/film/native-son.

73. Quoted in Rowley, 383.

74. *Native Son*, 39:48–39:54.

75. Wright, *12 Million Black Voices* (1941; Philadelphia: Perseus Books, 2008), 146–47.

76. Katznelson, *When Affirmative Action Was White* (New York: W. W. Norton, 2005), 143, 11.

77. *Native Son*, 1:45:47.

78. As Rowley notes, *Native Son* owed its early box office receipts almost entirely to people's curiosity about seeing Wright as Bigger Thomas (394).

79. Virginia Whatley Smith, "African American Travel Literature," in *The Cambridge Companion to American Travel Writing*, ed. Alfred Bendixen and Judith Hamara (New York: Cambridge University Press, 2009), 211.

80. Fussell, *Abroad*, 42.

81. Rowley, 401.

82. Fabre, *Quest*, 347.

83. Anna Shechtman, "'Native Son' and the Cinematic Aspirations of Richard Wright," *New Yorker* April 4, 2019, par. 9 (www.newyorker.com/books/page-turner/native-son-and-the-cinematic-aspirations-of-richard-wright).

84. Rowley, 384.

85. See Gates, "Writing 'Race' and the Difference It Makes," *Critical Inquiry* 12, no. 1 (1985): 1–20.

86. Thy Phu, "Bigger at the Movies: *Sangre Negra* and the Cinematic Projection of *Native Son*," *Black Camera* 2, no. 1 (2010): 49, 55.

87. Phu, 48.

88. Phu, 49.

89. Fabre, *Quest*, 344.

90. See Arthur M. Schlesinger Jr., *The Vital Center* (1949; New Brunswick, NJ: Transaction, 2017).

91. Wright, *White Man, Listen!* (1957), in *Three Books from Exile*, 705.

92. Quoted in Fabre, *Books and Writers* 93.

93. Wright, *Black Power*, in *Three Books from Exile*, 56. Hereafter cited parenthetically as *BP*.

94. See Hoffman, 148–82.

95. Quoted in Gruesser, *Black on Black*, 1. See also Wilson Jeremiah Moses, *Afrotopia* (New York: Cambridge University Press, 1998).

96. Gruesser, *Black on Black*, 7.

97. Gruesser, *Black on Black*, 140–41.

98. Several critics have noted Wright's similarity to Lerner; see Nina Kressner Cobb, "Richard Wright and the Third World," in *Critical Essays on Richard Wright*, ed. Yoshinobu Hakutani (Boston: G. K. Hall, 1982), 228; Rasberry, 321; Reynolds, 17–23. Lerner is singled out for criticism in Said's *Orientalism*, but as I indicated in the introduction, there is a convergence in postwar American models of cosmopolitan selfhood, which would include Said's as well as Lerner's and Wright's.

99. Hemant Shah, *The Production of Modernization: Daniel Lerner, Mass Media, and the Passing of Traditional Society* (Philadelphia: Temple University Press, 2011), 50.

100. Virginia Whatley Smith, "French West Africa," in Virginia Whatley Smith, *Richard Wright's Travel Writing*, 213.

101. Quoted in Pratt, *Imperial Eyes*, 218.

102. Pratt, *Imperial Eyes*, 218. A quarter-century after the publication of *Imperial Eyes*, Pratt's view remains unchanged: "postcolonial travel writers decolonize the self-consistent, authoritative, (white and male) voice of the travel writing convention. . . . Mastery and control cease to drive the text" (Afterword, *The Cambridge Companion to Postcolonial Travel Writing*, ed. Robert Clarke [New York: Cambridge University Press, 2018], 226).

103. Wright, "How," 462.

104. See Ngwarsungu Chiwengo, "Richard Wright's Africa," in Virginia Whatley Smith, *Richard Wright's Travel Writings*, 20–44, for a relation of *Black Power* to the slave narrative genre.

105. Kwame Anthony Appiah, "Wright in the Gold Coast," in Rampersad, ed., *Richard Wright* (Englewood Cliffs, NJ: Prentice-Hall, 1995), 102. For a favorable view of *Black Power* that argues Wright anticipated Nkrumah's undemocratic cult of personality, see Kevin K. Gaines, *African Americans in Ghana* (Chapel Hill: University of North Carolina Press, 2006), 52–68.

106. Manthia Diawara, *In Search of Africa* (Cambridge, MA: Harvard University Press, 1998), 70.

107. Sean McCann, *A Pinnacle of Feeling* (Princeton, NJ: Princeton University Press, 2008), 23.

108. Quoted in Fabre, *Books and Writers*, 73.

109. Franklin Roosevelt quoted in Jefferson Cowie, *The Great Exception: The New Deal and the Limits of American Politics* (Princeton, NJ: Princeton University Press, 2016), 94.

110. Wright quoted in James Campbell, *Middle Passages* (New York: Penguin, 2006), 300–301.

111. Virginia Whatley Smith, "African American Travel Literature," 205.

112. W. W. Rostow, *The Stages of Economic Growth* (1960; Eastford, CT: Martino, 2017), 162.

113. See Wilford, 197–224.

114. María DeGuzmán, *Spain's Long Shadow* (Minneapolis: University of Minnesota Press, 2005), 235–36, 240.

115. See Keneth Kinnamon, "Wright, Hemingway, and the Bullfight," in Virginia Whatley Smith, *Richard Wright's Travel Writings*, 157–64.

116. Bellow, "The Gonzaga Manuscripts," in *Mosby's Memoirs*, 116.

117. Frantz Fanon, *Black Skin, White Masks*, trans. Charles Lam Markmann (1952; New York: Grove Press, 1967), 111–12.

118. Wright, *Pagan Spain* (London: Bodley Head, 1960), 180.

119. For critiques of *Pagan Spain*, see DeGuzmán, 224–41; Nancy Dixon, "Did Richard Wright Get It Wrong? A Spanish Look at *Pagan Spain*," *Mississippi Quarterly* 61, no. 4 (2008): 581–91; Isabel Soto, "Black Atlantic (Dis)Entanglements: Langston Hughes, Richard Wright, and Spain," *Zeitschrift fur Anglistik und Amerikanistik* 65, no. 2 (2017): 212–25.

120. Chris Schmidt-Nowara, "Spain between the Black Atlantic and the Black Legend," *Arizona Journal of Hispanic Cultural Studies* 5 (2001): 152.

121. Charles Reagan Wilson, *Flashes of a Southern Spirit* (Athens: University of Georgia Press, 2011), 193.

122. M. Lynn Weiss, "*Para Usted*: Richard Wright's *Pagan Spain*," in *The Black Columbiad*, ed. Werner Sollors and Maria Diedrichs (Cambridge, MA: Harvard University Press, 1994), 221–22.

123. Quoted in Cobb, "Richard Wright: Individualism Reconsidered," *CLA Journal* 21, no. 3 (1978): 335. As Cobb observes, "This is the question that Wright addressed himself to in his autobiography and it dominated almost all of his writing" (335–36). Cobb briefly notes Wright's affinity with Weber (344), whom I shall discuss below.

124. Carl Sandburg, *Cornhuskers* (New York: Henry Holt, 1918), 11.

125. Walker, *For My People* (1942; New Haven, CT: Yale University Press, 2019), 14. "For My People" originally appeared in *Poetry* magazine in 1937.

126. Mangione, 123–24.

127. Wright quoted in *The Richard Wright Reader*, ed. Fabre and Ellen Wright (New York: Harper and Row, 1978), 110–11.

128. Wright, *White Man, Listen!*, 701, 712.

129. See Max Weber, *The Protestant Ethic and the Spirit of Capitalism* (1904–5), trans. Talcott Parsons (New York: Scribner's, 1976), 95–154.

130. Weber, 181, 182.

131. Wright, *White Man, Listen!*, 722.

132. Wright, *White Man, Listen!*, 727.

133. For a criticism of Wright's celebration of "the jackpot of Enlightenment rationalism," see Gates, "Third World of Theory," *Critical Inquiry* 34, suppl. (2008): S193.

134. Wright, "Memories," 164.
135. Wright, "Memories," 170.
136. Wright, *White Man, Listen!*, 714.
137. Wright, *White Man, Listen!*, 715, 716.
138. Wright, "Memories," 167.
139. Norman Mailer, "The White Negro," *Dissent* (Fall 1957): 278.
140. DeGuzmán, 232–33.
141. Wright, "Memories," 204.
142. Sandburg, 5, 11.
143. Quoted in Fabre, *Books and Writers*, 71.
144. See Wright, "Harlem Spanish Women Come Out of the Kitchen," in *Byline*, 102–104.
145. Dow, "The Literary Journalism of Richard Wright," in Dow and Craven, 241.

Conclusion

1. Kaplan, "'Left Alone with America': The Absence of Empire in the Study of American Culture," in Kaplan and Pease, 21 n. 17.
2. Lawrence Buell, "American Literary Emergence as a Postcolonial Phenomenon," *American Literary History* 4, no. 3 (1992): 417.
3. Buell, "American Literary Emergence," 428.
4. Buell, "American Literary Emergence," 411.
5. See Arjun Appadurai, *Modernity at Large* (Minneapolis: University of Minnesota Press, 1996), 33.
6. Michael Hardt and Antonio Negri, *Empire* (Cambridge, MA: Harvard University Press, 2000), 154. Hereafter cited parenthetically as *E*.
7. For the classic statement on the convergence of the transnational turn with corporate globalization, see Michael Bérubé, "American Studies without Exceptions," *PMLA* 118, no. 1 (2003): 103–13. For an excellent discussion of the welfare state in relation to transnationalism, see Robbins, *Feeling Global: Internationalism in Distress* (New York: New York University Press, 1999), 11–37.
8. Limerick, "Turnerians All," 698.
9. Fernand Braudel quoted in Hardt and Negri, 3.
10. Said, "Commencement June 2002," 9.
11. Said, "Commencement June 2002," 8.
12. Hollinger, 68.
13. Cowie, 7.
14. Cowie, 209, 229.
15. Cowie, 32.

Bibliography

Aarons, Victoria, ed. *The Cambridge Companion to Saul Bellow*. New York: Cambridge University Press, 2017.

Almeida, Sandra Regina Goulart, Glaucia Renate Goncalves, and Eliana Lourenco de Lima Reis, eds. *The Art of Elizabeth Bishop*. Belo Horizonte, Brazil: Editoria UFMG, 2002.

Alsen, Eberhard. *Romantic Postmodernism in American Fiction*. Atlanta: Rodopi, 1996.

Appadurai, Arjun. *Modernity at Large*. Minneapolis: University of Minnesota Press, 1996.

Arac, Jonathan. Huckleberry Finn *as Idol and Target*. Madison: University of Wisconsin Press, 1997.

Ashbery, John. "Second Presentation of Elizabeth Bishop." *World Literature Today* 51, no. 1 (1977): 8–11.

Atlas, James. *Bellow: A Biography*. New York: Random House, 2000.

Atlas, James. "Chicago's Grumpy Guru." *New York Times Magazine*, January 3, 1988.

Augspurger, Michael. "Archibald MacLeish and Professional Leadership." *College Literature* 36, no. 4 (2009): 1–24.

Axelrod, Steven Gould. "Elizabeth Bishop and Containment Policy." *American Literature* 75, no. 4 (2003): 843–67.

Axelrod, Steven Gould. "The Jewishness of Bellow's Henderson." *American Literature* 47, no. 3 (1975): 439–43.

Baker, Houston A., Jr. *Long Black Song*. Charlottesville: University of Virginia Press, 1972.

Baldwin, James. *Collected Essays*. Ed. Toni Morrison. New York: Library of America, 1998.

Banash, David. "From Advertising to the Avant-Garde: Rethinking the Invention of Collage." *Postmodern Culture* 14, no. 2 (2004).

Barnhisel, Greg. "Modernism and the MFA." In *After the Program Era*, ed. Loren Glass, 55–66. Iowa City: University of Iowa Press, 2016.

Barthes, Roland. *Mythologies*. 1957. Trans. Annette Lavers. London: Paladin, 1972.

Belletto, Steven. *The Beats*. New York: Cambridge University Press, 2020.

Bellow, Saul. *The Adventures of Augie March*. 1953. New York: Penguin, 2001.

Bellow, Saul. *Dangling Man*. 1944. New York: Penguin, 1996.

Bellow, Saul. "The Future of Fiction." In *To the Young Writer: Hopwood Lectures.* Ed. A. L. Bader. Ann Arbor: University of Michigan Press, 1965.

Bellow, Saul. *Henderson the Rain King.* New York: Viking, 1959.

Bellow, Saul. *It All Adds Up.* New York: Viking, 1994.

Bellow, Saul. *Mr. Sammler's Planet.* New York: Viking, 1970.

Bellow, Saul. *Mosby's Memoirs and Other Stories.* New York: Viking, 1968.

Bellow, Saul. *There Is Simply Too Much to Think About.* Ed. Benjamin Taylor. New York: Viking, 2015.

Bellow, Saul. *To Jerusalem and Back: A Personal Account.* New York: Viking, 1976.

Bennett, Eric. "How America Taught the World to Write Small." *Chronicle of Higher Education* (September 28, 2020). Web.

Bennett, Eric. "How Iowa Flattened Literature." *Chronicle of Higher Education* (February 10, 2014). Web.

Bennett, Eric. *Workshops of Empire.* Iowa City: University of Iowa Press, 2015.

Benson, Lee. "The Historical Background of Turner's Frontier Essay." *Agricultural History* 25, no. 2 (1951): 59–82.

Berkowitz, Michael. "A 'New Deal' for Leisure: Making Mass Tourism during the Great Depression." In *Being Elsewhere*, ed. Shelley Baranowski and Ellen Furlough, 185–212. Ann Arbor: University of Michigan Press, 2001.

Bérubé, Michael. "American Studies without Exceptions." *PMLA* 118, no. 1 (2003): 103–13.

Bevins, Vincent. "Brazil Exhumes Remains of Leftist President Deposed in 1964 Coup." *Los Angeles Times*, November 14, 2013.

Bhabha, Homi. *The Location of Culture.* New York: Routledge, 2004.

Bill, Roger. "Traveler or Tourist? Jack Kerouac and the Commodification of Culture." *Dialectical Anthropology* 34, no. 3 (2010): 395–417.

Billington, Ray Allen. *Frederick Jackson Turner.* New York: Oxford University Press, 1973.

Bishop, Elizabeth, trans. *The Diary of "Helena Morley."* 1957. New York: Farrar, Straus and Giroux, 1995.

Bishop, Elizabeth. *Elizabeth Bishop and* The New Yorker*: The Complete Correspondence.* Ed. Joelle Biele. New York: Farrar, Straus and Giroux, 2011.

Bishop, Elizabeth. *One Art: Letters.* Ed. Robert Giroux. New York: Farrar, Straus and Giroux, 1994.

Bishop, Elizabeth. *Poems, Prose, and Letters.* Ed. Giroux and Lloyd Schwartz. New York: Library of America, 2008.

Bishop, Elizabeth. *Prose.* Ed. Lloyd Schwartz. New York: Farrar, Straus and Giroux, 2011.

Bishop, Elizabeth, and Robert Lowell. *Words in Air: The Complete Correspondence between Elizabeth Bishop and Robert Lowell.* Ed. Thomas Travisano with Saskia Hamilton. New York: Farrar, Straus and Giroux, 2008.

Bledstein, Burton J. *The Culture of Professionalism*. New York: W. W. Norton, 1976.

Bold, Christine. *The WPA Guides*. Jackson: University Press of Mississippi, 1999.

Boorstin, Daniel. *The Image*. 1962. New York: Vintage, 1992.

Boot, Max. *The Road Not Taken: Edward Lansdale and the American Tragedy in Vietnam*. New York: W. W. Norton, 2018.

Borchert, Scott. *Republic of Detours*. New York: Farrar, Straus and Giroux, 2021.

Brennan, Timothy. *At Home in the World*. Cambridge, MA: Harvard University Press, 1997.

Brennan, Timothy. "Cosmopolitanism and Internationalism." *New Left Review* 7 (2001): 75–84.

Brennan, Timothy. *Places of Mind: A Life of Edward Said*. New York: Farrar, Straus and Giroux, 2021.

Brodkin, Karen. *How Jews Became White Folks and What That Says about Race in America*. New Brunswick, NJ: Rutgers University Press, 1998.

Brogan, Jacqueline Vaught. "Naming the Thief in 'Babylon.'" *Contemporary Literature* 42, no. 3 (2001): 514–34.

Budick, Emily Miller. "The Place of Israel in American Writing: Reflections on Saul Bellow's *To Jerusalem and Back*." *South Central Review* 8, no. 1 (1991): 59–70.

Buell, Lawrence. "American Literary Emergence as a Postcolonial Phenomenon." *American Literary History* 4, no. 3 (1992): 411–42.

Burdick, Eugene. "The Democratic Party." *Holiday* (June 1960): 60–62, 121–29.

Burdick, Eugene. "Political Theory and the Voting Studies." In *American Voting Behavior*, ed. Burdick and Arthur J. Brodbeck, 136–49. New York: Free Press, 1959.

Burdick, Eugene. "The Politics of the Beat Generation." *Western Political Quarterly* 12, no. 2 (1959): 553–55.

Burdick, Eugene. "Rest Camp on Maui." *Harper's Magazine* (July 1946): 83–90.

Burdick, Eugene, and Harvey Wheeler. *Fail-Safe*. New York: McGraw-Hill, 1962.

Burke, Seán. Introduction. *Authorship*. Ed. Burke. Edinburgh: Edinburgh University Press, 1995.

Burroughs, William S. "The Art of Fiction." Interview by Conrad Knickerbocker. *Paris Review* 35 (Fall 1965): 12–49.

Burroughs, William S. *Cities of the Red Night*. New York: Henry Holt, 1981.

Burroughs, William S. "In Search of Yage." In Harris, *William Burroughs and the Secret of Fascination*, 1–53.

Burroughs, William S. *The Job*. Ed. Daniel Odier. New York: Grove Press, 1969.

Burroughs, William S. *The Letters of William S. Burroughs, 1945–1959*. Ed. Oliver Harris. New York: Viking, 1993.

Burroughs, William S. "My Purpose Is to Write for the Space Age." In *William S. Burroughs at the Front*. Ed. Jennie Skerl and Robin Lydenberg, 265–68. Carbondale: Southern Illinois University Press, 1991.

Burroughs, William S. *Naked Lunch*. 1959. New York: Grove Press, 1997.

Burroughs, William S. *Nova Express*. New York: Grove Press, 1964.

Burroughs, William S. *Queer*. New York: Viking, 1985.

Burroughs, William S. *Roosevelt after Inauguration* (1953). New York: Fuck You Press, 1964.

Burroughs, William S. *The Soft Machine*. Restored text. Ed. Oliver Harris. New York: Grove Press, 2014.

Burroughs, William, and Allen Ginsberg. *The Yage Letters Redux*. Ed. Oliver Harris. San Francisco: City Lights Books, 2006.

Butler, Judith. *Gender Trouble*. New York: Routledge, 2014.

Butler, Robert James. "The American Quest for Pure Movement in Bellow's *Henderson the Rain King*." *Journal of Narrative Technique* 14, no. 1 (1984): 44–59.

Buttinger, Joseph. "Fact and Fiction on Foreign Aid: A Critique of *The Ugly American*." *Dissent* 6, no. 3 (Summer 1959): 317–67.

Campbell, James. *Exiled in Paris*. Berkeley: University of California Press, 2003.

Campbell, James T. *Middle Passages*. New York: Penguin, 2006.

Carpio, Glenda R., ed. *The Cambridge Companion to Richard Wright*. New York: Cambridge University Press, 2019.

Cayton, Horace R. *Long Old Road*. 1965. New York: Routledge, 2017.

Chenal, Pierre, director. *Native Son*. Sono Film, 1951. 1 hr., 48 min. https://www.kinolorber.com/film/native-son.

Chomsky, Noam. *Deterring Democracy*. New York: Hill and Wang, 1992.

Cleghorn, Angus. "The Politics of Editing Bishop's 1962 *Brazil* Volume for Life World Library." *Berfrois*, September 20, 2011. Web.

Cleghorn, Angus, and Jonathan Ellis, eds. *The Cambridge Companion to Elizabeth Bishop*. New York: Cambridge University Press, 2014.

Cleghorn, Angus, Bethany Hicok, and Thomas Travisano, eds. *Elizabeth Bishop in the 21st Century*. Charlottesville: University of Virginia Press, 2012.

Clifford, James. "Traveling Cultures." In *Cultural Studies*, ed. Lawrence Grossberg, 96–115. New York: Routledge, 1992.

Clune, Michael. *American Literature and the Free Market, 1945–2000*. New York: Cambridge University Press, 2010.

Cobb, Nina Kressner. "Richard Wright: Individualism Reconsidered." *CLA Journal* 21, no. 3 (1978): 335–54.

Conrad, Joseph. *Heart of Darkness*. Ed. Paul B. Armstrong. New York: Norton, 2006.

Cook, Eleanor. *Elizabeth Bishop at Work*. Cambridge, MA: Harvard University Press, 2016.

Cooney, Terry A. *The Rise of the New York Intellectuals*. Madison: University of Wisconsin Press, 1986.

Cowie, Jefferson. *The Great Exception*. Princeton, NJ: Princeton University Press, 2016.

Craven, Alice Mikal, and William E. Dow, eds. *Richard Wright: New Readings in the 21st Century*. New York: Palgrave Macmillan, 2011.

Cronin, Gloria L., and Lee Trepanier, eds. *A Political Companion to Saul Bellow*. Lexington: University Press of Kentucky, 2013.

Cullather, Nick. *Illusions of Influence*. Stanford, CA: Stanford University Press, 1994.

Culler, Jonathan. *Framing the Sign*. Oxford: Blackwell, 1988.

Curnutt, Kirk, and Gail Sinclair, eds. *Key West Hemingway*. Gainesville: University Press of Florida, 2009.

Darda, Joseph. *How White Men Won the Culture Wars*. Berkeley: University of California Press, 2021.

Davis, Elmer. "New World Symphony, with a Few Sour Notes." *Harper's* 170 (May 1935): 641–52.

Dean, Robert D. *Imperial Brotherhood*. Amherst: University of Massachusetts Press, 2001.

Debord, Guy. *The Society of the Spectacle*. 1967. Trans. Donald Nicholson-Smith. New York: Zone, 1994.

DeGuzmán, María. *Spain's Long Shadow*. Minneapolis: University of Minnesota Press, 2005.

DeMasi, Susan Rubenstein. *Henry Alsberg*. Jefferson, NC: McFarland & Company, 2016.

Denning, Michael. *The Cultural Front*. New York: Verso, 1997.

Denning, Michael. *Culture in the Age of Three Worlds*. New York: Verso, 2004.

De Saussure, Ferdinand. *Course in General Linguistics*. Trans. Wade Baskin. New York: McGraw-Hill, 1959.

DeWitt, John. "The Alliance for Progress." *Journal of Third World Studies* 26, no. 1 (2009): 57–76.

Diawara, Manthia. *In Search of Africa*. Cambridge, MA: Harvard University Press, 1998.

Dickstein, Morris. *Leopards in the Temple*. Cambridge, MA: Harvard University Press, 2002.

DiLeonardi, Sean. "Improbable Realism: The Postwar American Novel and the Digital Aesthetic." PhD diss., University of North Carolina, 2021.

Dolinar, Brian. "Editor's Introduction." *The Negro in Illinois: The WPA Papers*. Urbana: University of Illinois Press, 2013. ix–xliii.

Drinnon, Richard. *Facing West*. Minneapolis: University of Minnesota Press, 1980.

Edwards, Brent Hayes. *The Practice of Diaspora*. Cambridge, MA: Harvard University Press, 2003.

Edwards, Brian T. *Morocco Bound*. Durham, NC: Duke University Press, 2005.

Ehrenreich, Barbara, and John Ehrenreich. "The Professional-Managerial Class." *Between Labor and Capital*. Ed. Pat Walker. Boston: South End Press, 1979. 5–45.

Ekbladh, David. *The Great American Mission*. Princeton, NJ: Princeton University Press, 2010.

Ellison, Ralph. *Shadow and Act.* 1964. New York: Vintage, 1995.

Emre, Merve. *Paraliterary.* Chicago: University of Chicago Press, 2017.

Erkkila, Betsy. "Elizabeth Bishop, Modernism, and the Left." *American Literary History* 8, no. 2 (1996).

Fabre, Michel. *Richard Wright: Books and Writers.* Jackson: University Press of Mississippi, 1990.

Fabre, Michel. *The Unfinished Quest of Richard Wright,* 2nd ed. Urbana: University of Illinois Press, 1993.

Fabre, Michel. *The World of Richard Wright.* Jackson: University Press of Mississippi, 1985.

Fanon, Frantz. *Black Skin, White Masks* (1952). Trans. Charles Lam Markmann. New York: Grove Press, 1967.

Fanon, Frantz. *The Wretched of the Earth* (1961). Trans. Richard Philcox. New York: Grove Press, 2004.

Federal Writers' Project. *American Stuff.* New York: Viking, 1937.

Federal Writers' Project. *A Guide to Key West.* New York: Hastings, 1941.

Federal Writers' Project. *New York Panorama.* New York: Random House, 1938.

Fiedler, Leslie. "Come Back to the Raft Ag'in, Huck Honey!" *Partisan Review* 15, no. 6 (1948): 664–71.

Foley, Barbara. *Wrestling with the Left.* Durham, NC: Duke University Press, 2010.

Foucault, Michel. *Discipline and Punish* (1975). Trans. Alan Sheridan. New York: Vintage, 1995.

Frank, Thomas. *Commodify Your Dissent,* ed. Frank and Matt Weiland. New York: W. W. Norton, 1997.

Frank, Thomas. *The Conquest of Cool.* Chicago: University of Chicago Press, 1997.

Frank, Thomas. *One Market under God.* New York: Anchor, 2001.

Freedman, Jonathan. *The Temple of Culture.* New York: Oxford University Press, 2000.

Friedan, Betty. *The Feminine Mystique.* New York: W. W. Norton, 2013.

Fuchs, Daniel. *Saul Bellow.* Durham, NC: Duke University Press, 1984.

Fussell, Paul. *Abroad.* New York: Oxford University Press, 1980.

Fussell, Paul, ed. *The Norton Book of Travel.* New York: W. W. Norton, 1987.

Gates, Henry Louis, Jr. *The Signifying Monkey.* New York: Oxford University Press, 1988.

Gates, Henry Louis, Jr. "Writing 'Race' and the Difference It Makes." *Critical Inquiry* 12, no. 1 (1985): 1–20.

Gates, Henry Louis, Jr., and K. A. Appiah, eds. *Richard Wright: Critical Perspectives Past and Present.* New York: Amistad, 1993.

Geidel, Molly. *Peace Corps Fantasies.* Minneapolis: University of Minnesota Press, 2015.

Gershenhorn, Jerry. *Melville J. Herskovits and the Racial Politics of Knowledge.* Lincoln: University of Nebraska Press, 2004.

Gilroy, Paul. *The Black Atlantic*. Cambridge, MA: Harvard University Press, 1993.

Ginsberg, Allen. *Howl and Other Poems*. San Francisco: City Lights Books, 1956.

Gitlin, Todd. *The Sixties*. New York: Bantam, 1993.

Grace, Nancy M. "The Beats and Literary History." In *The Cambridge Companion to the Beats*, ed. Steven Belletto, 62–76. New York: Cambridge University Press, 2017.

Gray, Jeffrey. *Mastery's End*. Athens: University of Georgia Press, 2005.

Green, Fiona. "Elizabeth Bishop in Brazil and the *New Yorker*." *Journal of American Studies* 46 (2012): 803–829.

Greene, Graham. *The Quiet American*. 1955. New York: Penguin, 2004.

Greif, Mark. *The Age of the Crisis of Man*. Princeton, NJ: Princeton University Press, 2015.

Griswold, Wendy. *American Guides*. Chicago: University of Chicago Press, 2016.

Grossman, James R., ed. *The Frontier in American Culture*. Berkeley: University of California Press, 1994.

Gruesser, John Cullen. *Black on Black: Twentieth-Century African American Writing about Africa*. Lexington: University Press of Kentucky, 2000.

Gruesser, John Cullen. *White on Black: Contemporary Literature about Africa*. Urbana: University of Illinois Press, 1992.

Hakutani, Yoshinobu, ed. *Critical Essays on Richard Wright*. Boston: G. K. Hall, 1982.

Hardt, Michael and Antonio Negri. *Empire*. Cambridge, MA: Harvard University Press, 2000.

Harris, Oliver. *William Burroughs and the Secret of Fascination*. Carbondale: Southern Illinois University Press, 2003.

Harris, Oliver, and Ian MacFadyen, eds. *Naked Lunch @ 50: Anniversary Essays*. Carbondale: Southern Illinois University Press, 2009.

Harrison, Victoria. *Elizabeth Bishop's Poetics of Intimacy*. New York: Cambridge University Press, 1993.

Harvey, David. *The Condition of Postmodernity*. Oxford: Blackwell, 1990.

Hellmann, John. *American Myth and the Legacy of Vietnam*. New York: Columbia University Press, 1986.

Hemingway, Ernest. *The Sun Also Rises*. 1926. London: Arrow Books, 2004.

Herskovits, Melville J. *Cultural Relativism*. New York: Random House, 1972.

Herskovits, Melville J. *Franz Boas*. New York: Scribner's, 1953.

Hickey, Dennis, and Kenneth C. Wiley. *An Enchanting Darkness*. East Lansing: Michigan State University Press, 1993.

Hicok, Bethany. *Degrees of Freedom*. Lewisburg, PA: Bucknell University Press, 2008.

Hicok, Bethany. *Elizabeth Bishop's Brazil*. Charlottesville: University of Virginia Press, 2016.

Hicok, Bethany. "Elizabeth Bishop's 'Queer Birds.'" *Contemporary Literature* 40, no. 2 (1999): 286–310.

Hirsch, Jerrold. *Portrait of America*. Chapel Hill: University of North Carolina Press, 2003.

Hitchens, Christopher. *Arguably*. London: Atlantic, 2011.

Hofstadter, Richard. *The Progressive Historians*. New York: Alfred A. Knopf, 1969.

Hollinger, David. *Postethnic America*. Revised edition. New York: Basic Books, 2006.

Hollister, Susannah L. "Elizabeth Bishop's Geographic Feeling." *Twentieth-Century Literature* 58, no. 3 (2012): 399–438.

Homer, Sean. *Jacques Lacan*. New York: Routledge, 2005.

Hughes, Langston. *The Big Sea*. 1940. New York: Hill and Wang, 1993.

Immerwahr, Daniel. "*The Ugly American*: Peeling the Onion of an Iconic Cold War Text." *Journal of American-East Asian Relations* 26 (2019): 7–20.

Jackson, Lawrence P. *The Indignant Generation*. Princeton, NJ: Princeton University Press, 2011.

Jameson, Fredric. *Postmodernism*. Durham, NC: Duke University Press, 1991.

JanMohamed, Abdul R. "The Economy of Manichean Allegory." *Critical Inquiry* 12 (1985): 59–87.

Jarraway, David R. "'o canada!': The Spectral Lesbian Poetics of Elizabeth Bishop." *PMLA* 113, no. 2 (1998): 243–57.

Johnson, Rob. *The Lost Years of William S. Burroughs*. College Station: Texas A&M University Press, 2006.

Jurca, Catherine. *White Diaspora*. Princeton, NJ: Princeton University Press, 2001.

Kaplan, Amy. *The Anarchy of Empire in the Making of U.S. Culture*. Cambridge, MA: Harvard University Press, 2002.

Kaplan, Amy. "Left Alone with America." In *Cultures of United States Imperialism*. Ed. Kaplan and Donald E. Pease, 3–21. Durham, NC: Duke University Press, 1993.

Katznelson, Ira. *Fear Itself: The New Deal and the Origins of Our Time*. New York: Liveright, 2014.

Katznelson, Ira. *When Affirmative Action Was White*. New York: W. W. Norton, 2005.

Kerouac, Jack. *On the Road*. 1957. New York: Penguin, 2003.

Kindley, Evan. *Poet-Critics and the Administration of Culture*. Cambridge, MA: Harvard University Press, 2017.

Klein, Christina. *Cold War Orientalism*. Berkeley: University of California Press, 2003.

Kloppenberg, James T. *The Virtues of Liberalism*. New York: Oxford University Press, 1998.

Krebs, Edgardo C. "*Native Son*, Lost and Found." *Film Comment*, September–October 2012. Web.

Kurnick, David. "Is There a Gay Literature of Poverty?" *Politics/Letters*, March 2, 2018. Web.

LaFeber, Walter. *Inevitable Revolutions*. New York: W. W. Norton, 1984.

Lamont, Daniel. "'A Dark and Empty Continent': The Representation of Africa in Saul Bellow's *Henderson the Rain King.*" *Saul Bellow Journal* 16.2–17.2 (2000): 129–49.

Latham, Michael E. *Modernization as Ideology.* Chapel Hill: University of North Carolina Press, 2000.

Leader, Zachary. *The Life of Saul Bellow, 1915–1964.* New York: Alfred A. Knopf, 2015.

Leader, Zachary. *The Life of Saul Bellow, 1965–2005.* New York: Alfred A. Knopf, 2018.

Lederer, William J. "Hymie O'Toole Is Never Wrong." *Esquire* (February 1951): 73, 98.

Lederer, William J. *A Nation of Sheep.* New York: W. W. Norton, 1961.

Lederer, William J. "The Western Pacific." *Saturday Review* (October 17, 1959): 42, 55–57.

Lederer, William J., and Eugene Burdick. "Salute to Deeds of Non-Ugly Americans." *Life* (December 7, 1959). 148–63.

Lederer, William J., and Eugene Burdick. *The Ugly American.* New York: W. W. Norton, 1958.

Lerner, Daniel. "The Grocer and the Chief." *Harper's Magazine* (September 1955): 47–56.

Lerner, Daniel. *The Passing of Traditional Society.* New York: Free Press, 1958.

Leuchtenburg, William E. "Roosevelt, Norris and the 'Seven Little TVAs.'" *The Journal of Politics* 14, no. 3 (1952): 418–41.

Levine, Robert M. *Father of the Poor? Vargas and His Era.* New York: Cambridge University Press, 1998.

Lewis, David Levering. *W. E. B. Du Bois: The Fight for Equality and the American Century, 1919–1963.* New York: Henry Holt, 2000.

Limerick, Patricia Nelson. "The Adventures of the Frontier in the Twentieth Century." In *The Frontier in American Culture,* edited by James R. Grossman, 67–102. Berkeley: University of California Press, 1994.

Limerick, Patricia Nelson. *The Legacy of Conquest.* New York: W. W. Norton, 1987.

Limerick, Patricia Nelson. "Turnerians All." *American Historical Review* 100, no. 3 (1995): 697–716.

Lombardi, Marilyn May, ed. *Elizabeth Bishop: The Geography of Gender.* Charlottesville: University Press of Virginia, 1993.

Long, Durward. "Key West and the New Deal, 1934–1936." *Florida Historical Quarterly* 46, no. 3 (1968): 209–218.

Longenbach, James. *Modern Poetry after Modernism.* New York: Oxford University Press, 1997.

Lowney, John. *History, Memory, and the Literary Left.* Iowa City: University of Iowa Press, 2006.

Lydenberg, Robin. *Word Cultures*. Urbana: University of Illinois Press, 1987.

MacCannell, Dean. *The Tourist: A New Theory of the Leisure Class*. 1976. Berkeley: University of California Press, 2013.

Mangione, Jerre. *The Dream and the Deal*. 1972. Syracuse, NY: Syracuse University Press, 1996.

Marshall, Megan. *Elizabeth Bishop*. New York: Houghton Mifflin Harcourt, 2017.

Martin, William G., and Michael O. West. "The Ascent, Triumph, and Disintegration of the Africanist Enterprise, USA." In *Out of One, Many Africas*, 85–122. Urbana: University of Illinois Press, 1999.

Marx, Leo. *The Machine in the Garden*. New York: Oxford University Press, 1964.

Maxwell, William J. *F.B. Eyes*. Princeton, NJ: Princeton University Press, 2015.

McCann, Bryan. "Carlos Lacerda." *Hispanic American Historical Review* 83, no. 4 (2003): 661–96.

McCann, Sean. *A Pinnacle of Feeling*. Princeton, NJ: Princeton University Press, 2008.

McCann, Sean, and Michael Szalay. "Do You Believe in Magic? Literary Thinking after the New Left." *Yale Journal of Criticism* 18, no. 2 (2005): 435–68.

McCarthy, Mary. "Burroughs' *Naked Lunch*." In *The Writing on the Wall*, 42–53. New York: Harcourt, Brace & World, 1970.

McConnell, Frank D. *Four Postwar American Novelists*. Chicago: University of Chicago Press, 1977.

McCormick, Thomas J. *America's Half-Century*. 2nd ed. Baltimore: Johns Hopkins University Press, 1995.

McCoy, Alfred W. *The Politics of Heroin*. Chicago: Lawrence Hill, 1991.

McGurl, Mark. *The Program Era*. Cambridge, MA: Harvard University Press, 2009.

Melley, Timothy. *Empire of Conspiracy*. Ithaca, NY: Cornell University Press, 2000.

Miles, Barry. *Call Me Burroughs: A Life*. New York: Hachette, 2013.

Miller, Ruth. *Saul Bellow*. New York: St. Martin's, 1991.

Millier, Brett C. *Elizabeth Bishop*. Berkeley: University of California Press, 1993.

Mills, C. Wright. *White Collar*. New York: Oxford University Press, 1951.

Mills, Nathaniel. *Ragged Revolutionaries*. Amherst: University of Massachusetts Press, 2017.

Milne, David. *America's Rasputin: Walt Rostow and the Vietnam War*. New York: Hill and Wang, 2008.

Morgan, Ted. *Literary Outlaw: The Life and Times of William S. Burroughs*. New York: Henry Holt, 1988.

Morrison, Toni. *Playing in the Dark*. Cambridge, MA: Harvard University Press, 1992.

Mullins, Greg A. *Colonial Affairs*. Madison: University of Wisconsin Press, 2002.

Murphy, Timothy S. *Wising Up the Marks: The Amodern William S. Burroughs*. Berkeley: University of California Press, 1997.

Nadel, Alan. *Containment Culture*. Durham, NC: Duke University Press, 1995.

Nash, Gerald D. *Creating the West*. Albuquerque: University of New Mexico Press, 1991.

Nashel, Jonathan. "Modernization Theory in Fact and Fiction." In *Cold War Constructions*, ed. Christian G. Appy, 132–54. Amherst: University of Massachusetts Press, 2000.

"New Deal Awakens Key West, America's Tropical 'Problem City.'" *New York Times*, May 2, 1937, section R. p. 2.

Newman, Judie. *Saul Bellow and History*. New York: St. Martin's, 1984.

Newman, Judie. "Saul Bellow and Social Anthropology." In *Saul Bellow at Seventy-five*. Gerhard Bach, ed., 137–49. Tübingen: Gunter Narr Verlag, 1991.

Noll, Steven G. "When Government Really Mattered." Review of John A. Stuart and John F. Stack, eds., *The New Deal in South Florida*. H-Florida, H-Net Reviews, 2008.

Ogle, Maureen. *Key West*. Gainesville: University Press of Florida, 2003.

Oliveira, Carmen L. *Rare and Commonplace Flowers*. Trans. Neil K. Besner. New Brunswick, NJ: Rutgers University Press, 2003.

Parker, Phyllis R. *Brazil and the Quiet Intervention, 1964*. Austin: University of Texas Press, 1979.

Phu, Thy. "Bigger at the Movies: *Sangre Negra* and the Cinematic Projection of *Native Son*." *Black Camera* 2, no. 1 (2010). 36–57.

Potter, David. *People of Plenty*. Chicago: University of Chicago Press, 1954.

Pratt, Mary Louise. Afterword. In *The Cambridge Companion to Postcolonial Travel Writing*. Ed. Robert Clarke, 217–30. New York: Cambridge University Press, 2018.

Pratt, Mary Louise. *Imperial Eyes*. New York: Routledge, 1992.

Rampersad, Arnold. Introduction to *Native Son*. In Wright, *Native Son*, ix–xxii.

Rampersad, Arnold, ed. *Richard Wright: A Collection of Critical Essays*. Englewood Cliffs, NJ: Prentice-Hall, 1995.

Rasberry, Vaughn. *Race and the Totalitarian Century*. Cambridge, MA: Harvard University Press, 2016.

Reich, Robert B. *The Work of Nations*. New York: Alfred A. Knopf, 1991.

Reynolds, Guy. *Apostles of Modernity*. Lincoln: University of Nebraska Press, 2008

Rich, Adrienne. *Blood, Bread, and Poetry*. New York: W. W. Norton, 1986.

Riesman, David, with Nathan Glazer and Reuel Denney. *The Lonely Crowd*. Abridged ed., 1961. New Haven, CT: Yale University Press, 2001.

Robbins, Bruce. *Upward Mobility and the Common Good*. Princeton, NJ: Princeton University Press, 2007.

Rodgers, Daniel T. *Atlantic Crossings*. Cambridge, MA: Harvard University Press, 1998.

Rodrigues, Eusebio. "Bellow's Africa." *American Literature* 43, no. 2 (1971): 242–56.

Rodrigues, Eusebio. "Reichianism in *Henderson the Rain King*." *Criticism* 15, no. 3 (1973): 212–33.

Rook, Robert. "Race, Water, and Foreign Policy." *Diplomatic History* 28, no. 1 (2004): 55–81.

Rosenfeld, Isaac, and Saul Bellow. "Der shir hashirim fun Mendl Pumshtok." Trans. Barbara Mann. *Princeton University Library Chronicle* 63, no. 1–2 (2002): 23–25.

Ross, Andrew. *No Respect*. New York: Routledge, 1989.

Rossinow, Doug. *Visions of Progress*. Philadelphia: University of Pennsylvania Press, 2008.

Rostow, W. W. *The Stages of Economic Growth*. 1960. Eastford, CT: Martino, 2017.

Rowe, John Carlos. "Edward Said and American Studies." *American Quarterly* 56, no. 1 (2004): 33–47.

Rowley, Hazel. *Richard Wright*. Chicago: University of Chicago Press, 2001.

Rutkowski, Sara. *Literary Legacies of the Federal Writers' Project*. New York: Palgrave Macmillan, 2017.

Said, Edward W. *Culture and Imperialism*. New York: Vintage, 1993.

Said, Edward W. "Mount Hermon Commencement Speech." June 2002.

Said, Edward W. *Orientalism*. New York: Vintage, 1978.

Said, Edward W. *Out of Place*. New York: Alfred A. Knopf, 1999.

Said, Edward W. *Reflections on Exile and Other Essays*. Cambridge, MA: Harvard University Press, 2000.

Sandburg, Carl. *Cornhuskers*. New York: Henry Holt, 1918.

Saunders, Frances Stonor. *The Cultural Cold War*. New York: New Press, 1999.

Schaub, Thomas Hill. *American Fiction in the Cold War*. Madison: University of Wisconsin Press, 1991.

Schlesinger, Arthur M., Jr. *The Vital Center*. 1949. New Brunswick, NJ: Transaction, 2009.

Schmidt-Nowara, Chris. "Spain between the Black Atlantic and the Black Legend." *Arizona Journal of Hispanic Cultural Studies* 5 (2001): 149–60.

Schneiderman, Davis, and Philip Walsh, eds. *Retaking the Universe: William S. Burroughs in the Age of Globalization*. Sterling, VA: Pluto Press, 2004.

Schryer, Stephen. *Fantasies of the New Class*. New York: Columbia University Press, 2011.

Schwartz, Lloyd, and Sybil P. Estess, eds. *Elizabeth Bishop and Her Art*. Ann Arbor: University of Michigan Press, 1983.

Schweik, Susan. *A Gulf So Deeply Cut: American Women Poets and the Second World War*. Madison: University of Wisconsin Press, 1991.

Scott, Ellen. "Blacker Than Noir: The Making and Unmaking of Richard Wright's 'Ugly' *Native Son* (1951)." *Adaptation* 6, no. 1 (2012): 93–119.

Scott, James C. *Seeing Like a State*. New Haven, CT: Yale University Press, 1998.

Shah, Hemant. *The Production of Modernization: Daniel Lerner, Mass Media, and the Passing of Traditional Society*. Philadelphia: Temple University Press, 2011.

Shechtman, Anna. "'Native Son' and the Cinematic Aspirations of Richard Wright." *New Yorker*, April 4, 2019. Web.

Shelden, Michael. *Graham Greene*. New York: Random House, 1994.

Singh, Amritjit, and Peter Schmidt, eds. *Postcolonial Theory and the United States.* Jackson: University Press of Mississippi, 2001.

Singh, Sukhbir. "The Political Satire in *Henderson the Rain King.*" *Saul Bellow Journal* 18, no. 2 (2002): 23–39.

Sitkoff, Harvard. *A New Deal for Blacks*. New York: Oxford University Press, 1978.

Skerl, Jennie. *William S. Burroughs*. Boston: Twayne, 1985.

Skidmore, Thomas E. *Politics in Brazil, 1930–1964*. New York: Oxford University Press, 1967.

Skidmore, Thomas E. *The Politics of Military Rule in Brazil, 1964–85*. New York: Oxford University Press, 1988.

Slotkin, Richard. *The Fatal Environment*. 1985. Norman: University of Oklahoma Press, 1998.

Slotkin, Richard. *Gunfighter Nation*. 1992. Norman: University of Oklahoma Press, 1998.

Smith, Carol R. "The Jewish Atlantic—The Deployment of Blackness in Saul Bellow." *Saul Bellow Journal* 16.2–17.2 (2000): 253–79.

Smith, Chris. "Intellectual Action Hero," *California* (June 19, 2010). Web.

Smith, Henry Nash. *Virgin Land*. 1950. Cambridge, MA: Harvard University Press, 1978.

Smith, Valerie. *Self-Discovery and Authority in Afro-American Narrative*. Cambridge, MA: Harvard University Press, 1987.

Smith, Virginia Whatley. "African American Travel Literature." In *The Cambridge Companion to American Travel Writing*. Ed. Alfred Bendixen and Judith Hamara, 197–213. New York: Cambridge University Press, 2009.

Smith, Virginia Whatley, ed. *Richard Wright*. Jackson: University Press of Mississippi, 2016.

Smith, Virginia Whatley, ed. *Richard Wright's Travel Writings*. Jackson: University Press of Mississippi, 2001.

Spahr, Juliana. *Du Bois's Telegram*. Cambridge, MA: Harvard University Press, 2018.

Steinbeck, John. *Travels with Charley in Search of America* (1962). New York: Penguin, 2000.

Stone, Robert. Introduction to Greene, *The Quiet American*, vii–viii.

Susman, Warren I. "The Frontier Thesis and the American Intellectual." In *Culture as History*, 27–38. New York: Pantheon, 1984.

Szalay, Michael. *New Deal Modernism*. Durham, NC: Duke University Press, 2000.

Szalay, Michael. "'Nothing More Than Feelings': Generational Politics and the Authenticity of Alternative Culture." *Michigan Quarterly Review* 37, no. 4 (1998): 843–59.

Tanner, Tony. *City of Words*. New York: Harper & Row, 1971.

Taylor, David A. *Soul of a People*. Boston: John Wiley, 2009.

Taylor, Nick. *American-Made*. New York: Bantam, 2008.

Thomas, Brook. "Turner's 'Frontier Thesis' as a Narrative of Reconstruction." In *Centuries' Ends, Narrative Means*. Ed. Robert Newman, 117–37. Stanford, CA: Stanford University Press, 1996.

Travisano, Thomas J. *Elizabeth Bishop*. Charlottesville: University Press of Virginia, 1988.

Travisano, Thomas J. "The Elizabeth Bishop Phenomenon." *New Literary History* 26 (1995): 903–30.

Tucker-Abramson, Myka. *Novel Shocks: Urban Renewal and the Origins of Neoliberalism*. New York: Fordham University Press, 2019.

Turner, Frederick Jackson. *Rereading Frederick Jackson Turner*. Ed. John Mack Faragher. New Haven, CT: Yale University Press, 1998.

Veloso, Caetano. *Tropical Truth*. Trans. Isabel de Sena. New York: Alfred A. Knopf, 2002.

Vendler, Helen. "The Poems of Elizabeth Bishop." *Critical Inquiry* 13 (1987): 825–38.

Walker, Margaret. *For My People*. 1942. New Haven, CT: Yale University Press, 2019.

Walker, Margaret. *Richard Wright, Daemonic Genius*. New York: Warner Books, 1988.

Warner, Michael. Introduction. *Fear of a Queer Planet*, vii–xxxi. Minneapolis: University of Minnesota Press, 1993.

Webb, Walter Prescott. "Ended: 400 Year Boom." *Harper's Magazine* (October 1951): 25–33.

Weber, Max. *The Protestant Ethic and the Spirit of Capitalism*. Trans. Talcott Parsons. New York: Scribner's, 1976.

Weiss, M. Lynn. "*Para Usted*: Richard Wright's *Pagan Spain*." In *The Black Columbiad*. Ed. Werner Sollors and Maria Diedrichs, 212–25. Cambridge, MA: Harvard University Press, 1994.

Whyte, William H. *The Organization Man*. 1956. Philadelphia: University of Pennsylvania Press, 2002.

Wilford, Hugh. *The Mighty Wurlitzer: How the CIA Played America*. Cambridge, MA: Harvard University Press, 2009.

Wilkinson, Rupert. "Connections with Toughness: The Novels of Eugene Burdick." *Journal of American Studies* 11, no. 2 (1977): 223–39.

Williams, William Appleman. "The Frontier Thesis and American Foreign Policy." In *A William Appleman Williams Reader*. Ed. Henry W. Berger. Chicago: Ivan R. Dee, 1992.

Wilson, Charles Reagan. *Flashes of a Southern Spirit*. Athens: University of Georgia Press, 2011.

Wright, Richard. *Black Boy (American Hunger)*. New York: HarperCollins, 1998.

Wright, Richard. *Black Power* (1954). New York: HarperCollins, 2008.

Wright, Richard. "Blueprint for Negro Writing" (1937). In *The Richard Wright Reader*. Ed. Ellen Wright and Fabre, 36–49. New York: Harper & Row, 1978.

Wright, Richard. *Byline, Richard Wright*. Ed. Earle V. Bryant. Columbia: University of Missouri Press, 2015.

Wright, Richard. "How Bigger Was Born." In Wright, *Native Son*, 433–62.

Wright, Richard. Introduction. *Black Metropolis*. By St. Clair Drake and Cayton. New York: Harcourt, Brace, and Co., 1945.

Wright, Richard. "Memories of My Grandmother." In *The Man Who Lived Underground*, 161–211. New York: Library of America, 2021.

Wright, Richard. *Native Son*. Restored text. 1991. New York: HarperCollins, 2005.

Wright, Richard. "Not My People's War." *New Masses* (July 17, 1941): 8–9, 12.

Wright, Richard. *Pagan Spain*. 1957. New York: HarperCollins, 2008.

Wright, Richard. "Richard Wright on Relief: The Illinois Writers' Project Essays." *Southern Quarterly* 46, no. 2 (2009): 84–128.

Wright, Richard. *The Richard Wright Reader*, ed. Fabre and Ellen Wright. New York: Harper and Row, 1978.

Wright, Richard. *12 Million Black Voices*. 1941. Philadelphia: Perseus, 2008.

Wright, Richard. *Uncle Tom's Children*. 1940. New York: HarperCollins, 2008.

Wright, Richard. *White Man, Listen!* In Wright, *Black Power*, 631–812.

Wrobel, David. *The End of American Exceptionalism*. Lawrence: University Press of Kansas, 1993.

Young, Robert J. C. *Colonial Desire*. New York: Routledge, 1995.

Index

Burke, Seán, 71

Burroughs, Edgar Rice, 23

Burroughs, William S.: and anticolonial nationalism, 81–87, 90; *Cities of the Red Night*, 220n10, 222n50; cut-up method, 76–77; as farmer, 67–70; and Ginsberg, 66–70; and Kerouac, 1, 52–53, 67–70; "The Mayan Caper," 65, 83–86, 88, 112, 186; *Naked Lunch*, 28, 63–68, 74–82, 90; and New Deal, 220–221n17; and Nike advertisement, 88–90; *Nova Express*, 86–87; political beliefs of, 66–68; and postcolonial theory, 77–87; *The Soft Machine*, 28, 65, 81, 83–86; Talking Asshole routine, 68; "Twilight's Last Gleaming," 222n50; *The Yage Letters*, 66, 70–71

Butler, Judith, 129, 229n40

Buttinger, Joseph, 41, 48, 216n38

Castro, Fidel, 143–144

Cayton, Horace R., 166

Central Intelligence Agency (CIA), 21, 83, 112; and Bishop, 143, 146; and Burroughs, 84–85; and Kerouac, 51, 56; and *The Ugly American*, 27, 32, 34, 42, 45–49, 56–59; and Wright, 49, 170, 189

Chaplin, Charlie, 205

Chenal, Pierre, 170, 176–178, 180

Chomsky, Noam, 48, 217n66

Cincinnati Anti-Fluoride Society, 78

Civil Rights Movement, 21, 38, 112

Cleghorn, Angus, 123, 148

Clifford, James, 28, 92, 108

Clune, Michael, 75, 76

Cobb, Nina Kressner, 235n98, 236n123

Cohen, Milton A., 217n63

Communist Party USA (CP), 29, 95, 112, 125, 154, 156–159, 174, 179, 192

Conrad, Joseph, 40, 108; *Heart of Darkness*, 92–93, 99, 101, 183, 196–197

Cook, Eleanor, 124

Cooney, Terry A., 113

Cooper, James Fenimore, 40

Cowie, Jefferson, 188, 207

Crane, Louise, 123–124, 127

Cullather, Nick, 218n97

Culler, Jonathan, 72, 80

cultural hybridity, 2–3, 26, 56, 64, 79, 81, 109, 113–114, 202–206

Cultures of United States Imperialism, 4

Darda, Joseph, 54

Davis, Elmer, 123

Davis, Thadious T., 12

Dean, Robert D., 58

Death of a Salesman (Arthur Miller), 40

Debord, Guy, 79

DeGuzmán, María, 189, 196

DeMasi, Susan Rubenstein, 161, 167

Denning, Michael, 7, 49, 170

Derrida, Jacques, 28, 71, 73, 77

Devlin, Paul, 217n63

DeWitt, John, 143

Diawara, Manthia, 187

Dickstein, Morris, 2, 21–22, 26–27, 53

Dies, Martin, Jr., 161, 165, 167

Dirlik, Arif, 213n94

Dr. Benway, 79–80, 85–86, 221n17, 222n50

Dolinar, Brian, 8–9, 232n19

Dooley, Thomas A., 46

Dow, William E., 199

Drinnon, Richard, 59, 209n11

Du Bois, W. E. B., 8, 15–16, 33, 94, 100, 168, 206, 212n66, 221n17

Dulles, Allen, 58, 61

Edwards, Brian T., 63–64, 77–78, 80

Ehrenreich, Barbara, 210n20

Eisenhower, Dwight D., 33, 38–39, 51, 143

Ekbladh, David, 39

The New American Canon